"PLEASE, PLEASE," SARA CRIED. "PLEASE COME GET US, MOMMY."

I was trying to soothe her, reassure her. Iraj grabbed the receiver and shouted at her. I begged him to put Sara back on; I pleaded with him to let me talk to Cy. He didn't even respond, but started to harangue me about my failings as a wife, my flaws as a mother, my shortcomings as a daughter- and sister-in-law. And he screamed at me that I had upset Sara. Then he banged down the phone.

I was devastated. My children were desperate. They wanted me to rescue them, to pick them up as if they were finished with a play date at a child's house nearby. I would have crawled across Europe and the Middle East to get them. And in those moments after the call, all my emotions, hot and tumultuous, coalesced into one cold and hard feeling of determination. I would get my children back! Come hell or high water, I would get my children out of Iran and back home where they belonged.

RESCUED

JESSICA DOYLE
& CAROLYN NICHOLS

HarperPaperbacks
A Division of HarperCollinsPublishers

HarperPaperbacks   *A Division of* HarperCollins*Publishers*
10 East 53rd Street, New York, N.Y. 10022

Cover photograph is from the author's personal collection

First printing: July 1994

Printed in the United States of America

HarperPaperbacks and colophon are trademarks of HarperCollins*Publishers*

❖ 10 9 8 7 6 5 4 3 2 1

For my dearest Sara and Cy, my beautiful, brave children, full of laughter, goodness, and love, my joys forever.

For Mike, my courageous true love, my strength, my soul mate.

For Sue, my dear sister who gave herself to me for Sara and Cy's freedom.

For my parents, and for Rob and Beth; for their constant love and support in every way.

In memory of Aunt Mary, for her cherished prayers and words of hope.

"Real isn't how you are made," said the Skin Horse. "It's a thing that happens to you. When a child loves you for a long, long time, not just to play with, but REALLY loves you, then you become Real."

"Does it hurt?" asked the Rabbit.

"Sometimes," said the Skin Horse, for he was always truthful. "When you are Real you don't mind being hurt."

"Does it happen all at once, like being wound up," he asked, "or bit by bit?"

"It doesn't happen all at once," said the Skin Horse. "You become. It takes a long time. That's why it doesn't often happen to people who break easily, or have sharp edges, or who have to be carefully kept. Generally, by the time you are Real, most of your hair has been loved off, and your eyes drop out and you get loose in the joints and very shabby. But these things don't matter at all, because once you are Real you can't be ugly, except to people who don't understand . . . but once you are Real you can't become unreal again. It lasts for always."

—The Velveteen Rabbit
Margery Williams

ONE

IT WAS A BEAUTIFUL SPRING MORNING, FULL OF SUNSHINE and the promise of a mild wind that might blow away some of my fear and anxiety. I was rushing to leave the house for work when the phone rang at about nine. I raced to get the call, hoping it was from my children, who were on a brief vacation with their father in Canada.

It wasn't eight-year-old Sara or five-year-old Cy on the line. It was my ex-husband's brother, Jamshid. The moment I heard his voice, I panicked. Had there been an accident? Was one of the kids hurt? Sick? With Jamshid's chilling words, April 12, 1990, became the blackest day of my life.

"Iraj has taken the children to Iran," Jamshid said. "You'll never get them back."

My worst nightmares had become real. My ex-husband

had kidnapped our children. And he had taken them to a nation that had held my countrymen hostage and whose fanatic religious leader had declared that every American citizen was a mortal enemy.

In August 1977 I met Iraj Salimi. Little did I guess on that sultry summer night when the handsome Princeton grad student from Iran asked me to dance that he was the man I would marry, have two children with, be abused by, and divorce in 1989. And who could have imagined then that thirteen years after first setting eyes on Iraj, I would experience the worst possible torment and anguish at his hands when he abducted our young son and daughter, spiriting them back to Iran?

I knew Iraj for almost two years before I married him. I stayed married to him for almost ten years. Obviously I didn't enter into the relationship with him impulsively; I certainly didn't get out of it impulsively. So I don't have the excuse that I'd been swept off my feet, and I don't have the comfort of knowing I ended a bad marriage before it could deteriorate into something much worse. My childhood had prepared me to be cautious and to expect constant conflict, as well as a good deal of unhappiness.

I grew up in a dysfunctional family where bitter arguments and accusations, tears and fault-finding were only occasionally punctuated by bursts of euphoric "togetherness." Throughout my childhood I never knew what to expect from day to day, and I learned at a very early age that one of my most important responsibilities was to cope with the moods of my parents, especially my mother. My moods were unimportant. My needs just didn't matter very much.

RESCUED

The "Me generation"? I didn't know a thing about it. I was perfectly trained to put everyone ahead of myself. And I brought that attitude and behavior to my relationship with Iraj. His moodiness and suspiciousness and demands seemed normal to me. His temper tantrums and rages simply were to be endured, then forgotten as quickly as possible. But during the last few years of our marriage, I changed. Little by little. With the help of my sisters, a psychotherapist, and a women's support group, I slowly gained first self-esteem, then optimism and the courage to change. I became determined to make a better life, one that was happier and more stable, for my children and myself. After years of a marriage that was pure hell, I was finally able to break free and file for divorce.

When my divorce became final on March 2, 1989, I felt reborn. That spring was glorious. The judge had awarded me full custody of the children, and they were thriving. During the last miserable year of my marriage, the children had started school, and I had gained enough self-esteem to try to build a future for myself. I'd decided that I would love to teach social studies, so I'd investigated the graduate programs in secondary education at nearby colleges and universities and learned that I needed five more undergraduate courses to qualify. I applied at the local community college and was accepted.

My self-confidence began to soar as I successfully completed the first courses, even though the divorce proceedings were unbelievably awful. I had met a woman at the college who would become a source of great inspiration for me. She had hired me as a tutor, and I worked part time for about a year in the goals office. Shortly after the divorce decree was handed down, my mentor-friend recommended me for a position that had opened up; it was an even more challenging job than the one I had in the goals office. I got it! And I had completed the requirements for graduate work that would lead to certification as a teacher, so I started evening courses in the grad school that summer. I felt wonderfully satisfied; I was making enormous progress in building a good life, with the prospect of a job I really wanted on the horizon.

In early September my ex-husband moved a thousand miles away, to Chicago. I was exuberant with relief. I knew I was healing quickly, and I took a small step toward building a social life for myself by joining a group for single parents. But I was quite timid about going out on dates—until a friend in the office introduced me to Mike Doyle.

As kind as he was good-looking, Mike had a great sense of humor. He liked outdoor activities, hiking in particular. I'm an avid hiker, so we enjoyed tramping through the woods, trudging up mountain trails, walking along the river, as well as traditional dates, going to movies and out to dinner. There were many other activities we enjoyed, as a couple and with Sara and Cy. The children took to Mike as much as I did. We had a wonderful Thanksgiving and an even better Christmas that year with Mike in our lives. He was a godsend. And I was falling in love. For the first time.

The new year of 1990 dawned bright. I was feeling healthy, self-confident. Mike and I were growing closer with every passing day. He was teaching me a lot about respect, equality, and having fun in a relationship, about appreciating differences and expecting harmony and happiness. Even the relationship with my ex-husband seemed manageable then. I didn't want the children to feel they'd lost their father, and I was trying to foster a good rapport between them. Iraj spoke to them on the phone and visited them when his work brought him back to our area. His calls were erratic, though, and I asked him to try to make sure that he spoke with Sara and Cy more often and on a regular basis. (His child support payments were as erratic as the calls.)

When Iraj arranged a visit with the kids in February 1990, I was really glad, because I knew it meant a lot to Sara and Cy that their father wanted to see them. But at the end of their afternoon together, there was a brief, frightening episode that should have put me on guard.

During their time with their father, the kids had talked about Mike and all the things they enjoyed doing with him. When Iraj drove up to the house, I went out to meet him and the kids. I had a protection-from-abuse order still in effect against Iraj; it barred him from coming into the house, and my lawyer and the police urged me to meet him only outside on the drive, not even at the front door, when he picked up and dropped off the children. On that cold February afternoon as we walked up the path to the house, Iraj confronted me about the man in my life. In seconds he flew into a rage, turned, ran back to the car, and started kicking and beating on it. I felt as though I'd been jerked back in time. My heart sank and I was scared. Quickly, though, Iraj got himself under control. He apologized, explaining that he'd known I'd find someone else one day, but he hadn't expected it to happen so soon. He said he was seeing other women and was hoping for a good relationship too.

"I love you like a sister now," he said, "so I don't really understand why I got mad a minute ago. Your good news about finding a man like Mike is my good news too."

Why didn't I question his motive for saying this? Why

did I shrug off my doubts about his sincerity? Maybe because Iraj seemed so contrite, so generous with his wishes for my happiness. Or maybe I'd just forgotten what a good actor he was.

He conned me that day, and he went on conning me in the days that followed. I can't imagine why I was so blind. I can only guess that I wanted his relationship with the children to work, and my wish was so strong that I couldn't allow myself to perceive that anything might be wrong. Or I might have been slipping back into the patterns so firmly established during my marriage, accepting Iraj's apologies and believing in his promises of good behavior. But I was alert and alarmed about ten days later when he called and asked me to let Sara and Cy spend their spring break with him in Canada. I said no.

Over the next few weeks Iraj waged a campaign that a consummate politician could have been proud of to get my permission for the kids to vacation with him at his brother Jamshid's home in Toronto. Iraj was all sweet reason. He didn't want the children to lose touch with their aunt and uncle, with their cousins. He wanted them to continue to know and love his side of the family. That was only right, wasn't it? Of course it was, but Mike and I were worried. The phone calls started to pour in from Jamshid and his wife. They begged to have Sara and Cy come for that week. They talked about how much their daughters wanted to play with their cousins. They all missed the kids, and family meant so much. How could I deny them the opportunity to be with Sara and Cy for one short week? No harm could come to the children in their own uncle and aunt's home, they kept reminding me.

There was precedent for this visit. Some months

before, shortly after the divorce, Iraj and his brother and sister-in-law had been on this same kick. Iraj's point then had been that the visit with his brother and sister-in-law was the only vacation he could afford, since I had "taken him to the cleaners" in the divorce. That certainly was not the case! At any rate, the persistence of Iraj, Lelah, and Jamshid in trying to get my permission for the children to visit had almost driven me around the bend. Finally, Jamshid had suggested that I supervise the visit, and I'd given in. He and his wife had been great, very warm. Iraj and I had nothing to do with each other; he entertained all the kids, I entertained myself with long walks around the neighborhood and sightseeing in Toronto. Sara and Cy had a wonderful time, especially playing with their three cousins. Jamshid and Lelah's daughters really were adorable, and my children just loved being with them.

The only dark cloud, aside from the presence of Iraj, was his younger brother, Nasser, whom I'd never liked. A couple of years before the divorce Nasser had stayed in my home after Iraj had smuggled him out of Iran. He was still as cocky as he'd been during those few weeks he'd lived with us and had tried to order me around as if I were his slave. Nasser had the attitude that the West owed him something—God only knows how he came to that conclusion—and he was disturbingly similar to Iraj in his arrogance. I considered Nasser an obnoxious little brat, but he certainly didn't have that effect on everyone; a lot of people found him very attractive, perhaps because he was very handsome and self-assured. Iraj practically worshipped him. I had avoided Nasser in Canada, and except for his annoying presence and Iraj's irritating manner, the trip had been a success.

So in this campaign to get me to let the kids go alone with their father to Toronto, the Salimis reminded me frequently of the success of the previous visit. Iraj's cousin Bobek, a college student in Chicago who'd visited us a lot in the past and was well liked by the kids and me, called several times. He wanted me to understand that he would be going on the trip as "an escort to the kids," and that he'd watch over them every second. He said he loved Sara and Cy very much and I could count on him to take wonderful care of them.

More than anything, I wanted to be a good and constructive parent, not tainting the children's feelings for their father with my own deep dislike of him. I was torn. And questioning myself: I wasn't sure why I was so worried. I wondered if deep down I might be afraid that Iraj would charm the kids into preferring him to me. Was my apprehension coming from my own insecurity? Was I being neurotically distrustful?

In fact, I had good reason to distrust Iraj after twelve long years of enduring his manipulative behavior, his deceit, his violent outbursts. But what was I really afraid he might do? He'd never taken care of the children, always shunning responsibility for doing anything for them, because men did not bathe babies or touch diapers or feed infants where he came from. By all accounts he was enjoying his bachelor life in Chicago to the hilt. It was inconceivable to me that he'd want to have the children living with him there. And he was very outspoken about how much he hated the anarchy and repression that gripped his homeland. Often during the last several years he'd said, "Iran is the last place on earth I'd want to live right now." I summarily ruled out any notion that he would try to take Sara and Cy away from me. But still, I was nervous while I packed their bags, and I found myself praying fervently for their safety when I waved good-bye to them, Iraj, and his cousin Bobek.

I felt a lot better when I got a telephone call in the wee hours of the morning from Sara saying they had arrived safely at their uncle's house. After all, I kept telling myself, I was doing the right thing by encouraging Iraj to be a good father and making sure that Sara and Cy respected and liked him. And anyway, the children would be back home in just a few days.

On that sunny morning when Jamshid called to tell me Iraj had abducted the children, I think I went into shock. His words sank in slowly . . . *taken Sara and Cy to Iran . . . never get them back.* I vaguely recall screaming at Jamshid that he and his wife had promised to care for my children as if they were their own. I asked over and over how they could have broken their word to me and worse, let Iraj do such a terrible thing. Most of all I was wild with fury at myself for letting Sara and Cy go off with their father on an unsupervised trip across the Canadian border. Why, oh why had I gone against my instincts?

After I hung up I was speechless at Iraj's actions and the treachery of Bobek, Lelah, and Jamshid—especially Jamshid. Then I went numb with horror at the thought of what Sara and Cy must be feeling. How were they reacting to being wrenched away from everything that was familiar and dear to them?

I'd always prided myself on my control over my emotions, but after learning that my children had been stolen away from their home and from their country and were being held by their father in Iran, I lost all control. I cried, I pounded my fists on the floor. My younger sister, Beth, who'd been staying at my house, was also shocked and crying. My older sister, Sue, who happened to stop by shortly after the phone call from Jamshid, was furious. Periodically she would shout, "How could he be such a maniac? How could he do such a thing?" I called the police, the State Department, my congressman, both my senators. I called the FBI and the lawyer who had handled my divorce and the court orders for my protection from Iraj's harassment. He promised to start all the necessary legal work immediately. As soon as I hung up, I fell apart. I began to howl with pain and scream in outrage.

Suddenly Mike was there, thank God. He held me as I sobbed and shouted. I can't remember much about the next few hours beyond feeling paralyzed by grief. My babies were half a world away with a man who at best could be described as unstable. A man who had never lifted a finger to walk them or wipe their noses or dry their tears. I hurt, I just ached to hold my children, to rock them, to stroke their hair and tell them everything was going to be all right. I was in agony over what they must be going through after what could only have been a grueling trip. They would be frightened in an Iranian house, primitive by their American standards, with its strange furniture and odors. All the customs—when to eat, sleep, play—would be so incredibly hard for them to adjust to. The people around them would be speaking a language that Sara and Cy didn't understand. Who would comfort them and guide them? I couldn't stand all these thoughts and questions. But I also couldn't stop them, and I do remember wondering if a person could die from feeling so much pain.

I haunted the children's rooms, running my hands

over their toys and clothes, visualizing Sara playing with her dolls, Cy with his fleet of matchbox cars. I could almost see them drawing at their little desks, standing by their beds in their pajamas. Sara is vivacious and clever; she's a beautiful little girl, tall for her age, with the kind of lanky, muscular body that's just right for gymnastics, which she loves. Like her brother, she has dark hair, big brown eyes, and tawny skin. Cy is a handsome little imp with the most mischievous smile and the brightest twinkle in his eyes. They are both spirited and sweet, and utterly precious to me. I curled up on Sara's bed and cuddled her teddy bear; I went to Cy's room and sorted his transformers, so sorry that I had used the vacation to clean the children's rooms. Cy's elaborate Lego constructions of roadways, bridges, and tunnels and his fleets of little cars and trucks no longer covered his bedroom floor. Sara's artwork, crayons, and paints had been tidied; her party scene for Barbie and Ken had been cleared away. The life was gone from their rooms . . . and the children were gone from my life. I hurt so much then that I couldn't even cry. After a while I had to shut the doors to their bedrooms; I found no comfort in looking at their things, only pain.

I had withdrawn far into myself during the first twelve hours after Jamshid's call. Those who had gathered around by that time tell me that I looked as if I were in a stupor. Occasionally my grief would break, and I would fly into a fit of rage, wishing I could get my hands around Iraj's neck and strangle the life out of him.

Traumatized, none of us could shake the idea that this was all a nightmare from which we could wake by appealing to Iraj to come to his senses and bring the children home. We were trying to end the nightmare by daydreaming. But in one respect we were lucky, and even then I was dimly aware of just how lucky. Jamshid had told me in a second call that Iraj had taken Sara and Cy directly to the family farm in Iran. At least I knew exactly where my children were.

I had traveled to the Salimi farm both times I'd gone to visit Iraj's family before our marriage. It was about an hour's drive from Tabriz, the fourth-largest city in Iran, with a population of almost half a million people. But as soon as you leave Tabriz, you see very few people. The villages are tiny, and the farm is in one of them. The area is mountainous, surrounded by hot springs—and right in the middle of an active earthquake zone! A farm in the Azerbaijan Province of Iran looks nothing at all like a farm in Iowa or Maryland. In her book *The Women of Deh Koh: Lives in an Iranian Village*, Erika Friedl might just as well be describing the site of the Salimi farm. It is one of many "oases of huddled houses surrounded by fields and, as the people say, lonely barren wilderness beyond. . . . mud, dust, walls of adobe bricks, walls of stones, hedges of brambles, donkeys, sheep, goats, cows. . . . Poplar-lined water channels run like lifelines along roads, across alleys, through gardens and fields."

I had been surprised at how bleak the landscape was; I had expected lush greenery. The houses were packed together in the small village and had few outbuildings. The odors were awful, until, thankfully, one's olfactory nerve went dead to them. But, miracle of all miracles, the farm did have a telephone—and I had the number.

Trembling, I placed a call. The phone rang . . . and rang . . . and rang.

No sooner had I hung up than I got a call—but not from Iraj. When Jamshid had given me the hideous news about the abduction, he'd also told me that Iraj had left a letter for me spelling out his demands. The letter was being held by Nasser, who would call me and read it to me. It was Nasser on the phone now. His voice, so unlike Iraj's, was high-pitched; it always had shredded my nerves like a fingernail across a blackboard. But even his voice couldn't put me off at that moment, because I was so eager to hear Iraj's message, which I prayed would give me all the information I needed to get my children back.

The conversation with Nasser tested my control to the limit. He was giddy with glee over the success of the kidnapping, which, he boasted, had been a family-wide conspiracy, weeks in the making. I was gritting my teeth, and when I couldn't stand to listen to him anymore, I interrupted and insisted he read Iraj's letter. If I'd been able to think clearly, I would have anticipated what my ex-husband had to say, and what he wanted. But still in shock and disoriented, I was surprised by the contents of the letter. Iraj had written a string of rambling, almost incoherent indictments, saying that I was "inferior" in everything I'd done during our marriage, "unworthy" of being his wife and the mother of his children. There were overblown lines of sloppy sentiment about his love for Sara and Cy and his duty to them.

Embedded in all this crazy stuff were his demands. If I'd ever had any doubts about Iraj's venality or his disturbed personality, they were wiped away by that letter. Fueled by jealousy over Mike, many of his demands grew out of his conviction that the divorce settlement had been unfair to him. Reviewing the evidence about Iraj's abusive behavior, the judge had granted me custody of the children, giving me half the equity in the house we'd shared. I'd had to buy out Iraj's half in order to remain in the home we'd lived in for over two years; to do this I'd had to borrow about $50,000 from my father. The judge had also ordered Iraj to pay alimony and child support, and to return half of a large sum he'd squandered on schemes to get members of his family out of Iran. This large sum was credited toward my purchase of Iraj's half of the house.

The letter from Iraj that Nasser read instructed me to go to court and have the custody and support payment orders overturned. He made wild statements about how much the house was worth and about the value of two small trusts in the children's names. Based on his demented calculations, he assumed I could get $200,000 right away—only the dear Lord knows how or from where he thought I could get this huge amount of money. There wasn't even that much equity in the house, which Iraj would have realized if he'd been in his right mind. And how could I borrow on the equity in the house anyway? My small income certainly wouldn't convince a bank officer to give me a second mortgage or home equity loan. Petty, insignificant requests followed, jumbled together with huge, impossible demands—all the product of an unhinged mind.

My sisters, Mike, and I felt one point was paramount: Iraj wanted money from me, and he wanted it immediately. He'd actually said in the letter that if I turned over the $200,000 right away, he would allow me to visit the children in Iran! My first reaction was that his letter was really a ransom note. Then I realized it was far worse. He wasn't suggesting a way I could "buy back" the children; he only offered me the chance to "rent" a visit with them in a hostile country.

* * *

My thoughts churning, unable to sit still, I paced, periodically calling the farm in Iran. The phone there rang . . . and rang . . . until I thought I'd go out of my mind if it wasn't answered. I couldn't sleep or eat. At last, on Saturday, April 14, Iraj answered, and for a moment I was afraid I might not be able to speak—or even breathe. Somehow I managed a few words.

I needn't have worried about speaking; Iraj was more than willing to do all the talking. He was triumphant. He gloated about how clever he'd been, how clever everyone in his family had been. He seemed to relish telling me every detail of how he'd been able to get the children away from me. He kept repeating that the kids would be with him forever, that I would never get them back.

"But you *are* their mother, Jess," he conceded magnanimously. "You could visit them here." His tone was so calm, so superior and infuriating that I think my blood pressure must have shot off the top charts.

Somehow managing to hold my temper, I asked to speak to the children. He refused. My heart sank as I heard a child screaming in the background. Suddenly, Sara was on the phone—she had taken the receiver from her father.

"Please, please," she sobbed. "Please come get us, Mommy. I want to come home. Please pick us up."

I tried to soothe her, to reassure her. Iraj grabbed the receiver and shouted at her. I begged him to put Sara back on; I pleaded with him to let me speak to Cy. He didn't even respond but started to harangue me about my failings as a wife, my flaws as a mother, my shortcomings as a daughter- and sister-in-law. And he screamed at me that I had upset Sara. Then he banged down the phone.

I was devastated. My children were desperate. They wanted me to rescue them, to pick them up as if they'd gone to play at a child's house nearby. I would have crawled across Europe and the Middle East to get them. And in those moments after the call, all my emotions, hot and tumultuous, coalesced into one cold and hard feeling of determination. *I would get my children back*. Come hell or high water, I would get my children out of Iran and back home where they belonged.

TWO

I FACED MY THIRD SLEEPLESS NIGHT, ALTERNATELY BLAMING myself for encouraging any sort of relationship between the children and their father and trying to come up with solutions to this terrible situation. I would grow upset and frustrated when I looked at the clock and realized there was no one I could call, no work I could do in the dark of night to help get Sara and Cy back home.

And I couldn't help thinking back to other times with Iraj. How naive I'd been when I first got involved with him—but could I have known what he was really like? Could I have guessed even if I'd been older, more experienced, less needy, that he was so unstable and would become abusive?

I don't think so. I really don't believe that at first there was a hint of anything negative about Iraj, not to mention disturbed. Not a hint of anything other than his intelligence, swarthy good looks, romantic appeal, ambition, and a certain air of mystery. But even his aura of mystery didn't seem in the least dark then. It could have been called charm, a natural part of a man from an exotic land whose culture dated back more than 2,500 years. But I *was* naive and had been sheltered in a peculiarly insulated, home-centered life, so that meeting a man who seemed as worldly as Iraj was a heady experience for me at twenty-one.

It was a hot, humid night in August 1977 when I met him. I had graduated in June from Penn State, taken a summer job, and was trying to figure out what I was going to do with my life. In short, I was asking myself all those questions a young woman with a brand new college degree in her pocket asks herself. Several of my friends were going out to a popular dance spot in Princeton that evening and asked me to come along. I'd been working on my résumé and jumped at the chance to leave it on my desk and go out and have some fun.

We hadn't been seated for more than ten minutes when a handsome, very well-dressed young man asked me to dance. He introduced himself as Iraj Salimi, a graduate student at Princeton. We danced together awkwardly, and I felt self-conscious. When I said that he was no Fred Astaire and I sure wasn't Ginger Rogers, he laughed. That broke the ice, and we began to enjoy ourselves. I asked him to join me and my friends at our table. We talked for a long time.

I found him very interesting. Six years older than I, he seemed sensitive as well as smart. I was impressed by his descriptions of his Iranian homeland, particularly by the fervor with which he spoke about the hopes and dreams of those working for change there, and by the affection that colored his beautifully modulated voice when he told me about his family. I suppose I was ready for a person like Iraj to come into my life. Right from the beginning, he seemed to fit in perfectly with my expectation that I'd meet all sorts of unique and fascinating people as an independent adult. When we parted that first evening, he asked me to join him the following weekend for a tour of the Princeton campus. I was pleased and quickly agreed.

Did I give much thought to Iraj during the following days? I don't think I did. It certainly wasn't a case of love at first sight; he was simply an interesting man with whom I'd had a very engaging conversation.

The tour of Princeton put me in a romantic mood, though not one directly connected to Iraj. The beautiful campus made me envision a life lived happily on its academic fringe. A fulfilling job for myself, a husband involved with the university, and after a couple of years, a child. Romantic fantasy, indeed. But I was prone to daydreaming about having a good relationship with a man, a relationship that would lead to a happy family life. I wanted to be very different from my parents. Their problems had created so much tension and unhappiness; their arguments and constant threats to divorce each other made life too sad and uncertain. My dream was to have a good marriage and a happy, peaceful home life.

Iraj pursued me, at times almost weaving a spell around me. He had the most intent way of holding my gaze, his big, brown eyes full of what I perceived as tenderness and love. He complimented me on my looks extravagantly. And that voice of his—low, mesmerizing, with an accent that was cultured and had a musical quality. He told me in every way possible through words and actions that he enjoyed being with me, that he was falling in love with me. I had never been courted before; I had had lots of friends, but not boyfriends. And I had only dreamed of experiencing this level of attention and admiration.

I stifled any doubts that came to mind. And a few did. He was so sure of himself, so persuasive—and so vehement about the correctness of every opinion he held, every decision he made. But I refused to heed these warning signs or to confront him about much of anything.

Taking a big step into a relationship with Iraj, I accepted a job in Princeton and moved into a small apartment in Palmer Square. He was deeply involved in his graduate studies and working hard, but he always had plenty of time for me. In fact, he made his life revolve around me. He included me in all his activities with his friends in graduate school, most of whom were foreign students. They accepted me warmly as part of the gang, which made me very happy. We had spaghetti dinners with jug wine picnic-style on the floors of our apartments; we went out to clubs or discos and off on hikes. We went to the movies together, to lectures; we sat around listening to music and talking late into the night. And in this group I saw several cross-cultural couples who seemed to be making their relationships work despite their many differences. So whenever I became aware of a conflict between Iraj and me, I dismissed it as "a cultural thing" that we could work out in time. I cringe now when I think about how careless I was about such matters. It's almost as if I was determined to blot out any recognition of the important differences between us and to ignore any sign that some of Iraj's traits were unattractive.

But I was just floating on cloud nine then. Iraj made no secret whatsoever of his attraction, telling me constantly that I was the most desirable woman he'd ever met. And he introduced me to so many new things. We had a lot of fun, mostly, I think, because Iraj had a real talent for finding out about places and activities, exploring and sharing them with me. Our dates were always fun and a good example of this was the way he guided me around New York City.

I'd lived all my life in the suburbs of New Jersey and Pennsylvania, only an hour and a half from Manhattan by train, but I had only come into the city a few times as a child when my parents treated us to a holiday show at Radio City Music Hall or my mother brought us in to see an exhibit at one of the museums. When Iraj found out that New York City was foreign territory to me, he got excited. He would be my romantic guide in opening up the world to me, starting with the Big Apple, and so he planned a series of dates there to prowl the museums and attend the theater. We drank hot chocolate while watching the ice skaters at Rockefeller Center; we explored Chinatown, Little Italy, Greenwich Village, and Soho. I was terribly impressed with how adept Iraj was at getting around a new place. And I was touched that he cared enough to figure out what things would appeal to me and organize dates around them. We had wonderful times together then, and how sweet and loving Iraj seemed as he enthusiastically went about expanding my horizons.

Somebody loved me. Somebody wanted to be with me all the time. I felt wonderful. Now, looking back, I'm a little embarrassed by all that. Was I really so needy and so unaware? I believe I fell in love with Iraj's falling in love with me, not with the man himself. His devotion and rapt attention—and flattery—were irresistible.

Some aspects of Iraj's background made me feel a lot of admiration for him. They still do. His crimes can't wipe out the things I still respect. He came from a nomadic tribal family of modest means whose members had virtually no formal education. He worked hard, determined from a very young age to get an education, to better himself and do everything possible to raise his family's standard of living. He excelled and got scholarships from the Iranian government, finally landing in Princeton, where he was working on a master's degree in electrical engineering and computer science. It is no small achievement to burst through the boundaries of a culture more ancient than the recorded history of Persia and get all the way to a prestigious Ivy League university. Along the way he helped his brothers, got consulting jobs, sent money and gifts back home, and supported his family in every conceivable way.

Iraj met my parents and my sisters and brother and enthusiastically took them to heart. Of course I was delighted that he thought my family was such an attractive, intelligent, lively bunch. He got along well with my brother Rob, six years my senior and almost to the day the same age as Iraj. Rob's a lawyer, and a good one, who is a lot of fun and loves to play all kinds of sports. My sister Beth is two years younger than I, and we look very much alike; Sue, two years older than I, is quite fair and lovely. Two brunettes and a blonde and three of the closest sisters in the world. Iraj said he was crazy about

Beth and Sue, and he plied them with compliments and seemed to love to tease them. He liked my mom, too, but the person in the family that he most loved and admired was my father. He often commented about how smart and hardworking my father was, and how successful. Iraj was not only in awe of my dad's abilities, but also of the warmth and affection he received from my brother, sisters, and me.

Nadir Salimi, Iraj's father, was a quiet, passive man, essentially sweet, but with little drive or personality. Iraj confessed that he'd always wished he had a father like mine. His mother, Homa, was the force to be reckoned with in the family, he said. It was she who'd struggled to arrange excellent matches for her daughters. Most of all she had pushed her sons, Iraj especially, to work hard and move up in the world in order to raise up the entire family. And while Iraj merely tolerated Nadir, he adored Homa.

I was flattered that Iraj spoke so openly to me about his family, confiding in me about the problems he had with his parents and his three brothers and four sisters. (I'd always thought I had a large family, but with seven siblings, Iraj really had one!) He told me of his doubts about whether he could live up to his mother's expectations. I grew to trust him emotionally and shared with him some of the difficulties I'd faced growing up. This was a first for me, as I'd never really talked with an outsider about our family's problems.

I'm part of an exuberant family that from the outside looks as though it inherited the American Dream. In some respects this is true. My mother is Jewish, and her Hungarian parents immigrated to America shortly after they were married in the early twenties. At almost the same time, my father's Catholic parents met on the boat coming over from Italy. Both my mom, Gloria, and my dad, Ralph, are bright and attractive—and quite strong-willed. A photograph would capture the image of a large family blessed with health, good looks, and prosperity. But inside our sprawling contemporary redwood and glass home with its swimming pool and beautiful landscaping, the atmosphere was thick with hostility, tension, and the emotional poverty caused by anger and mental illness.

My mother suffered from manic-depressive illness, a type of mood disorder characterized by swings between inappropriate highs and awful lows. She is a fantastic woman with a lot of courage and a lot of talent, and I love her dearly, but I hate her illness. Probably the only thing as bad as being a manic-depressive is living with one!

Now that I'm older, I see that my mom was a fish out of water. Creative and flamboyant, she didn't live easily in a traditional suburban community. I often wonder what her life—and the course of her illness—might have been if she had lived in New York's Greenwich Village or London's West End. And, of course, I wonder what my life and my sisters' lives might have been like if Mom had raised us in an environment that supported and applauded her original mind and her love of the arts. But mom didn't raise us in a Bohemian community. And in suburban New Jersey, she embarrassed all of us except Rob, who'd somehow managed to turn away from the troubles with Mom at an early age. She made Sue, Beth, and me feel like freaks in many ways. One of the worst was how she made us dress for school. Mom designed and sewed a lot of our clothes. Today I'd love to wear some of those outfits. They'd be called funky, cool. Back in the late sixties and early seventies, they were called weird. Confronting Mom about being teased for this or about any other matter was useless.

"Those kids are just jealous," she'd say stoutly. "Don't pay a bit of attention." And that was the end of it as far as she was concerned.

Life with Mom was totally unpredictable. She could go to bed feeling that all was right in her world and wake up in a numbing, black despair. She spoke then, when she spoke at all, of hopelessness and helplessness, of meaninglessness and death—though, thank God, she never threatened or attempted suicide. But her depression was total, and the episodes could last for weeks.

I've learned that depression is the most common of all mental illnesses, and in any given six-month period, about ten million Americans suffer from it. The good news today is that doctors consider depression one of the most treatable of illnesses, but this was not the case while I was growing up. I don't think there was much, if any, understanding that this was a biologically-based disorder where the patient, like a diabetic, is missing at least one crucial, naturally occurring substance in the body. Biomedical research indicates that a person suffering from depression has an imbalance of neurotransmitters, substances that allow brain cells to communicate with one another. Two such transmitters are serotonin and norepinephrine. Unlike insulin, however, serotonin and norepinephrine can't be injected to make the patient function normally. But now there are drugs that seem to help the body either produce the neurotransmitters or pep up and keep in balance the ones they have.

Thank God for lithium, the drug now used to treat manic-depressive illness. Lithium has made a great difference to my mother, and to all of us who know her and love her.

Unfortunately, though, it wasn't until I was well into my teens that Mom was somewhat successfully treated with lithium, and while it stabilized her moods so the highs weren't so high and the lows so low, it did nothing to cure the problems in her marriage. My father, a graduate of MIT, owned his own commercial-industrial development company with two partners. He was a workaholic who spent a good deal of time from home— more and more time away as my mother grew angrier with him. She criticized him, he criticized her, and their shouting matches were volcanic, and frequent. Mom was obsessed with her poor relationship with Dad, and she made us girls her allies, her confidantes in her war with him and his parents, whom she detested. For their part, my paternal grandparents weren't thrilled with my mother's side of the family. I guess I liked my father's parents a little better than my mother's, but I had to rely on my Hungarian grandparents because they lived close by and helped in our home. Unfortunately, though, Beth, Rob, and I didn't quite meet with their approval. Brunettes with brown eyes and dark skin, we too much resembled my father's Italian family to please them. Sue came closer to their ideal in terms of looks and got favored treatment. It hurt. A lot.

Naturally this atmosphere did not encourage us to bring friends home from school or have parties, or in fact to be very sociable at all. We three girls turned to each other. We were best friends then, and we are best friends today.

In rare moments of stability Mom would design hats for her parents' boutique in Trenton, New Jersey. She would become an involved, concerned mother, cook and keep house, and fight with her husband. Her manic episodes were almost more intolerable than her depressive ones. She would go wild with activity, cleaning like a fury from the top of the house to the basement, cooking unbelievably huge amounts of food that filled the refrigerator and choked the freezer; she'd sew all night, plan enormous parties, take my sisters and me to art exhibits and out skating and off to movies, and she'd shop until she dropped. For a while. Then she would go still and silent. A big broken doll, she would stay slumped in a chair or curled on the sofa or propped up in bed in her darkened room. "Unable to function"; I must have heard that phrase a thousand times during my childhood. When Mom was depressed, Beth, Sue, and I were the three little nannies, worrying about her and taking care of her with the help of her parents.

In those days before lithium, Mom saw psychiatrists—many psychiatrists. A major result was that from a very early age my sisters and I were pulled into the analytic approach that came to rule our homelife. We were encouraged to analyze all the emotions churning around and within Mother. There were two Great Quests for Beth, Sue, and me during most of our childhood—to keep the peace between our parents and to try to help Mom discover what, beyond her problems with Dad, was making her so miserable.

In the first quest my sisters and I were go-betweens for our parents; we were their communicators, negotiators, manipulators. In the second quest, we were ceaseless analyzers. We could always turn a situation or problem on its side and examine it from a new perspective. There was nothing we wouldn't ponder or discuss; our skills at ruminating were completely overdeveloped. I think this preoccupation with analyzing played a critical part in my relationship with Iraj, as did my sense of responsibility for trying to fix anything that wasn't going well.

I vividly remember a day during our honeymoon in Germany when Iraj woke up as grumpy as a centipede with tiny splinters in each of his little feet. My first thought was that he was in a bad mood because of something I had done or failed to do. I brought him a fresh-brewed cup of coffee. Wrong. I got him a glass of orange juice. He snarled. Maybe I should have brought him apple juice? He was as cross as two sticks by then. Maybe I should make a nice breakfast. I did. That wasn't right either. I asked what was the matter. He muttered and said he didn't want to talk. I shrank from confrontation. By the time he was shaved, showered, and dressed, he was truly angry and he stormed out. I had a bad hour or so of castigating myself for being insensitive, and planning what I would do to get him into a better mood and make him happy. Of course when he returned, he reeled off a set of complaints about the world at large and me in particular. And while the world wasn't the least bit ready to take the blame for his bad mood, I was. For years I responded to his displeasure and criticism with self-blame: "If only I hadn't . . ." "If only I had thought to . . ." "If only I . . ."

There's no doubt in my mind that this was a straight continuation of the mentality I'd grown up with. My sisters and I had been responsible for Mom; I was responsible for Iraj. I had felt frustrated and inadequate because I couldn't make everything right in my mother's life, so it was as natural, as automatic to me as breathing to shoulder the blame when Iraj was even a little bit unhappy. It was a long, long time before I came to see that he always blamed others for his problems, that he was a confused and angry man who vented his disappointment and rage on those closest to him. I'm keenly aware, though, that it was I who leapt into the role of scapegoat and whipping girl for Iraj. My guess is that early on in our courtship he'd picked up on this tendency in me, and without my being the least bit aware of it, he had begun to exploit it long before our marriage.

The sharing and the sympathy are what I most remember about the early days with Iraj. The ugly arguments and his violence are what I recall of our last few years together.

As I wandered through the house in the middle of the night, full of dread and fear and despair over the kidnapping, I seemed to find a terrible memory of Iraj's abuse in every room. There were the replastered kitchen walls, so smooth now under my fingertips, that he had bashed holes in. There was the door into the powder room, hanging beautifully now, that he had yanked and slammed so hard that it had listed drunkenly on its damaged hinges.

The staircase represented a strategy of terror Iraj had used in the last days of our marriage, to extract something he desperately wanted from me—money. I had watched our savings account dwindle from $70,000 to nothing. He had used the money in a very secretive fashion, saying it went to his family and to get his brothers out of Iran. And he wanted more cash. For weeks he'd insisted that I cosign papers with him at the bank to refinance the mortgage on our house so that he could free up $50,000 for his purposes. I would not do it. The house was all I had left for my children. He used his full arsenal of tactics to coerce me into signing.

First, he tried to break me with anger and surliness, harassing me for days and nights on end. I ignored him. He tried to "discipline" me by withholding household money. I humbled myself and borrowed from my friends and family. He sweet-talked me, treated me like a princess, begged for forgiveness, and promised a bright future if I would only give in and go along with the mortgage scheme. I had heard this song from him too many times before and knew he was singing off key.

When none of his strategies was successful, he resorted to the tactics of a terrorist, using sleep deprivation, surprise, and fear to try to get what he wanted, and that's where the staircase played such an important part.

On one night Iraj would wake me up just after I went to sleep; the next night he might wake me at three A.M.; the next he might get me up right before dawn. I never knew when he would strike, and the unexpected or erratic nature of this tactic was probably the worst aspect of it. By then I had moved out of the room we'd shared; he would creep to my bedside and suddenly wake me by pulling me up and shaking me. He would immediately start to rage at me, as I blinked and cringed from his touch. While I was still disoriented, he would yank me out of bed and drag me down that staircase, screaming at me all the while. His harangues could go on nonstop for as long as an hour; he demanded and begged and ordered that I agree to the refinancing. Sometimes he would throw things at me; sometimes he would shove me hard onto a chair or sofa. But the night he yanked me down the stairs, pushed me against the foyer wall, and threatened my life if I didn't sign over the house to him, was the end—for Iraj, not for me. The next morning, exhausted and bedraggled, I bundled my kids into the car, drove straight to a lawyer, and filed for divorce.

But that hadn't stopped the terror. Staking his financial claim, he refused to leave the house. He had his half, he said, and intended to stay there. The war was on—until one workday when Iraj came home early. The children were playing at a neighbor's house. I was showering in the bath off the master bedroom. When I opened the door, I saw him on my bed wearing only his shorts. He had not been in this room for weeks, and frightened, I closed and locked the bathroom door and dressed. I was trapped. My only escape, I decided, was to bolt from the room, race down the stairs, grab my car keys from the hook in the kitchen, and make a run for the front door. I tried it.

Iraj was on my heels and pounced on me as I started out of the kitchen with car keys in hand. Twisting my wrists, he pushed me into the family room. I screamed and kicked him. He threw me down on the sofa, hurled himself on top of me, and tried to secure my arms above my head. I fought him.

"I'm going to rape you," he shouted. "I have nothing to lose, bitch."

And he tried. I was blind with fear and rage and determination. I fought him with a strength I didn't even know I had. He clawed my thighs. I pounded him with my fists; the right one still held my car keys, and I knew they were hurting him so I hit harder. He pressed my shoulders down so hard that I thought he'd dislocate them. With my hands and arms and torso immobilized, I used my feet and legs to fight him and was finally able to knee him in the groin. He recoiled, giving me my chance to get away. I squirmed out from under him and fled.

•

Bruised, disheveled, trembling, I went to my sister's house, though how I drove in that condition I'll never know. My sister let out a shriek when she saw me, then helped me into her family room, where she made me lie down on the sofa. She ran to get cold cloths and some ice before she even asked what had happened. And when she found out, she was as furious as I was hurt and dazed. She helped me get calm and organized enough to telephone the police and my lawyer.

Within days a judge awarded me a protection-from-abuse order and Iraj was forced to leave the house, the house where we still lived.

Since then I had repaired the house he'd damaged so badly, erasing more than the physical signs of Iraj's abuse, and the children and I had made it a home filled with peace, happy times, and love. Now that monster had snatched my children from this home, and the ghost of his presence was haunting every room.

On my third sleepless night since the abduction, I paced, wracking my brain, determined to find a way to undo his actions and exorcise his ghost.

THREE

THE VERY NEXT DAY THE ORIGINAL OF IRAJ'S LETTER OF demands arrived—I'd insisted that Nasser send me the *original*. We needed to study it, and I wanted it for evidence. I vowed that someday I would make this criminal and his conspirators in his family pay dearly for what they had done; at the moment, though, I cared only about the children. My sisters, Mike, and I read and analyzed the letter until it was dog-eared.

It boggled the mind. Some of the letter was pure invective; large parts read like a lawyer's memo or a technical paper. He had a list of five demands, all regarding bank accounts, possessions, and money. For example, the fourth was "Deposit, every month, 25% of your monthly income, as the child support, equally to their trust accounts [sic]." Couched in terms of the children, what they were due and would be due in the future, his argument started with a statement about his paternal responsibilities.

"Sara and Cy will be living with me," the letter stated.

"You are unfit to have the custody of my children. Even your own court, considering the circumstances, would rule accordingly. However, as far as I am concerned, Sara and Cy are my children, I am their father, and I will take care of them and raise them in a healthy environment; and I do not need a judge to tell me that. . . . I do not need child support from you, as I did not and still do not need the $200,000 equity of the house that you (legally) stole from me. However, I cannot give away what was supposed to benefit my children." Shortly after this came his five demands and the "suggestion" that I go to court and get an order granting him custody of the children and vacating the alimony and child support orders. "This way," he wrote, "we would not have to stay away from the United States."

He went on, "By the way, what I am about to do may sound and is indeed extreme. However, extreme circumstances require extreme measures. You went too far. . . . My children will understand my action; it is the only option I have. What I have suggested to you, on the other hand, is the least you could do. You, with your support group and everything else, had all the answers. How could you be so sure that you are so right about everything? Well, you were wrong; you did not understand me, you did not understand your own children, you did not understand the concept of family, and you did not understand love. That is it."

He was right about only one thing: I did not understand him, did not understand how he could do such a criminal and damaging thing to his own flesh and blood. And my crime, which made me "unfit," my having gone "too far"? Daring to try to make a life for myself, daring to start a relationship with Mike. Thirteen years of my life hadn't been enough for Iraj. The divorce had not been real to him. He had intended all along to keep me in some kind of emotional bondage, if not under his physical domination. But, in his terms, I'd had the audacity to break free of his shackles, so he would punish me in the most cruel way imaginable—through the children I loved with my whole heart.

Beth had to go back to work, but Sue got a baby-sitter and stayed by my side. Mike canceled his jobs—he has his own tile contracting company—and stayed with me too. The three of us fell into a pattern on the morning of April 15 that would last throughout the ordeal. We gathered around the kitchen table to analyze everything that had happened and brainstorm about what our next move might be. We became a task force, the kitchen table our command center. We used pads of paper and pencils at first: shortly we added more high-tech equipment to our arsenal: the telephone and tape recorders.

As soon as it became obvious to us that I might be talking on the telephone with Iraj, we realized it could be helpful to have tapes of conversations with him and with any of his relatives he chose to have deliver messages. Then we could analyze the spoken word as we'd been analyzing the letter. Actually, the idea for recording conversations came from past experience with Iraj. During and after the divorce proceedings, he had made a lot of disturbingly threatening, nasty calls to the house, and my brother-in-law had given me an answering machine so I could screen calls; my lawyer too had urged me to screen incoming calls. So Mike went to Radio Shack, got the equipment we needed to do this taping, and hooked it up.

We worked like crazy, putting in eight straight hours, breaking for dinner, then setting to work again. We made lists of possible sources of help, and took notes on conversations we had with the close friends to whom we turned for ideas. We went to the library and looked up *parental abduction* in the index, then brought home every book, paper, and magazine with even the slightest reference to the subject. And we kept analyzing the letter from Iraj, as we would analyze the letters that we couldn't know then would pour in during the days and weeks ahead. We looked for his weaknesses, for a hidden agenda, for anything that might help.

When we were all talked out, we read the material from the library. There were many case histories of children abducted and hidden both in the United States and abroad. I discovered to my horror that experts estimate that fewer than twenty percent of the almost 350,000 children kidnapped each year are ever recovered. I quaked. God, oh God, I had to make sure that Sara and Cy were two of that small number of kids who *were* recovered. The dismal facts about abduction scared me to death. I searched hard for success stories; I needed them as a source of hope, as well as of information and ideas. The first I came across was that of a woman named Betty Mahmoody, who had been held prisoner in Teheran by her Iranian husband and had made a harrowing escape with her young daughter through the mountains into Turkey. Her experiences, chronicled in her best-selling book, *Not Without My Daughter*, really inspired me. Betty was high on the list I was putting together of people I wanted to contact.

The case histories of kidnapped children made me angry as hell, not only at the kidnappers but also at my government. Those case histories revealed that there was little official help to be had. This was exactly the wall I had been running into. Because of the large number of international abductions, the State Department had set up a desk within the Bureau of Consular Affairs about a year or so before to assist parents. The international law behind the State Department's efforts is the Hague Treaty, negotiated in 1980 and signed by the United States in July 1988. This treaty obligates nations that "harbor wrongfully removed or retained children" to return them to the country they lived in before the abduction. Unfortunately, only thirteen countries, including the U.S., have signed: Australia, Austria, Canada, France, Hungary, Luxembourg, Norway, Portugal, Spain, Sweden, Switzerland, and the United Kingdom. West Germany, Mexico, and Italy, the countries topping the list of those where children are taken, aren't signatories to the treaty. In my case the situation was even worse—not only were the children in a country in the Middle East, but in Iran!

The person I spoke with in the Bureau of Consular Affairs let out an audible sigh when I explained that my ex-husband was holding the children in Iran. She asked a few questions so she could fill out her forms, then told me she was sending me the State Department's booklet outlining what steps I should take. A booklet. So cool, so bureaucratic. I was too surprised and disappointed at that moment to do anything more than accept what she said and hang up. In succeeding days, however, I was constantly in touch with State.

If I hadn't done my homework, I'd have believed that State wasn't more helpful only because Sara and Cy were in Iran, and they considered my children to be in a situation that was as impossible as the hostage crisis under the Ayatollah. Unfortunately, I discovered that State's performance is just as lackluster and sluggish whether a child has been abducted to Ecuador or Egypt, or even to one of the countries that's a signatory to the Hague Treaty. Later I would get the impression from people I talked to at State that they thought if one married a foreign national and the relationship soured, one should expect just this kind of a situation!

We continued to work the phones, making contact with people and organizations from which we might get some help or leads to help. Most of the groups were headed by parents of abducted children. Child Find of America, Inc., is a New York–based group; Vanished Children's Alliance is headquartered in San Jose, California; Children's Rights of America is located in the Florida Keys. From the people in these groups we talked to and from our reading, we discovered an astonishing and depressing fact: United States law does not include parental abduction under federal *felony* statutes. If the law in our country doesn't treat this as a serious crime, how can we expect the State Department to do so, much less other countries of the world?

Most of my calls led to dead ends. I spoke with people at Amnesty International, the Family and Children's Services of Catholic Charities, and International Social Services, whose avowed purpose is to help with international family problems. I reached across national borders to speak with people at Terre des Hommes, people of the earth, an organization similar to the Red Cross that could check on the children. I got in touch with RE-UNITE, an organization in London headed by Lucy Jacy, which is a support group for women whose children have

•

been abducted. And I spoke with a Swiss journalist, Liesl Graz, who tried to get information for me from people in her embassy in Teheran.

I also got interesting counsel from two individuals. An Iranian psychologist, a woman, advised me to behave in a very cooperative fashion with Iraj, keeping every option open in every discussion. Under no circumstances, she said, should I go to Iran, because I had no rights there and might encounter personal danger. I spoke with a British recoverer of children who had worked for seven years in the Middle East and maintained all his contacts there. He was wonderfully supportive and followed up our conversation with a letter a couple of days later. First of all, he cautioned me about having anyone check on the children in Iran. "Iranians have a paranoid mistrust of everyone not Iranian. This makes even inquiries about the children by outsiders fraught." He went on to write, "Negotiation is the best thing. Progressing by other than negotiation could be a protracted business, and costly. People will require to be paid up front at every stage, and neither you nor I would have a guarantee that we were getting anywhere."

I called my congressman and senators again. They were no help.

I soon learned that most parents in my situation felt they had no option but to take the law into their own hands.

I heard and read countless stories about reabduction in the next few days. "I hate to say it," one U.S. senator was quoted as having said, "but the parents who do get their kids back are the ones who put some money together and hire a soldier of fortune to do the job. Of course you can get your head blown off doing that."

I shuddered. My God, would I have to go that route? I couldn't bear to think of putting Sara and Cy in any more danger than they were already in. Aside from the physical risks, there was the psychological damage, which might be even greater than what they'd experienced in the initial abduction. And the cost of a recovery was astronomical, ranging from $50,000 to $200,000, according to the articles I read. Where was a person supposed to get a sum like that? Still, reabduction was the course that almost everyone advocated in a situation like mine. And so just days after I'd learned Iraj had kidnapped the children, I had my first brush with the subterranean world of "operatives."

A friend arranged for me to meet Dave Christian, a local businessman and politician who had a reputation for getting things done. One of the most decorated Vietnam veterans, Dave was in touch with former military men who specialized in commando-style operations, which he advocated in situations like mine. I was wary but very impressed with this blond, blue-eyed, well-built man of action.

Dave read Iraj's letter carefully.

"This guy went ballistic when he found out that things were getting serious between you and Mike," Dave said. "See?" And he pointed to several references in Iraj's letter. "He probably thought he could get you back. I think your best bet is to convince him you've sent Mike packing. Then you come on to him. Come on like a sexpot. Use every feminine wile you've got, and then make up a few. You'll get results, you'll see."

The mere thought of "coming on" to Iraj turned my

stomach. I challenged Dave, pointing out that Iraj and I had been divorced for almost a year before Mike was seriously in the picture.

Dave argued his case, and very convincingly too, but I wasn't ready at that moment to accept it.

Before we parted that day he gave me some advice that was invaluable. He told me he'd always been successful in battle when he took the offensive; he'd never had much success when he was on the defensive.

"Remind yourself over and over that you're in battle, Jess," he said. "Be on the offensive, the person in control. Convince yourself you're going to be the winner in a situation where there is definitely going to be a winner and a loser."

I didn't forget. And I tried to act on Dave's advice every day, in every way.

I suppose that after my conversation with Dave I should have had a glimmer of understanding that it might be a very long time before I saw Sara and Cy again. But I didn't. Perhaps in these early days my blindness to the possibility of living through months of anguish and torment protected me from being overwhelmed. I couldn't begin to imagine then what I would face. Thank God. If I'd been confronted all at once with what was in store, I don't think I could have coped.

At this point I was determined to use legal means to get my children back. I am a traditional person, law-abiding, with a lot of faith in my country and the legal system. I was convinced that local, national, and international law would offer staunch support. I didn't have an inkling then that there were challenges ahead of me that I'd never even dreamed I might encounter in my lifetime. I would be forced to develop an ability to think shrewdly and make judgments about strangers quickly. To learn to act roles that were totally alien to me . . . to summon the courage to outwit the madman I'd divorced. I would be plunged into a world I had believed existed only in books and movies and the highest reaches of government, a world peopled by soldiers of fortune, former secret agents, "recoverers," and "operatives." I would learn to talk easily about surveillance, safe houses, escape routes, ruses and disguises, "the mission," and "the grab."

Me. A very ordinary woman. But, I learned, there is no end to what an ordinary woman can do when her children are in danger and suffering.

We were lucky. Dave Christian knew Betty Mahmoody— one of those small-world occurrences that shouldn't surprise me anymore but always do—and put us in touch.

Betty telephoned me, and just the sound of her voice made me feel optimistic. After she expressed sympathy and began to get into the issues of the abduction, I also felt a surge of relief. Here was a person who could really understand the situation.

Betty's strongest advice was to keep open the lines of communication, direct and indirect—no matter what. The biggest problem for a lot of parents who are trying to get their abducted children back is finding out where they are. The kidnapping parent often lives with the child or children as a fugitive and under an assumed name. If Iraj broke off contact with me and hid himself and the children at the home of a distant relative or friend in, say, Isfahan or Mashad or some other city in that hostile country, I'd never be able to locate them. He might be just as hard to track down if he fled to some other country altogether. If I didn't even know where Sara and Cy were, then what would I do?

Betty volunteered to fly to my hometown and meet with me. She couldn't schedule the trip immediately but promised to keep in touch by telephone until she could arrange to travel. Her generosity overwhelmed me, as did her ability to empathize. It was such a relief to talk to someone who knew Iran and had suffered through a situation similar to mine. One anecdote that I shared with Betty had her clucking with sympathy throughout and ending up in stitches.

Iraj had insisted on representing himself in the divorce proceedings, and my lawyer felt the court had bent over backward so as not to be accused of treating an underrepresented person unjustly. Iraj had played holy hell with the system—and they let him get away with it. My poor lawyer had to endure endless abusive phone calls from Iraj. But finally he went too far. He began to write long letters to the judges in the court. Betty understood the source of all this very well, because in Iran the Imams, the Muslim clerics, adjudicate many of these kinds of domestic matters and may be treated somewhat like father figures in the proceedings. When Iraj wrote to a judge begging him not to grant me the divorce because he wouldn't be able to bear losing my dad as his father-in-law, the court said enough! Iraj was sent a very firm, very formal letter telling him to cease and desist bothering the judges and to adhere to normal legal procedure.

Betty was very supportive, too, in backing my idea that I should play to Iraj's vanity to persuade him to bring the kids back. He'd always been egocentric, bragging unashamedly about his intelligence and accomplishments. And he was always right; I'd always been wrong or "inferior" during our marriage. His expertise extended to every area—why, he even knew the correct way to nurse a baby and I didn't! It was essential that I continually get myself into a frame of mind that enabled me to agree with his absurd positions and stay calm. I couldn't afford to antagonize him now under any circumstances.

We went to see a former psychology professor of mine, Dr. Henry Kranshawe. He knew Iraj fairly well from a number of encounters with him while we were married, and he was willing to put together a psychological profile based on his general knowledge, the letter of demands, and discussion with us. Dr. K felt that underneath the boasting, puffed-up person was a fragile man who had cracked when he'd learned that Mike was in my life in a serious way. It had brought home to him that he really had been rejected, divorced, and no longer had power over me. And he was sexually jealous, violently so. Certainly that incident in February when he'd flown off the handle and pounded on the car supported this. But how masterful he'd been at covering up his real feelings and faking an acceptance of our changed relationship.

"There's a maxim that's been kicking around a few hundred years that seems to me to apply here," Dr. K said. "'Jealousy is always born together with love, but it does not always die when love dies.' So Iraj may not love you, but he's jealous of you.

"One way to reach him, I think, is to claim you've renounced Mike. Or that Mike has renounced you."

He went on to explain that he believed Iraj was locked in an Oedipal struggle, trying to win his mother from his passive father, whom he hated. Therefore, he was compelled to behave aggressively with me rather than to act in any way that might remind him of Nadir, who had won out over him with his mother.

The matter of Iraj's father reminded us of mine, and how much Iraj liked and respected him—idolized him really. Working my father into the equation had possibilities, we agreed, but we would have to explore those later. Dr. K left us with the idea that it was vital for me to appear utterly contrite and conciliatory in my dealings with Iraj—in other words, to give him all the support Homa did without any of the nagging, complaints, or criticisms about his inadequacies. Fine with me. If being Iraj's good mother would help to disarm him psychologically so that I could get the kids out of his hands, then "good mother" I would be!

We had developed some key elements of our strategy. That night Rob, Sue and her husband, Beth, Mike, and a couple of friends came over to help hash out and refine it. My brother and sisters and I had talked privately and decided it was best not to let our parents know about the kidnapping yet. My father would be distraught, and God only knew how my mother might react. We just couldn't deal with them at the moment.

We reviewed our position. Iraj was demanding money, and that it be coughed up fast. He believed his actions were totally justified and wanted me to say that I had been the guilty party in the divorce—he wanted his pound of my flesh. He wanted to be acclaimed the victor by me and see me apologetic and humble before him. In short, he wanted to have unambiguous power over me. Okay. But, all of us wondered, even if he had every one of his demands and desires were met, how could we get him to turn over the kids? It was clear the money wasn't a quid pro quo for their return, so how could we engineer things so that we got them back?

Rob made the point that Iraj was a materialist, quite accustomed to all that the West had to offer, so he'd be smarting soon, if he wasn't already, at the deprivations he'd have to endure in his homeland. Rob's guess was that Iraj never intended to return permanently to Iran and bring up the children there; he was only using the country, hostile and off limits to Americans, to get what he wanted from me. Iraj might believe that he'd be back in the States very soon, ensconced in our house or a similar one, back at a good job with AT&T or another such company and happy as a clam.

That was pretty much what the rest of us had been thinking, but leave it to Rob to articulate it so well. It made especially good sense, too, because of Iraj's very consistent, long-term position that he really hated his country. Everyone in the room had heard him over the years denounce again and again the "backwardness" of many of the people and most of the institutions there; the repressive nature of the religion and the culture; the stifling and depressing lack of opportunity for a technological wizard like himself. A large and comfortable house, silver Audi, well-paying job, singles bars and the nightlife of Chicago, if not suburban Philadelphia, were what Iraj Salimi wanted in his everyday life.

He was a man who liked luxury.

He thought his ace in the hole was Iran; we were very sure it was ours.

Our strategy then had to be to convince him he was going to get the huge amount of money he demanded, and to persuade him Mike was long gone from my life and that I realized the error of my ways. Naturally, I desperately wanted him back as my husband. A great deal would have to be played by ear, but basically this was the way to go.

There were lots of obvious pitfalls, and one that couldn't be minimized was the constant need for me to control my emotions, hiding them and acting a part that was totally different from the way I really felt.

I thought of how I'd blown up on the phone that very day while talking to one of Iraj's old friends who had just moved to Washington, D.C. This man claimed to be shocked and appalled by the abduction and had spoken with Iraj in Tabriz. Trying to remain neutral about the issues between me and Iraj, he'd repeated in an almost hushed voice what he'd been told. The justifications Iraj was using made me livid, and I exploded. I called Iraj a criminal, nothing more than a low criminal who hadn't a shred of genuine concern for his children. That was just for starters. Well, now I knew I couldn't do a thing like that again. That man might very well have called Iraj back and told him how outraged I was. With anyone connected to Iraj in any way, I had to play my role, be sweet and conciliatory, watch every word I said so that I'd be convincing. I couldn't be accusatory or angry or show any negative emotion. This was going to be tough. It's hard to deny real emotion. Beyond that, I am straightforward almost to a fault. I would have to weigh and analyze every single syllable I uttered to Iraj, to any member of his family and to his friends. With tears in my eyes I vowed to do it, no matter the cost to my sense of honesty and integrity. But there was a greater challenge still.

I was going to have to say that Mike was out of the

picture and that I was glad. This caused me a great deal of anguish. I love Mike, cherish him. I did not even want to mention his name to Iraj, much less pretend he was something he was not. We started to work on a tall tale about Mike, and everyone was endlessly supportive in helping me get over my repugnance so I could do what I had to do. While discussing this, it became perfectly clear that I'd need help in these conversations with Iraj. He might be a braggart, but that didn't mean he wasn't very smart. He certainly was, and he was cunning, shrewd, as well. I would have to be constantly alert to how devious he was—and become more devious myself.

Someone suggested that we write out some scripts for arguments and pleas I could make to Iraj, with big notes at the top reminding me to be sweet, conciliatory, humble, apologetic, and complimentary.

There was so much to do, so many changes to bring about in myself. Still, I felt a great sense of accomplishment when the evening ended.

That night all of us got some much needed rest, but the following morning we were all working like demons on the scripts. My speeches weren't difficult to plan, though we did have to be very careful that there weren't any false notes in them. Anticipating what Iraj might throw at me was the hard part and took the most time. Sue helped me rehearse my lines, and Mike came in at the end to give us a fresh opinion on how well I was doing. At last I felt prepared. And for the first time in my life, I was looking forward to getting on the telephone and telling lie after lie.

Biting my lip, stomach queasy, I still felt as though my mind was clearer than it had been since the abduction; I got Iraj on the phone and launched the performance of my life. It was April 18. I was full of adrenaline, psyched to play my role. I tried to sound depressed and contrite as I told Iraj that Mike hadn't been willing to cope with this situation, that he'd called it a mess, said he didn't want to get mixed up in it, and had walked out on me. Beth gave my hand an encouraging squeeze and from the expression on Sue's face and Mike's thumbs-up, I knew I was succeeding in my debut as an actress.

Even though Iraj claimed that he didn't believe me, he demanded details.

My heart started to hammer. I took a deep breath. I condemned Mike, said he had disappointed me deeply, but that it wasn't a total surprise, as I'd been questioning the relationship for some time.

"Why," he asked, "didn't you dump that guy before he had a chance to dump you?" He sounded pretty damned outraged.

Wonderful! Iraj was a genius at turning things upside down. The very idea that his ex-wife was the one who'd been dumped instead of the one doing the dumping wounded Iraj's vanity, and, of course, gave him the opportunity to blame me for being an "unworthy fool." "How dare you," he screamed "let that dumb, lowlife Lumber Guy do such a thing?"

Iraj was scornful of anyone who worked with his hands; on one visit with the children he had caught a glimpse of Mike wearing a Black Watch plaid wool shirt. For both these reasons he had dubbed him "the Lumber Guy" some months before. I shouldn't have been surprised at Iraj's response, but I was. After just a beat, I said, "Oh, Iraj, I'm so sorry. I know I was a fool." I heard him grunt and knew I'd put the right amount of humility into my voice and words. Still, I knew I couldn't let down my guard. I went on with my fabrications about the situation with Mike.

Iraj either lost interest or was satisfied, soon interrupting to outline again what I must do. He emphasized that I must get the cash together for him, and quickly. Now, however, he was calling the money "rightfully mine." Before he'd been saying "it rightfully belongs to the children." The truth on that matter was out!

I stalled by telling him I was doing the paperwork to get the court orders rescinded, going into a song and dance about how complicated it was, with all the red tape, the legal formalities. He became furious, screaming that he wanted the money the next day.

I gulped, genuinely almost in tears at this point, and told him I would have great difficulty getting together the large sum he wanted.

"Get it from your rich family!" he jeered.

I burned. Iraj knew very well that my family wasn't rich. My father and brother and sisters are hardworking people, and everyone in the family is proud of them. They are well-off, but not rich by any means. Of course, I couldn't argue with Iraj, so I meekly repeated that I would do everything humanly possible to get the $200,000 as soon as I could.

This first foray into acting was difficult enough, but what came next was no act, and it almost broke me—an exchange with my tearful children, with Iraj warning me before he put them on that he would never let me speak to them again if I told them I loved them. The rotten bastard. He let each child say only a few words, then took the receiver back. Why in God's name he decided to lash out at me then, I'll never know. I can only guess that it was because the children were so sad to be separated from me and yearning so much to be back home. They'd said how much they missed their friends and toys and games and their cat, Benjamin Franklin, whom they sometimes called Benji. They had been crying while telling me they missed me and wanted to come home. Cy had said flatly, "I don't like it here! Come get me, Mom, and bring Benji with you."

My heart was breaking, and I took Iraj's angry words on the chin. But my stomach felt as if it was on a fast, downward elevator ride. Irrational, bitter, cruel man— and my children and I were at his mercy. At last he paused in his tirade. I swallowed my anger and begged him to let me speak to the children the next day. He arrogantly said that he might answer the phone if it rang. Then abruptly, he hung up.

I collapsed. I didn't feel I'd made much progress with him, if any, and I was berating myself for not being more clever, but Sue and Mike thought I'd done a great job.

"Hey," Mike said, "go easy on yourself. You've never had to do anything like this before."

"Jess," Sue added, "you were wonderful."

No, *they* were wonderful. What would I have done if I hadn't had such love and support?

FOUR

IF I'D FEARED THAT I'D FAILED TO MAKE PROGRESS IN MY conversation with Iraj on April 18, on the following day I was sure of it. He did decide to answer the phone, but he was more curt and nasty than ever. He wouldn't discuss any of the items on my agenda. He said that if I wanted to see the children again I would have to come to Iran. I began to plead for him to understand that what he was suggesting just wasn't possible. How could I go to Iran when the State Department had a ban on travel and I couldn't get a visa?

He sneered. "State Department? State Department? You don't need the State Department. You can get here if you want to. Don't be stupid. These laws mean nothing."

Utterly frustrating. He refused to deal with real issues of any kind—and, yes, laws meant nothing to him. Not Iranian laws or U.S. laws. But why should I think they would? He'd scoffed at and broken laws in the past. And he was a kidnapper.

"Iraj, please be reasonable," I said. "I would be stopped

at the airport. I wouldn't even be able to get into the country without papers."

"Don't be an idiot," he shouted. "All can be arranged, and you know it." Suddenly he changed gears. "What about the money? Why hasn't the Bank Melli account been set up?"

He sounded different, more frantic. Was he simply impatient because his wishes hadn't been satisfied as quickly as he'd expected? Or was it something else? Just how desperate was he for that $200,000? Before I could probe, he ended the day's conversation—with a bomb.

"Make up your mind! Do everything I said in my letter or else. I am taking the kids on a trip, Jess."

"Where?"

No answer.

"How long will you be away, Iraj?"

No answer.

"Please," I said, "tell me where you're going and how I can reach you."

"You won't be able to phone for a while."

Moving the children from the farm? I panicked. This could be the beginning of a new strategy on his part— and it could be the beginning of what all of us most feared. It was possible he'd decided it had been a mistake to have his brother tell me where he was so that I could communicate by phone. Did he intend to move to another location and break off telephone contact until I let Jamshid or someone else know I was ready with the money? I was scared, and I anxiously pressed for more details about his trip, specifically where they were going and when they'd be back.

"That is none of your goddamned business," he finally shrieked. "I go where I want to go, do what I want to do.

And I take the children when and where I like. Understand?"

"But will you be back at the farm with them soon?"

"Shut up, bitch. Didn't you understand what I told you? I said that was none of your business." Iraj was interested only in giving me an ultimatum: "Get the paperwork done for the transfer of the money. Do you hear me? Obey me on this," he said. "Get that paperwork done and be ready to bring the money to Iran."

"Please, Iraj, we've already talked about the visa problem, but besides all that, you know I can't bring huge amounts of cash across borders. It isn't legal."

Iraj's response was to slam down the phone.

Sue, Mike, and I tried to figure out what was going on with Iraj. His need for the money seemed to be overshadowing even his need for emotional revenge. I transcribed the tape of this conversation and we went over the pages again and again. He had sounded desperate about getting the money, and his words in black ink on cold white paper made the impression a reality. Iraj was crazed to get his hands on a large sum. But why? We knew things were bad in Iran. Engineers waited in lines to drive cabs. Rice, the staple food of the country, was selling for ten dollars a pound. People were using raisins to sweeten their tea instead of lumps of sugar, which was priced astronomically due to shortages. Most items from the West had disappeared from shelves.

Eleven years after the shah had been forced out, the country was still in chaos, the economy in ruins. This was mostly because of the disastrous war with Iraq, in which the two ancient enemies squared off for a fight that killed millions and cost billions. The Khomeini regime had been successful in ending foreign domination and eradicating Western secularism, but it was nearly impossible to make fundamentalist Islamic doctrine work in everyday matters, especially when it came to the economy. Things were so bad that in 1987 Khomeini had made a move that was dramatic and must have been very difficult for him: he had given the government the power to overrule Islamic law in secular matters when they felt it was necessary.

And what were Iraj's prospects? Probably pretty poor. He hadn't finished the work in Iran that he'd been expected to do in order to pay off his scholarship aid; perhaps he couldn't work because of that. If the revolutionary government had kept up with the records from the shah's regime and it was known he'd reneged on his agreement, Iraj might even be considered a traitor and be in terrible trouble. The country was full of corrupt officials, and he might need money for bribes.

Looking back at the U.S., Iraj's situation was equally bad. He'd burned his bridges to America, leaving behind a good job with AT&T, a house, his car. Perhaps he was bent on total self-destruction. But would he destroy the children as well?

I fantasized a lot when I was confronted with questions like these. I knew it was ridiculous, but it comforted me to imagine myself flying into Iran, making my way to Tabriz, snatching the children out of the farmhouse, and getting the three of us back to the U.S. safe and sound. If only that were possible. If only . . .

I decided to try the idea out on a couple of people. Mike and Sue thought it was unreasonable but played out a few scenarios with me, until I could see that it was absurd to suppose I could reabduct the children. Ah, but could I get them out legally? What if I went to Iran armed with all my papers from our courts and fought for custody. Ridiculous. Not even worth wasting time or breath on. I wouldn't get a hearing, much less a fair one, in a Muslim country that didn't belong to the Hague Convention, didn't recognize the rights of women, and had such antipathy toward anyone, male or female, from the United States.

I wanted to use traditional means to tackle and solve this problem. I didn't want to get involved with "recovery specialists," the inhabitants of that subterranean world with which I'd had a brief encounter, and I didn't want to waste time daydreaming about becoming some kind of superwoman and rescuing the kids. I wanted my State Department to help me fight this battle; I wanted the FBI and Interpol on the case. Yet not one of the people I talked to at those agencies offered even the slightest assistance, except for an officer at State who said he would request that a Swiss diplomat check on the children in Tabriz and give me a report on their health and living conditions.

I knew about this "Swiss check" from Betty Mahmoody and Liesl Graz. First of all, the diplomat wasn't representing one of his own countrymen and didn't have much of a vested interest in the duty. A perfunctory call would be made by a Swiss representative; he would interview the children, but with Iraj and others of the Salimi family present, the kids would be cowed. Then he would report back that everything seemed okay. What good could that possibly do? None, as far as I could see. And it had an extremely destructive side: it would alert Iraj that I was contacting government officials about his abduction of the children. I didn't have to use much imagination to envision his response to that!

RESCUED

I couldn't believe that my own government wouldn't help. Perhaps it was me, my approach to those officials, my failure to explain the situation adequately. Rob, our legal beagle, tried . . . with no success. We made inquiries through our congressman and an influential family friend. Nothing. We had found the names of a couple of people whose children had been abducted to the Middle East. I got their telephone numbers and called.

I was able to reach Holly Planels, who had set up a group called American Children Held Hostage after her son had been kidnapped by his father. Holly's son had been in Jordan, his father's homeland, for many years. She had spent untold amounts of time and money trying to regain custody, even getting the support of the American ambassador in Jordan and persuading him to accompany her into the home in Amman where the boy was being held. The ambassador had given her a great deal of moral support but hadn't been able to help her any more than an ordinary citizen could have. Holly had exhausted every conceivable legal method for getting authorities in Jordan to honor her court-awarded custody. Her experiences with the State Department had been frustrating, and futile. I would talk to Holly and her mother, who also worked for American Children Held Hostage, quite a few times over the next few weeks.

My conversations with Holly and the cases I read almost confirmed that there was little if any official help to be had, and certainly none would be forthcoming from the Department of State.

Why wouldn't these agencies help? A judge had given me custody of my children. My ex-husband had broken the law. He was a criminal, pure and simple—and a particularly loathsome criminal, because he'd violated a trust that goes beyond the courts: the trust in their parents that all children have a right to. Angry at me for rejecting him, bitter because I'd "replaced" him with Mike, he'd used his own son and daughter for revenge, knowing that was how to drive a knife into my heart. Nothing—not a violent attack on me, not the destruction of all my possessions—could hurt me except this abduction of the children.

He didn't give a damn about Sara and Cy's welfare. If he had loved them at all, even a little bit, he wouldn't have snatched them from their home and taken them to a dismal and alien place. What were they but hostages to his absurd pride and remorseless desire to see me suffer? What were they but victims of his criminal effort to get hundreds of thousands of dollars out of me and my family? I wanted to see him in hell for all this. But more, I wanted—no, I felt I *deserved* official support. As an American citizen I was entitled to advice from my State Department about how to use diplomatic means and international law to help me recover my children. I got nothing, not even polite treatment.

Many people have tried to explain the State Department's position to me: State can't get involved in these kinds of problems, which are personal in origin. Not true. They're *legal* in origin. State can't do anything in a situation where the U.S. has broken off diplomatic relations. Perhaps not, but they *can* try to do something through the channels available to the country representing U.S. interests, such as Switzerland in the case of Iran. One person who thought it was particularly unreasonable of me to want the support of my government through the State Department asked, "What do you want them to do, Jess? Send in the marines to get Sara

and Cy? Start World War Three over your children?"
That was infuriating. While I certainly didn't expect our
government to go to war to solve my problem, I did
expect counsel and support. I began to wonder what the
hell my tax dollars designated for the Department of
State were really getting me.

The major difficulty with parental abductions is that
they're viewed as "domestic relations problems," an area
that the local, national, and international law enforcement people want to have nothing to do with. Just as
local police want nothing to do with stalkings or threats
of beatings or murder by ex-spouses, the FBI and
Interpol and other international law enforcement people want nothing to do with parental kidnappings. This
reluctance has led to much tragedy for Americans. It
simply isn't right, in my opinion, to view these or outright violations of law as "mere domestic squabbles,"
which, believe it or not, was what one official called
them in front of me.

Frustrated, I went over all this when Rob and
Beth joined us that evening. Our discussion led us back
to the beginning. Our only option seemed to be to go on
with the attempt to turn Iraj around and persuade him to
bring the children back. My heart was sinking. This
seemed to be an impossible goal, now that Iraj was being
so vicious and tyrannical. But then someone, I can't
remember which one of us, asked a brilliant question
that led us in a new direction.

What if I could coax Iraj into bringing Sara and Cy
out of Iran and into a neutral third country for the visit
with them he had promised? No matter what Iraj had
said, it was virtually impossible for me to get into Iran.
Face to face with him and with the children at my side, I

thought I just might be able to persuade him to turn them over to me.

The more we talked about this, the better I felt. I felt fairly confident that if I could look straight into Iraj's eyes, with the children in my arms, I could persuade him to let them come home with me—or, more probably, bribe him with all that money he wanted. I was exhilarated. Get them all into a third country, any country. That was it!

But something else became perfectly clear that night. It might take quite a while to get the children back, and in any case, short or long, it was going to be terribly expensive. With no help from the State Department or law enforcement agencies, I'd have to spend a lot of money. Why, just the cost of the telephone calls to Iran was sky high. What was I going to do?

After a long, anxious time, I forced myself to face facts. I'd have to borrow money. A great deal of money. My brother had offered to help me financially, but I'd also have to turn to my father. He always had been generosity itself with all his children, but I did not want to ask him for money. I had to bite the bullet. I had to tell my parents that their grandchildren had been kidnapped and were being held by their father in Iran. And I had to ask my dad to loan me money, when there was no guarantee that even a fortune would do the trick and bring the children back.

We went over to see my parents. They were unexpectedly wonderful. My mother didn't fall apart; my father didn't get all outraged and furious. They both said they'd do anything to help, and before I asked, my father offered to loan me all the money I would need.

RESCUED

In a real dark night of the soul
it is always three o'clock in the morning.
—F. Scott Fitzgerald, *The Crack-up*

My children were going through a terrible experience. Was the water and food making them sick? Were they lonely and frightened? Where had their father taken them? And, oh God, could they be living in terror of him?

I remembered times during our marriage when Iraj had flown into rages that had terrified me, a grown woman in my own country with family nearby and police I could call and neighbors who would help. I trembled for Sara and Cy. All alone, they might be going through one of those episodes at that very moment, one as scary as the horrible one that took place in the waning days of my marriage.

It was near Christmas in 1984. Tension had been so thick that it should have been visible, and Iraj's temper had gone past all the bounds of his control and my endurance. His parents had come from Iran for a visit of a few weeks—and had stayed three months. The strain their presence placed on the household was enormous. But the pressure had started to build before their arrival. They didn't come directly to America; traveling with Jamshid, his wife, and their daughters, they had flown to Zurich, Switzerland, and applied for visas at the American embassy. Homa and Nadir got theirs immediately, but visas for the others were denied. Iraj asked my father and me to intervene, which we did, but the consular official there flatly refused to grant the visas. The official minced no words with me: he felt sure that

Jamshid and his family intended to stay in the U.S., illegally, if necessary, once they got in. This made Iraj blow up, of course, and he vehemently denied it, accusing the officer of being vindictive because of the hostage crisis. Almost two years later Iraj confessed that he had lied to me: in fact the consular official had correctly surmised the intentions of the Salimis. Had Jamshid and his family entered the country then, they would not have left.

Homa was by turns brooding and distraught over this turn of events, miserable about the fate of her youngest, Nasser. Prodded by his mother, Iraj too was terribly upset, and soon he became obsessed with getting Nasser out of Iran. I was very sympathetic. In the bloody war with Iraq, thousands of young men were being killed and maimed each day. Iraq seemed to have the most weapons—tanks, missiles, aircraft, and poison gas—and Iran relied on manpower. That meant young men were marching into deadly fire, being slaughtered in an attempt to gain mere tactical advantage. It was a hideous war, and I was all for getting Iraj's brothers out of Iran so they might avoid military service. There was a great sense of urgency, because we had heard that Iran, having been driven back after invading Iraq, was about to launch a "final offensive."

For me the stress grew daily. Completely dependent on the rest of us because of language and cultural barriers, Homa and Nadir stayed inside the house almost all the time. They and Iraj insisted on turning our American home into an Iranian one, complete with their traditional foods, schedules, routines. My mother-in-law's attitude toward me had changed dramatically. She was hostile, suspicious, condemnatory. I don't know if this was because of what Iraj had been communicating about his life with me or if she simply was behaving more like the traditional Iranian mother-in-law. I had noticed in my visits to Tabriz that when a son married, his mother's status seemed to be elevated in relation to her daughter-in-law. She became the judge of the younger woman's performance, the arbiter of rules, norms. Whatever the cause for the way Homa was acting, it was really trying. The tone for her entire stay had been set on her very first afternoon in my home, when she smacked me on the chest and declared in her guttural Turkish-laced Farsi that I couldn't nurse her grandson properly because my breasts were too small!

Iraj began to neglect his job. Soon he was spending hour upon hour, day after day, sitting on the sofa, surrounded by stacks of legal, immigration, and other papers. His mood grew darker and angrier. Everything got on his nerves—except his mother, to whom he actually cooed rather than spoke. She followed him around the house as if she were a servant awaiting an order. It was all very strange, impossible for me to understand. Iraj's irritation with his father and me and the children was constant. "How dare that baby cry?" he actually yelled one evening. "How dare anyone in this household laugh or play?" "How dare you turn on that television?" "Can't you keep your children under control, Jess?" He was tyrannical in enforcing his proclamation that a solemn atmosphere was to prevail until his brother was free.

Nasser was in a dank Iranian prison for no reason at all, Iraj told me and anyone else who would listen. The government, he said, was so fanatical that it rounded up teenagers willy-nilly. I would learn that this was a bald lie. Nasser was guilty of political crimes against his government and common crimes against his own people as a member of the Mujahedin, the left-wing organization related to the Marxist Fedayeen-e-Khalq movement. Like many groups of this kind, it attracted some people who weren't the least bit interested in its true purposes. Nasser was, I eventually discovered, one of those who had seen membership in the Mujahedin as an opportunity to act like a thug and get away with it. He primarily did courier duty in his political role for the Mujahedin; personally, he used the association as cover and support for his hooliganism.

Truth was of little consequence to Iraj, however. His determination to get Nasser out was the most important thing—after his own mood. He demanded we "honor" him and his jailed brother by behaving as if we were mourning. Only after Nasser was free could any of us enjoy life again. I was forbidden to talk for more than a minute or two on the phone; there was hell to pay if I danced and sang and played with the children in front of him. I took care of the children as usual when he was at work, and I frequently took them out when he got home so they wouldn't be oppressed.

Iraj lectured me at least twice a day about my faults, often after reports from his mother on my daily activities. He gave me ever increasing lists of calls to make and letters to write in his name on Nasser's behalf. With a stupendous amount of housework to do, I was his maid as well as his secretary. Homa wouldn't have anything to do with helping out in the house. She did spend time with the children, in particular Cy, an infant then. In Persian fashion she would sit on the floor, rest the baby on her extended leg, and jiggle him and chatter to him as she knit. She knit constantly, making sweaters for all of us; I believe she finished twelve or fourteen sweaters while she was with us.

The only other thing Homa liked to do for herself was prepare henna for her hair. She'd brought with her everything she needed: mortar and pestle, pouches of dried henna leaves and powered dye, and some metallic substance. She would pound and grind, grind and pound these ingredients, then add water to make a greenish-looking paste, which she slathered on her hair to give it deep reddish-orange streaks. The Persians have been fond of hennaed hair for centuries; there are references to it in tablets from the period of Cyrus the Great.

Preparing the special dishes Homa demanded—and refused to make for herself—was a job in itself. She wouldn't set foot in the kitchen. Among many physical complaints, she claimed she had a "bad stomach" that could be controlled only if she ate rice and sweet potatoes at every meal. After three months of cooking them, I never wanted to see another grain of rice or slice of sweet potato again as long as I lived.

But here again Iraj doted on her. When he went to the office, he would call several times a day to check on Homa's stomach pains. He took her to several specialists, who never found anything to treat; he insisted I nurse her as if she were an invalid.

In those trying days, the only thing I loved and enjoyed was being a mother to Sara and Cy, who were healthy and bright. They were all I was living for.

Why didn't I just leave? Dress the children in their snowsuits, put them in the car, and drive to one of my sisters' homes. Lots of reasons—shame and guilt at the base of every one of them. I was drenched with shame that I was under the thumb of Iraj, that I no longer had much courage or strength to act against him. I died a thousand deaths at the thought of my family's learning how bad life was for me every day. I just couldn't face them. And I felt guilty. I *did* care what happened to Nasser, and to all the young men in Iran whom the Ayatollah used as human mine sweepers at the front of his army or cannon fodder at the rear. I felt guilty that I couldn't deal with Iraj in this situation, and that I was growing cold to the plight of Nasser. Shame and guilt were keeping me as much a prisoner as the revolutionary forces were keeping Nasser a prisoner.

Iraj was behaving in ways that grew more and more bizarre. He was so obsessed with Nasser's release that I thought he might be having some kind of breakdown. But he'd always been odd about his youngest brother, attributing his own characteristics to Nasser, whom he seemed to see as his clone. He adored him. And Iraj was aggrandizing himself. He was at the center of a piece of high drama and relishing every minute of it. He smoked and drank Scotch incessantly—after his mother and father had gone to bed, of course.

Tiptoeing around, I nonetheless persisted in preparing for the holidays and having some fun with Sara. Iraj had enjoyed our Christmas celebrations in the past; they weren't offensive to him, he said, because he was an atheist. So it wasn't a religious or cultural problem for him that I was going ahead with Christmas, it was that I was violating his edict of solemnity. We decorated while Iraj was at the office, even his father taking pleasure in joining Sara and me or watching baby Cy while we worked. Iraj would sneer at a garland or wreath when he got home, and I cringed, afraid he might explode. Quietly, though, I forged ahead.

One snowy afternoon, Sara and I spent a couple of hours collecting evergreen boughs and pine cones in the woods around our house. My father-in-law gaily joined us at the dining room table to glue and wire and glitter our finds into decorations.

When Iraj stormed into the house, he passed us without speaking and went directly into the kitchen. Not seeing any food on the stove, he started to rage at me for being the worst kind of wife, a frivolous woman who was wasting her time when she should have been cooking his dinner. He threw pots and pans onto the floor. He slammed the refrigerator and freezer doors with such force that the dining room wall shuddered. He slammed the refrigerator doors again—and again, the doors and inside compartments creaking and cracking, plastic and hinges and glass bottles breaking. He turned over the central work island. I can't imagine how he could have done it; the piece was huge, heavy, and braced into the flooring. Only wild fury could have given him such strength. Then he began to kick and strike the walls. We could hear wood splintering, plaster crunching.

He tore into the dining room, a madman, snatched up all the decorations he could carry, and took them to the front door, where he heaved them out into the snow. My daughter and I cowered, and Iraj's father looked horrified and frightened. I grabbed Sara's hand and we ran through the living room. Iraj caught me and pushed me down on the sofa, telling me I would be thrown out in the snow next if I didn't get into the bedroom that minute and stay there. The fiery look in his eyes and the ferocity of the set of his mouth convinced me that he was capable of murdering me. I fled upstairs with Sara.

Witness to her father's abuse of me and also an object of it herself, Sara was crying.

"Daddy's so mean, so mean to you," she sobbed. "But I won't let him hurt you, Mommy."

My humiliation was complete. But I swore that very soon I would get out of that house and out of that marriage with my children, neither of whom would ever again think they had to parent me. And suddenly I had an awful insight, connecting my past to my present. My mother had made her children into her allies against our father; I was putting Sara in the same position I'd been in as a child. The only difference was that I had come to learn that my father wasn't the villain, my mother's illness was. But however it compared to my past, the present situation had changed. Iraj wasn't confining his abuse to me any longer; he was including the children. I might not be able to stand up for myself, but I could and would stand up for them. I determined then and there that my kids were not going to grow up in such an environment. This insanity had to come to an end.

And it had come to an end—until Iraj abducted the children. What if Sara and Cy were the victims of their father's insane temper right at that moment, far away in Iran with no one to turn to?

Several days passed, days full of an anxiety that grew out of not knowing where the children were and not being able to contact them or Iraj by phone. It was almost unbearable. I couldn't keep down a bite of food, and I couldn't sleep. My hands began to tremble all the time. And so when Iraj answered the telephone on April 23 I almost cried with relief. But he was so hostile it took my breath away. He wanted to know where the completed paperwork for rescinding the court orders was and why the $200,000 wasn't yet deposited in an account in Bank Melli. I should have sent all this documentation to Canada; it shoud have been in Jamshid's hands days before.

Jamshid? In Canada? He hadn't mentioned using his brother as a contact. I pointed it out, stalling, but he wouldn't buy that or any other explanation from me. He said he wouldn't speak to me again until he heard from Jamshid that everything had been done to his satisfaction. I humbled myself, I promised to move faster. I begged to speak to Sara and Cy.

He wouldn't put the kids on the phone, claiming that I upset them too much. Then he contradicted himself by saying he didn't care if they were upset or unhappy any more than he cared about stomach problems or anything else.

Alarms sounded in my head. Stomach problems? The children must be sick.

I confronted him on the issue. He refused to discuss it at first, then admitted that they were having problems adjusting to the food and water and had been nauseated and had diarrhea. He immediately changed the subject, making a new demand. He insisted that I would have to hand deliver the $200,000 in cash to him in Iran.

Hand deliver? Impossible. But there was no reasoning with him; he wouldn't let me finish a sentence, interrupting to accuse me of "doing something with the law about my bringing Sara and Cy here." He asked if I'd gotten an international arrest warrant out on him for kidnapping.

I was so astonished I could hardly breathe. The very day I learned about the kidnapping I had called the lawyer who'd handled our divorce. He was helping me explore every legal means of getting the children back.

Under his direction I'd filed a number of reports and complaints, as well as swearing out national and international forms that would lead to issuance of arrest warrants when the time was right. One reason that warrants weren't already out was that we were afraid of what Iraj would do if he somehow discovered that I'd taken such action. Now here he was suspecting just that! Of course, I vehemently denied that I even knew anything about warrants.

"Can I talk to the kids? Hear their voices?"

"No," he said. "You have to do certain things before you can talk to the kids."

"When can I talk with them?" Silence. "Send my love and kisses to them." Silence. "Did you take the kids to a doctor for their vaccinations?"

"I don't care if they're sick. Hear this. I made this decision and am happy with it. I don't care what psychologists say. There are many foreigners here. I would have rather lived in the U.S., but I don't care. The decision is how I made it."

"Let's talk about things, talk tomorrow," I said in a pleading tone. "I don't feel Iran is a good place for our family to live. Political conditions worry me. Freedom is not accepted."

"Don't command me to do things," Iraj shouted. "You do what I said with the dollars."

"We can come up with a solution."

"I'm not negotiating anything, and I am not blackmailing you."

"Can I see the kids?"

"Here. After you do what I said."

"Iraj, can I talk to them?"

"They're going to get upset this way or that way. They have plenty here. I want the money."

I could only think what a greedy jerk he was. But I said nothing. Then he started again, seeming to get angrier with every word. He began to call me names—"worthless whore," "bitch."

Picturing Sara and Cy's faces to keep myself under control, I said softly, "And I had so much hoped we could talk, get together somewhere and really try to understand each other, try to work things out."

That surprised him. I could hear it in his voice as he wound up the conversation, saying, less fiercely, "Once I have the cold hard cash in my hands, Jess, we can talk about the future." He hung up.

Was I getting anywhere with this man? That was the big question Sue, Mike, and I tried to answer over the next couple of days. We listened to the tape of the phone call, analyzing every word, every nuance. Iraj sounded to us like a man who was cornered. We decided he might be in some kind of trouble, because he seemed to have a lot more worries than having to take care of sick children. What could his problem be? He'd particularly emphasized the business about my showing up soon in Iran with $200,000 cash in hand. All right, he needed money; we'd come to that conclusion before. What else could it mean?

Sue and Mike became convinced that Iraj wanted to kidnap me. They thought he'd like to have me in Iran as his wife and the mother of his children in order to impress his family and friends. He probably felt, they reasoned, that I'd humiliated him, and having me back would restore his self-image. I agreed that he'd probably love to have me in a subservient position for all to see, but I thought that if he wanted to keep me in Iran it was to have me be maid, nurse, nanny, and housekeeper—in short, a slave. Finally, we decided the best course was for me to continue to try to convince him I wanted to see if we could get back together, making sure I didn't miss any chance to find out more about what kind of trouble Iraj might have gotten into.

For the first time I started to doubt my ability to manipulate the manipulator. As the fear of failure crept through me, I began to wonder if we weren't on the wrong course altogether. Maybe persuasion would never work, no matter how cool and crafty I became. Maybe the only answer was the one I hadn't even wanted to think about—hiring experts in covert work, men and women capable of using physical force if necessary to take the children from their father and bring them home.

Holly Planels had anticipated this, and she followed up a phone call during which I talked extensively with her mother by sending me an encouraging note and a short list of professional child recovery specialists. One of the names on her list was Patrick Buckman.

I'm not a mystical person. I don't believe in Fate or crystals or any of that. But I have to say that when I saw that name, I got goose bumps. We had just bought a copy of the April issue of the magazine *Parenting*, because its cover story was an article entitled "Parents Who Kidnap Their Own Children." When I found that the article described the successful recoveries of abducted children by Patrick Buckman, I knew some kind of fate was operating. I had to get in touch with him.

Patrick made an unforgettable first impression on me. Warm, experienced, he exuded confidence in himself and his abilities. He was a San Francisco–based private detective, about fifty years old. He listened to my story and asked excellent questions. Then he told me straight out that he would mount an operation to rescue a child anywhere in the world—except Iran.

He felt the strategy we were pursuing was the best one and I had to push forward with it, not letting myself get discouraged by what he thought might be a temporary setback. He wholeheartedly agreed with Dave Christian that the surefire way to lure Iraj was by "seducing" him. He too felt I would have to be very sexy with my ex-husband and make him believe I was still crazy about him and as eager to be married to him again as I was to get him into bed!

I told Patrick I was doing my very best, but the role of Jezebel or Delilah, never a natural one for me, was darned hard to play under the circumstances.

His pep talk on the subject made me laugh, for the first time in days. "Listen," he said, "be careful when you talk to other people in my line. I'm not saying this to be self-serving, but to be helpful. I've seen too many desperate parents throw away their last penny on people who lack the experience and the know-how to help them get their kids back. You're going to run into a lot of weirdos and charlatans, so be on guard."

I assured him I would, got a few more pointers on that score from him, and was about to say good-bye when he said something that really buoyed me.

"When it looks like you've convinced your ex-husband to come out of Iran with the children, think about giving me a call. I can get 'em back for you wherever he decides to meet you."

He didn't sound the least bit boastful, just self-assured. And he had a right to be. He had recovered more than one hundred children. "With a track record as terrific as yours," I told him, "you can bet I'll call you, if—*when* things work out."

I wouldn't know for four long months what a stroke of luck it had been that I had gotten through on the phone to Holly Planels, bought a magazine off the rack, and placed that call to Patrick Buckman.

FIVE

APRIL 29 WAS ONLY A FEW DAYS AWAY. CY WOULD TURN six on that day. I'd always made a big fuss over Sara and Cy's birthdays. We had traditional parties with all their friends, followed by a family party. Balloons and games, prizes and presents, the big cake and candles—but not this year. This year Cy would celebrate his birthday very differently. And I would be eight thousand miles away from him. I cried. A lot. Then my sadness turned to anger. I wanted to throttle Iraj for robbing me of all the precious days, especially this one, with my children.

Cy's birthday, the fact that the kids were sick, Iraj ordering me to bring money to Tabriz—all made me think a lot about the conditions in which my children were living. I remembered the farm, which I'd visited on my first trip to Iran.

* * *

Iraj was nearing the end of his master's program and talking about going on to get a Ph.D. at Princeton when he started getting distress calls from his mother in Iran. The family needed him at home, she said. They had countless problems they couldn't solve. Only he could take care of them. For quite a while Iraj seemed torn. He asked me what I thought he should do. What could I say? I wasn't sure I was in love with him and had a right to ask him to stay, and I didn't understand why he was needed to solve the family's problems. Couldn't one of his brothers take care of things? The answer was a resounding no. This is when I learned that Iraj, not his father, was considered the head of the family. At last, after a lot of pressure from Homa, Iraj went home, reluctantly. Our good-bye was a wrenching experience.

We corresponded faithfully and talked on the phone. Almost a year to the day after I'd met Iraj, I got a very emotional letter from him. He wrote of how much he missed me, how desperately he wanted me to visit him and meet his family. I was overjoyed and immediately started to plan the trip. We had been apart for three months, and I was thrilled about seeing him and his family, but I was nervous about making such a long trip alone to an exotic destination. I'd spent my first twenty-one years in suburban Pennsylvania and the last year just a score of miles away in New Jersey. A fairly staid existence. My sense of adventure was stimulated, and I was eager to see the world.

Since I'd been hoping for an invitation from Iraj to his homeland, I'd taken a course in Farsi, the Persian language, from a tutor in Princeton during the spring.

·

Perhaps because I'd grown up hearing my grandparents speak Hungarian and Italian, I'd developed an ear for languages. Whatever the reason, I seemed to have a talent for Farsi and had been having a lot of fun studying it. So, feeling as well-prepared as possible for my great adventure, I set out in the late summer of 1978, my family seeing me off at Kennedy Airport.

The flight across the mountains of Turkey and the vast stretch of Iranian desert reminded me just how different and faraway a place my destination was. Myriad shades of brown and gray earth undulated below the clouds through which the Boeing 747 flew. As the plane descended nearing Teheran, I could see enormous ridges running for miles along the taupe-colored ground. The ridges looked as if a gigantic worm had burrowed just beneath the surface. Later I learned that these long wriggling lines were the earthworks above the ancient, still vitally important tunnels called qanats that carry precious water to cities and villages throughout the country. It is said that they are filled with fish that are blind and white because of centuries of evolution within the pitch black tunnels. The men who must be lowered into these *qanats* to do the vital work of inspecting and repairing them are considered heroes in their villages, for it's an extremely hazardous job, and quite a few are killed each year doing it.

As we prepared to land in Teheran, I started to feel nervous—very nervous. I'd traveled halfway around the world alone and had been feeling quite grown-up and responsible. But it really hit me then that I wasn't reading an article in *National Geographic*, I was living it! Something very foreign lay waiting for me beyond those great long undulating lines stretching across the desert below. On the one hand I couldn't wait to see and experience it all, on the other hand I wanted the plane to turn around and fly at supersonic speed back to Philadelphia.

My worst fears about being able to cope with the foreignness of what I would face were confirmed as I walked into the airport terminal. The late evening sun gleaming off the light-colored tarmac had been blinding, and by contrast the interior of the building seemed very dark. The noise was overwhelming, the crowd intimidating. I couldn't understand a word of what I heard in the din of high-pitched, rapid chatter. There seemed to be a thousand men who might be Iraj milling about in the large throng of women, many of whom were covered from head to foot in the traditional dark veil, the *chador*, who moved together in groups like small flocks of big, black birds. There were few officials or signs giving directions. I was jostled and pushed by the other passengers toward the large chain link fence that bounded the cages of the immigration officials. I was really jumpy. And then I spotted Iraj and felt incredibly relieved. He was my anchor in the alien sea.

After what seemed an awfully long time in processing, I was on the other side of the customs barrier and in Iraj's arms. We hugged and kissed, not giving a thought to his country's traditions. But we didn't have much time to get reacquainted then because we had to catch the next bus bound for Tabriz, a ten-hour drive from the Teheran airport.

The windows of the bus were decorated with tassels; baggage was stacked precariously on the roof and threatened to topple off; pictures of popular Middle Eastern singers were plastered on the outside and inside of the bus. It was the Iranian version of the Toonerville Trolley. I was enchanted with this colorful vehicle and with the variety of people in traditional and Western clothing who crowded onto it. But I was a whole lot less than enchanted with the bus driver. The trip was hair-raising. The bus hurtled along at high speed, swaying on straightaways, lurching and thudding over huge potholes, taking hairpin turns breathtakingly fast, coming to stops with bone-jarring swiftness and the deafening squeal of brakes.

As we bounced along, Iraj and I talked animatedly. He stopped every few minutes to point out something I should look at before night fell. We were traveling mostly through desert, but desert that wasn't anything like the beaches I knew on New Jersey's Cape May or the scenes with those great sand dunes in *Lawrence of Arabia*. There's no golden sand at all, just grainy-looking gray soil in which very little grew and what did seem to be the same drab colors as the earth. The landscape gave me a whole new meaning to the word *bleak*.

At last we arrived—in one piece, thankfully—in Tabriz. The city wasn't taupe-colored, as it had appeared from a distance, but reddish-brown. Thick smog hung in the early morning air, and the streets were as congested as Philadelphia at rush hour. The drivers of all those cars and small trucks couldn't seem to find anywhere to rest their elbows and hands except on their horns. I would soon become accustomed to the noise and crowds, to the pollution and open sewers running through the middle or along the sides of the streets, but just then I felt as if I'd been thrust into a high-tech Samarkand or Timbuktu.

We took a taxi from the bus station to Iraj's family's house. The taxi ride taught me that the bus driver had been fairly conservative by Iranian standards. I'd say that the Iranian concept of driving is based on Indy 500 rules. Speed is essential; stopping might cause loss of face. So no lawn or sidewalk or traffic light or sign is a deterrent to passing or speeding. This is not funny. I saw the consequences in the monstrous wrecks left along the sides of the roads. When I asked later, I learned that thousands of Iranians are killed each year in traffic accidents.

Iraj had briefed me during our long bus trip about etiquette and expectations regarding my behavior, and I felt prepared to meet his family and friends. But I hadn't expected so many of them to turn out to welcome me— and with such enthusiasm! They were curious, smiling, friendly, and made me feel as though I was a very special, very honored guest.

The welcoming group included Iraj's parents, all his three brothers and four sisters, numerous aunts, uncles, and cousins, and a swarm of children. Neighbors joined the group outdoors but hung back when we entered the house. I saw the family take off their shoes before entering and slipped out of mine. The house was one of a long row of houses that fronted on the narrow dirt street. This block of houses was made of adobe brick, smoothly plastered over with a lovely pale honey-colored mud. I thought it was beautifully exotic, like all the people around me.

I was shown through the three rooms of the house and into a courtyard where there was a shallow ornamental pool. At the back of the courtyard was the kitchen and an outhouse. There was no indoor plumbing. A shower was attached to the rear of the house. Despite a lack of modern amenities, the family was well off, high in the middle class of Iran. They had risen in economic status from modest means through the help of their sons, primarily Iraj and Jamshid. Their new prosperity was obvious in the lovely furnishings of their house. Exquisite rugs covered every inch of the floors; plump cushions and beautifully embroidered pillows were strewn about and stacked for people to rest against. A great deal of the family's wealth was represented by the fine quality of these handmade carpets, some antique, and the pillow coverings. The reason for leaving shoes outside was immediately clear. The streets were muddy in places and quite filthy near the open sewers; one didn't want to track any of that onto the rugs and cushions where one sat and ate and lounged.

We had a spectacular feast that day, which introduced me to the delights of Iranian food. I was used to a "groaning board" at home, since my mother cooked well and in large quantities and loved to entertain with lavish meals, but the feast in Tabriz was especially big and impressive. Bowls of cut fruit surrounded a tray of two-foot-long wedges of Persian melon. Baskets heaped with wonderful unleavened breads, crisp to soft-textured, sat next to bowls of sweet butter and plates of pungent white goat cheese. There was *abgusht adas*, a sort of Persian lentil soup, *abgusht miveh*, dried fruit soup, and *borani*, a spinach salad with nuts, lemon juice, yogurt, and fresh mint. The entrees included *morgh polo*, chicken in a casserole with rice, and what became my favorite dish, *chelo kebab*, well-seasoned lamb, skewered and broiled over charcoal, and served with delicious steamed rice that had been mixed with butter, egg yolk, and powdered sumac and baked until it had a golden crust. And there were bowls and bowls of cooked and raw vegetables. Honeyed sweets and nuts and more fruit followed, all washed down with one's choice of soda, bottled water, tea, or thin and tart yogurt that isn't the least bit like the kind we have in America.

My mouth waters remembering the great Persian cuisine, but as much as I love the food, I feel sorry for the women who have to prepare it; shopping for meals and cooking takes up most of their time. In the following days we had many more such feasts at the homes of relatives and friends, and I had to urge Iraj to join me on lots of brisk walks to work off some of the calories I was consuming. But on that first day of meeting the family, I wasn't worried about calories or anything else. I was too busy being the center of attention, and when Iraj grew tired of translating and wandered off, too busy trying to understand and be understood. Some of Iraj's relatives spoke a little bit more English than I spoke Farsi, and they saved me. Everyone studied me as intently as I studied them. And they were full of questions about life in the West. It was fun trying to communicate, to use my few words and sentences of Farsi, and it was fun to be in such an exciting atmosphere.

Iraj and his family proved to be wonderful hosts, making sure I saw all the interesting things in and around Tabriz. We made excursions to the bazaars, which were so lively and full of fabulous goods and skilled craftsmen that I could hardly drag myself away. I was fascinated by the main bazaar, crowded with stalls where merchants sold antiques, sweets, jewelry, nuts—mostly pistachios— olives still on the vine, teas, cotton, rugs, and everything else under the sun, it seemed. Craftsmen squatted on the ground by their stalls making boxes or sat on stools in rays of sunlight, etching elaborate designs on metal plates. Some of these plates were actually the tops of oil drums made of very heavy aluminum; they were turned into surprisingly beautiful trays.

Tabriz is in the Azerbaijan province of Iran, which borders Turkey and Russia, and it seemed to me that the clothing and crafts were richer in color and design than those from other parts of the country. And since of course the Caspian Sea is in Azerbaijan and is the source of Iran's world-famous caviar, I saw kiosks in the bazaar where huge tins of caviar were sold at prices that Iraj told me would make consumers in the export markets weep.

We visited mosques of great beauty and profound serenity. Although I was told the names of all the designs in the mosaic work, it would be weeks before I made a breakthrough and actually could see how different one was from another. The exquisite mosaics covering walls and domes inside and out were for me an undifferentiated and absolutely dazzling sea of all the blues of the spectrum—aquamarine and cerulean, cobalt and peacock, sapphire and azure. These colors and the intricacy of the mosaics moved me very much, in a way I still can't quite express in words.

I was exhilarated. I felt as if I'd turned into a sponge and my mind and senses were soaking everything up. I was endlessly interested in all I saw and everyone I met.

Young cousins and siblings accompanied Iraj and me on hikes and picnics in the surrounding foothills, and on visits to the family farm some miles from Tabriz. It was rustic, to say the least; smelly and raw and primitive would be more like it. How could I have guessed then that this place would be so important to me in the future?

After a week or so Iraj had to return to his job as a systems analyst at the Central Bank in Teheran, and as prearranged, I remained with his family. I was very comfortable, all my self-confidence restored, and felt I could meet any cultural or personal challenge that came my way. And I was proud that I could be independent of Iraj. But the Farsi I'd learned was proving less useful to me in Tabriz than I'd hoped, because everyone I knew there spoke a dialect that was heavily laced with Turkish. Still, I liked trying to use what Farsi I had, trying to pick up some of the dialect. When I was understood and got a reply that I could understand, I was happy. I mostly relied on the children to help with the language; for them it was a fun game to talk to me, and they seemed never to tire of it.

I really wanted some freedom to explore on my own, to walk and shop and meander without feeling I was imposing on a family member. The women, Homa especially, were horrified by the idea. But I persisted, and they finally gave in, agreeing it might be all right for me to do a few things alone—only, however, after they'd taught me what they thought was vital. So they tutored me on bargaining at food and clothing shops and made sure I was deft in counting out my *rials* (about sixty-seven or sixty-eight *rials* were the equivalent of one U.S. dollar) and my *tomans* (ten *rials* equaled one *toman*). They already had made sure I understood that it would be insulting if I left the house in "immodest" clothing, so I always tried to wear conservative dresses or slacks, and not wanting to be disrespectful, I never went into the streets without covering my head. One of Iraj's female cousins had given me a voluminous black silk scarf for this purpose.

On my very first outing I discovered that what I'd heard about men in this culture was too true: many

Middle Eastern men perceive a woman alone as fair game and have no qualms about grabbing or pinching her fanny! The first time I was goosed, I couldn't believe it. The second time taught me a lesson. From then on I gave a wide berth to passing men and kept well ahead and out of the reach of trailing ones. But the intent way men stared at me was so unnerving that I never got used to it.

Busy in those first weeks, I had few pangs of homesickness. In addition to helping Homa as much as she would allow, I read a lot and wrote letters to family and friends. I was learning a great deal about the customs of the country and of Iraj's family. Most of it was fascinating, but some was quite unsettling.

In my first month in Tabriz I think I reacted to everything around me in a polarized way, either romanticizing it or being judgmental in a very American fashion. The culture into which I was being submerged really challenged me. Many customs bewildered me, while the roles and treatment of women, young and old, offended me. Most women made food and babies and lived only for their husbands and families. I saw very few professional women. Of course I knew all about the patriarchal culture of Iran, but it's far different discussing such things in animated conversations in Princeton with men and women who are getting graduate degrees than it is living intimately with the effects of such age-old traditions. As time passed, I grew more and more deeply aware of how different this way of life was from mine; these weren't people just like me only wearing unusual clothes and speaking another language. The society into which they'd been born had very different values; these people saw and dealt with the world in ways that weren't at all like mine. I realized I had to figure things out very carefully for myself.

Never were the contradictions more apparent than when I visited a carpet "factory" in Tabriz.

If you say Iran, most people think of oil and ayatollahs, of the struggle for modernization and of mosques. Say Persia and most people think of mosaics, paintings in miniature, melons, minarets, poetry—and carpets. The Persian carpet industry traces its origins back more than three thousand years to nomads who made carpets to cover the ground inside their *yurts*, large domed tents. The Iranians developed carpets into works of art as long as twenty-five hundred years ago. A fine, large Persian carpet, painstakingly handwoven, takes about three years to make. Its quality depends on the color and fastness of the vegetable and plant dyes and on the fineness of the silk or wool used, the artistry of the design and the precision of its execution. But the most common criterion for judging a carpet's quality is how many knots it has per square inch. An average rug has about 182 knots per square inch, an exceptional one has something like 625. There are even more in the finest silk prayer rugs. The more knots per square inch, the smaller each knot has to be, obviously. And the hands that make the highest quality, most expensive and prized carpets are the tiniest hands—the hands of little children.

There are a number of carpet factories which employ hundreds of people, but these are of relatively recent origin—recent in Iranian terms: they date from the thirties when the shah's father revived the industry. In fact there's a big one in Tabriz. But most good carpets are still made cottage-industry style. The adults prepare materials and designs, but the children of the very extended family live and work together as knot tiers. Most of these workers are girls; in some of the great holy cities like Qom and Mashad, though, boys as young as three years of age sit at the base of the looms all day making the tiny silk knots that distinguish these carpets. And, I was told, it was not unusual to see these little ones with permanently bent, crooked fingers.

I was horrified by this information—until I visited a family loom. It wasn't at all what I expected. The loom was built around three sides of a one-room building with very high ceilings, maybe the equivalent of three or four stories high. A skylight and large windows provided natural light to supplement the light from bare bulbs in sockets on the walls. The center of the room was open, its dirt floor well swept, and in the middle was a charcoal brazier on which tea was kept warm and food cooked. Under the loom all around the room was a platform, on which the children sat and worked—and chattered and giggled and poked each other while their small fingers flew. The day I was there an old man walked about straightening a wooden bar here, running his fingers through long bundles of strands of wool there, generally overseeing the weaving process. An elderly woman tended the brazier and occasionally made a comment to the girls. The girls were fascinated by me. They teased and called out questions. This was child labor. Awful, right? I was dead set against it. But the little girls were as gay and lively and naughty as any group I'd ever encountered. Later I would see young Iranian teenagers dressed in jeans and T-shirts and sandals hanging out on the street corners, at loose ends, some looking lost, and I'd be reminded of the scene in the home carpet factory. Those little girls had known who they were, where they belonged, and that they were contributing to an important economic, cultural, and artistic effort that went back through all the generations of the members of their tribe. And that seemed to me to sum up the wrenching dilemmas that had to be confronted by all Iranians, including the Salimis, who were doing their best to adjust.

The shah's stated goal was to have Iran join the ranks of the fully industrialized nations of the world within the next decade. And in fact he'd been pushing development so fast that it sometimes seemed reckless. The newspapers were full of reports of the "progress" the shah's government was making in economic programs and in bringing about far-reaching political, social, and cultural changes. In the past decade the gross national product had more than tripled, and industrialization had proceeded at a rate that some termed "epic." Annual growth in the industrial and mining sectors was at almost 13 percent, as it had been for the last ten years, and was outstripped only by the oil sector, which had an annual growth rate of 15 percent. Significant as this growth was, it paled in comparison to the social and cultural changes the shah had been making since he'd gained support through referendum in January 1963 for what he called the "White Revolution."

"The shah is the shadow of God," according to an Iranian proverb, and no one seemed to believe it more than Mohammed Reza Pahlavi, shah of Iran, King of Kings, Light of the Aryans, whose vision for his country was as big as his ego. In his determination to yank Iran out of the camel age and push it up to the heights of the jet age, he appeared to want to create an economic and military superpower that was the twentieth-century equivalent of the Persian Empire of Cyrus the Great. The twenty billion or so dollars a year of oil revenues gave him the money to try it. But I must say that all I'd heard about Iran being so "oil rich" baffled me, because the country I was visiting was very poor indeed. And the poverty I saw all around me made my heart ache. What, I often asked myself, could this place have been like before?

The centerpiece of the first phase of the shah's White Revolution was redistribution of land. In this he particularly fought against absentee feudal landlords to break up their holdings and give plots to peasants. This brought him to a direct, bloody confrontation with the religious establishment, which happened to be the second largest landholder in the country. The shah won the first round, scattering the mullahs back to their mosques, arresting and exiling their leader, Ayatollah Ruhollah Khomeini. But how many people were really benefiting from land reform? I didn't see much happening on this score with the Salimis and their acquaintances.

The shah's government had built almost nine hundred clinics and other medical facilities, and through the literacy corps the shah claimed to have increased the literacy rate by 30 percent. He reorganized the arbitration courts, again clashing head on with the clergy. His herculean efforts at modernization created great controversy, though, as all change, even change for the better, can be very frightening. Many people felt they were being westernized against their will and that their traditional religious beliefs were being demeaned. There was little freedom of expression; the newspapers, radio, and television were government controlled, there weren't real opposition political parties, and there was a lot of corruption and inefficiency in government. Quite a few people in the new middle class, especially those who like Iraj had been well educated in the West, focused on the lack of rights and on the corruption; they thought progress was too slow in some areas, too insensitively fast in others. Criticism wasn't a public thing for most people, though. It was reserved for discussions in the privacy of the home, and in the mosques. I remember once bringing a noisy party to pin-drop silence by asking about the Savak, the savage and much feared secret police. Suddenly everyone in the room was stone deaf—and totally mute.

But I was a cheering fan of one of the shah's programs: the upgrading of education and extension of rights for women. His father had outlawed the veil and opened the universities to women; the shah himself had given women the vote and the right to divorce their husbands. During my visit I learned that 38 percent of the students in Iran's universities were female. Victory—for some at least. But not for many of the women around me.

At first the women in the Salimi family and their neighbors and friends seemed to me to be anchored in the concrete roles that were stifling and depressing. Soon, however, I began to see beyond the day-to-day stuff—their household drudgery and obsession with discussing marriages, births, deaths, and financial success or lack of it. Like Western women, they were dealing with the fundamental things in life. And they had power; not directly in the outside world and not in the terms I'd grown up with, but power nonetheless. Homa, for example, was the family boss, no doubt about it. After a few weeks with her, I became convinced that if she'd been born and raised in Detroit she'd have been a prime candidate at any age for CEO of General Motors. Homa didn't suffer from manic-depressive disease, but she was much like my mother in the way she ran her household. While it was almost impossible for me, a free and independent American, to accept what appeared to be oppression or domination of women by men in public, I did try to be open-minded. And perhaps I took a first step toward wisdom. I learned how much I had to learn. Things were not always what they seemed to be, but they were always more complicated.

Iraj's visits on weekends—Friday and Saturday in Iran; their Sunday is back-to-work day, like our Monday—were treated as celebrations, with much food, and family coming from all over. Iraj was so sweet to me and so attentive that I was in heaven. Perhaps inspired by the celebrated poets of his homeland such as Hafiz, Sadi, and Omar Khayyam, he recited poetry to me and brought me flowers. I felt very special, very pretty, and loved. When Iraj was able to get a few extra days off, we would take trips so I could see more of the country.

One of the most exciting trips I took was to visit Iraj in Teheran, the thriving capital of a little over three and a half million people. Some of the avenues were wider than the widest ones in Paris, but more clogged than the narrow streets of Manhattan. And the noise of the traffic was even more deafening than in Tabriz.

Iraj's brother had come with me. The three of us toured until we were ready to drop from exhaustion, and much of what I saw then is a blur in my mind. What I do remember as clearly as if I'd seen them yesterday are the mirrored walls and grand staircase of the Golestan Palace, both a state guest house and a museum, which housed one of the two or three Peacock thrones in the country. There are several legends about the Peacock Throne. One says that the original jewel-encrusted throne was lowered from heaven; another says it was made by a German jeweler! *The* Peacock Throne had stood in the Great Mogul Palace in Delhi, India, and was brought to Persia by a conquering shah in the eighteenth century. Reza Pahlavi's was a copy made during the reign of Fath Ali Shah in the late 1700s and early 1800s and named after one of his favorites, Tavous Khanoum, or Lady Peacock. And how could I ever forget seeing the Crown Jewels?

The Iranian Crown Jewels are the most valuable and spectacular single collection of gems in the world. The collection backed the currency, just as the gold in Fort Knox and elsewhere backs ours. This incredible and matchless collection was maintained by the Bank Markazi and housed deep in a vault of the Bank Melli on Ferdowsi Street. I joined scores of people in line, and we filed down the red-carpeted steps to see the jewels.

The overall light level in the vault was surprisingly low, with spotlights illuminating the contents of the dozens of individual glass cases and display areas. And it was hushed. No sound reached it from the honking, gear-grinding, snarled traffic on the street above. I could hear only slight purring from the machinery that kept the humidity controlled and the temperature constant. Nothing distracted the viewer from the collection. And the collection was breathtaking.

Huge, exquisite unset gems were heaped on platters, brimmed over the edges of wide-lipped bowls, spilled out of boxes onto velvet mats. One case featured only emeralds, another only diamonds, another rubies, and so on. There were shelves full of magnificently set pieces—traditional jewelry, jewel-encrusted crowns, scabbards, scepters, boxes, tableware. There was a large gold and enamel throne, another Peacock Throne, that was studded with 26,733 gems, emeralds and rubies most prominently. The world's most precious emerald, 175 carats and perfect, was there, as was the world's largest collection of natural pearls, which took up almost one long wall of the vault, and the world's largest known diamond of its type and color, the inch-and-a-half-long, inch-wide, flat pink diamond of 182 carats known as the Darya-i-Nur, the Sea of Light, sitting in a case with lots of other huge diamonds. What a long and romantic history the Darya-i-Nur had!

But two things dazzled me more than the brilliance of the stones and their obvious value: the artistry of the set pieces and the history of them and of the loose stones. It brought home to me as nothing else had to this point just how ancient the Iranian civilization is. It's one thing to read or hear that Iran has a recorded history that dates back 2,500 years. It's a different matter entirely to be surrounded with precious things that have survived hundreds of years, a thousand or more years in a couple instances, and played such an important role in matters of political power and intrigue.

And then it was time to leave. Iraj had to go to work and so did his brother. I'd thought Tabriz had lots of kiosks where I could get reading material in English, but Teheran had even more, so I loaded up on magazines, journals, and newspapers. I needed the help of reliable news reports in papers like *The International Herald-*

Tribune to make sense of what I was seeing, hearing, and sensing all around me.

Tension was mounting as political opponents of the shah consolidated and gained power, heading for a confrontation. No one could fail to see the evidence of these rising tensions, not just in Teheran, but in Tabriz. More and more soldiers, bandoliers of ammunition crisscrossing their chests and machine guns at the ready, filled the streets in the Salimis' neighborhood and around the bazaars and mosques. I didn't like to walk near these armed men, many of whom were baby-faced and seemed to be very nervous. It was a wonder to me each day as I did errands and shopped that someone wasn't shot accidentally by one of the youthful, apparently inexperienced soldiers. And tanks rolled in the streets. The English-language newspapers reported daily confrontations. As it became obvious that there was going to be violence in the country, that the shah might be tumbled from his throne, I felt threatened. I was torn about staying. Iraj was pressing me to marry him and live in Iran, at least for a year or so. I was uncertain about marrying him, and by then I was really homesick, though I wouldn't have admitted it to anyone. Furthermore, I knew that I didn't want to live in Iran. I cared about his family, all of whom I liked, some of whom I was beginning to love. My heart went out to the people around me who endured so much hardship with such dignity. Even the poorest person I met was generous in a way that touched and impressed me. There was so very much I loved about Iran —and so much I disliked intensely.

In early November my three-month visitor's visa would expire. I decided not to have it renewed. I loved Iraj, or thought I did. He had become even more romantic, and he was showing enormous compassion and understanding about the predicament I was in. I was filled with guilt about leaving him at such a dangerous time, but I wanted to go home. There were numerous displays of anti-Americanism in graffiti and pamphlets and on banners, yet I never was threatened personally. I was treated with respect and kindness by all who knew who I was; strangers might have mistaken me for an Iranian because of my dark hair, eyes, and coloring, the product of my Mediterranean heritage. But even if I was safe, the government was not. I became convinced that the shah was going to fall at any minute, and I was equally convinced that bad as his government had been in terms of human rights violations, no one could be sure that a new regime would be any better. Finally, in very early November, I made arrangements to return to the United States. My parting with Iraj was bittersweet; the reunion with my family was joyous.

The Christmas holiday passed, and a little over two weeks after the dawning of the New Year 1979, the Pahlavi regime came to an end. Just about three weeks later an Air France 747 circled three times over Teheran and the nearby Elburz Mountains before landing at Mehrabad Airport. An old man, hunched inside black robes that swept the ground, walked down the ramp in the chill of the early February morning. The moment was historic as his foot touched the earth in the country from which he'd been exiled fifteen years before, which for the last several weeks had been in the grip of out-of-control, violent mobs. To shouts of "The holy one has come!" and "He is the light of our lives!" the Ayatollah Khomeini began a new era in Iran.

* * *

It was the middle of the night. As I stared out at the moonlit yard of my modern suburban house, my heart and soul were with my sick children eight thousand miles away. Were they still in that farmhouse with no running water or central heating? Oh, God, it could get so cold even in the spring and summer in the mountainous area where the farm was located. I had visions not of the generosity and gaiety of the Salimis and their neighbors, but of their rough ways. As a rule they weren't tender and gentle in their treatment of children. Were Sara and Cy scared? Did they know they'd been kidnapped? Or did they think they were only visiting and I might join them soon?

I couldn't see the yard any longer because of the tears that filled my eyes. My thoughts about Iraj were as black as the sky. He'd done such a terrible and destructive thing to his own children that I wanted him punished within an inch of his life. I've never hated Iraj Salimi more than I did that night.

SIX

THE LAST DAYS OF APRIL WERE DREARY. THE ONLY RAY of sunshine came from learning that the children had recovered from the vomiting and diarrhea they'd suffered.

Mail started to arrive from Iraj. Hen-scratched, with crossed-out words and writing running up the sides of the page and over the top, his first letter was dated "In the middle of the night as my children sleep." It was full of bombastic, pompous language. And threats. He ranted about my relationship with Mike, whom he called a "sicko." He raved that I was a "disgrace to the concept of motherhood." And he demanded—money, new clothes for the children, lots of things from "home"—by which he meant America!

I had written many reminders to myself on the tops of the scripts for my calls to Iraj. *Act respectful. Be conciliatory. Softly, softly catches the monkey.* This came from an article

I'd read about an Englishman who specialized in child recovery; it was his motto, and a good one for me to adopt, I thought. *Be sweet, sweet, sweet! Pretend you love him.* And believe me, I needed every single one of those reminders.

When I got a chance to speak to the children, I tried to accomplish two things: to let them know I loved and missed them, and to make them understand that we had to meet in a country other than Iran.

To Sara I said, "Sweetheart, no matter what Daddy says, I'm not allowed to got to the country you are in, because it's not safe. Ask Daddy if we can all meet in any other country. I want to be with you. I love you and miss you very much."

And to Cy I said, "Ask Daddy to meet with Mommy and you and Sara in a safe place, not in the country where you are. Lovey, I want to see you. I miss you so much."

Another letter from Iraj came on the heels of the first. He ordered me to wire $100,000, "half my money," immediately because the children were unhappy living where they were, and he needed the money right away to buy a house for them. Again, we realized there was something other than a house for which he needed money. (The value of the house we had shared would soon be inflated by him to $300,000!) In the next letter he called me a thief who'd stolen all the children's money, but in the same paragraph he wrote, "The fact is the children need their mother now and here, and you know it. However, your priorities are different, and you, in order to justify your priorities, have to make up this justification. Otherwise, you would feel guilty and guilt is not good for your health. Of course you cannot carry the guilt of putting the Lumber Guy in a higher priority compared to your children. Think back. Do you know what you have done? You have chosen a Low Life against your children."

Someone once said that the test of a first-rate intelligence is the ability to hold two opposed ideas in the mind at the same time and still retain the ability to function. Whether Iraj's intelligence was first-rate was in doubt and his ability to function could be questioned, but his ability to hold two opposing ideas in his mind at the same time was undeniable. After reading the following scribbled passage in this latest letter, I thought he had gone over the edge, his intellect and personality disintegrating:

Jess, when you made me to leave my home, I did not like it, but I accepted. . . . When you used a team of lawyers, accountants, and family members and practically took all my assets from me . . . I did not like it, but it was only money; besides, I thought Sara and Cy will continue living in a nice house.

When you humiliated me and broke my heart, on countless occasions, I swallowed my pride and did not mind. I kept hoping one day you will come back to me and we will be a family again—Mom, Dad, Sara, and Cy. As time went on, I realized how much I loved you, how deep I loved you; you were my life. . . . My success at work was important to you, being away from you and waiting for you to come back to me, I put my mind into work. . . . In just a few months I was the star of my department. Every organization in Bell Labs and AT&T that I had interaction with, wanted me in their organization; and in the recent months the company was counting on me. My 1989 total compensation was

*over $80,000. . . . I was being prepared for the senior
management positions. Next summer, as part of my
Executive MBA Program of Northwestern University,
I was supposed to take a two-month trip to Europe,
meeting European financial and corporate executives,
which involves a lot of receptions and parties. I was
dreaming that by then you will come back to me and we
will take the trip together. Yes, I was dreaming. I have
dreamed a lot. . . .*

He certainly had been dreaming. I had been in touch
with an Iranian friend of Iraj's who worked with him at
AT&T; he reported that Iraj had sent them a letter of
resignation, which had arrived on April 15, but before
that he had been having a great deal of difficulty getting
along with coworkers and his boss. Ever since I had
known him, Iraj had had difficulty getting along with the
people with whom he worked. "The star" of his department? That couldn't have been farther from reality.
"How deep I loved you; you were my life"? When he had
tyrannized me, abducted the children?

My campaign to get Sara and Cy back was to succeed
or fail on the whim of a man whose actions, whose words
in these letters and on the phone made him seem more
certifiable than in the past—and, God knows, he'd been
crazy enough then. And I had a new worry. Iraj had no
practice taking care of the kids. He'd played the traditional Iranian male role and had never seen to their
needs. But even discounting his lack of experience, he
seemed to be in such bad shape that he might not be able
to care for the children now even if he knew what to do
for them. He'd said Homa was ill. Old and traditional,
Nadir couldn't do anything for Sara and Cy. The farm

was somewhat isolated from the rest of the family, though there was a sister not too far away. Was anyone around to feed and bathe the kids, put them to bed, and supervise their play?

Sara was very capable for an eight-year-old, and I knew I could count on her to do her best in a bad situation. She had always shown a lot of responsibility for her little brother, and a lot of curiosity about everything around her. I'd often called her "our reporter," because of the way she would go about getting the details of a situation that interested her in the neighborhood or the family. So I knew Sara would try to be Cy's little mother in my absence, but who would be her mother? And I was concerned about Sara in another way. She's a sweet child and easy to get along with, but she's spunky and frank and straightforward, traits which usually delighted me. Now those qualities were a source of anxiety. I was sure she knew a lot about what was happening and was probably saying a lot about it too. She certainly would be punished for her outspokenness. In the Salimi family, children are to be seen and not heard. The notion that Sara might be punished reminded me of Betty Mahmoody. She and her daughter had been punished quite harshly for criticizing anything about Iran. One punishment had been being locked in a room, a sort of solitary confinement. I shuddered to think how such treatment would affect my lively little Sara.

Betty had telephoned a few days before and said she was coming to meet me on April 29. We picked her and her associate up at the airport, and they spent the entire day with us. Until this point Betty had been a voice on the phone. Now she was a real flesh-and-blood person for me—and a person who understood in a way others could not the culture that had produced Iraj and what the children might be going through. In many ways our Iranian ex-husbands seemed to have spoken and behaved identically.

We filled her in on what had been happening, and she listened to a couple of the tapes of my telephone conversations with Iraj. She suggested that I act a little more helpless, a bit more subservient. No easy thing for me. We had lots to talk about concerning current conditions in Iran. The children couldn't be enrolled in an English-speaking school these days; the Ayatollah had outlawed it. Since education was high on Iraj's list of the important things in life, this was a fact to work with in my conversations with him. Betty and I shared ideas on economic conditions in Iran.

The war with Iraq, which was proving to be unwinnable, had cost innumerable lives and wrecked the Iranian economy. Two important things had happened in 1988: a new Iranian parliament had been more concerned with economic reform than the war, which was turning in Iraq's favor, and the Ayatollah had reluctantly accepted the United Nations's call for a truce. For the last year and a half there'd been sharp conflicts between traditionalists, reformists, and radicals as to how to improve the economy, but the reformists had been most successful, and the country had been in the throes of widespread nationalization and redistribution of agricultural lands. This was disruptive and nervous-making, and people were hurting. Prices were still soaring, goods were scarce, and nobody could be sure where the economy was heading.

Betty was excited to learn that Iraj was a computer expert who adored his technological toys and gadgets in America. She thought I should push him regarding the limits on his ambitions imposed by the miserable economic situation in Iran. And the country had vaulted backward in terms of modernization, so there weren't many opportunities for him there. We thought that if we could manage to get his old employer, AT&T, or some other company to offer him a job, in Europe perhaps, he might jump at it. It was definitely something to think about and try to arrange—but with a big proviso. We'd have to come up with a way to do it that wouldn't get back to Iraj through one of his friends or colleagues, or he would know the job offer hadn't been quite legitimate.

It was a fruitful meeting, and I hated to see Betty go that evening. She'd contributed a lot to our longer-range planning. She'd been a comfort to me—and she had helped me get through this day, Cy's birthday, without giving way to despair.

When I got back from dropping off Betty and her associate at the airport, I was able to reach Iraj in Tabriz. They had gone there for a family celebration of Cy's birthday. He wouldn't allow me to speak to Cy. Somehow I managed to resist the almost overwhelming urge to shriek at him for denying such a simple request, that a mother be allowed to speak to her son on his birthday.

"I would like to wish Cy a happy birthday. I want to say hello, tell the children I love them. I would like to hear their voices. I miss them so much."

"No," Iraj said flatly. "They don't want to talk to you. And I don't want them to talk to you. You're a pig."

"Do you think that if you were Cy you would want to hear your mom wish you a happy birthday? Can you put yourself in his place?"

"No, bitch."

In the background I could hear Sara screaming for the

phone. In case she was able to grab the receiver, I shouted, "Sara, you're the best daughter in the world."

There were sounds of shuffling and Iraj saying something in a harsh tone that I couldn't quite make out. I heard Cy crying and yelled, "Happy birthday, Cy."

There was a loud click. Iraj had hung up.

That was a terrible night for me. I cried buckets as I remembered birthday parties in the past and yearned to be with Cy and Sara. I reread a letter from Holly Planels, whose own son was still held in Jordan. "You *must* never give up hope that you will be reunited *somehow*," she had written. "Be strong. And, if you're at all religious, ask God's constant guidance and strength. You are going to need a ton!" I prayed. A lot.

I called the next day, steeling myself, determined to turn this conversation to my advantage. This was harder than I thought it would be, for Iraj told me he'd been explaining to the children what a bad mommy I was. He'd been telling them that if I really loved them I would have come to Tabriz with their things and some money—that in fact I would have rushed there to be with them instead of staying back in the United States.

Money, money, money. He talked about it for several more minutes. Finally I was able to get him onto a couple of the subjects I wanted to discuss. I had really prepared for this call. We had scripted a lot of material for me, to get just the right tone. My goal was to begin to manipulate Iraj in earnest, and to start by trying to pull his thoughts and desires out of him. And, of course, I was aware that it was time to send out those lures.

I talked about how much I cared about him, and about

my belief that what had been good at first in our marriage had been undermined by our inability to communicate with each other. I emphasized the word communication, using it a lot to lead into the suggestion that we meet somewhere to talk. He started to discuss this possibility seriously, conceding that he'd often been closed-minded and explosive during our years together. Progress, I thought, until Iraj's next remark.

"There's no need for us to meet in some other country. If you come to Iran, I will take good care of you."

That sounded so sinister to me that for the first time I decided those who suggested Iraj wanted to kidnap me and hold me prisoner were right. Was it just for revenge? Or did he want me as well as Sara and Cy, so that he could get an even bigger ransom from my family? Probably both.

I called the next day. There was no answer at the farm. I tried his sister. She said Iraj was away and wouldn't be back for a while; she acted as though the children weren't with her. I didn't know what to believe.

I practiced my script for the next conversation I'd have with Iraj. Tone was important. I rehearsed speaking in a calm, sincere-sounding voice. My sisters and Mike tried to play Iraj's role, anticipating the irrational things he might spring on me. I practiced fielding unexpected points a lot. We decided that I was going to be "sick." Then if I was having trouble steering Iraj in the direction I wanted him to go, I could say I had to get off the phone because I didn't feel well. This proved to be an effective tool, because Iraj had answers for everything. Rather than get into a situation where we locked horns or I followed his train of thought, I needed to be able to break off a conversation, take a breather, regroup, and try again from a slightly different angle. I was going for broke now, trying to convince him how sincere I was in saying that I could see I'd made a big mistake divorcing him and that I still cared for him. Acting sincere when you're lying is tough; pretending to love a person you despise takes powerful motivation—and, for me, a lot of rehearsing!

On May 1, I started my talk with Iraj by trying to convince him that I really, really cared about him and wanted to explore the possibility of us getting together again. I thought he believed me.

On May 2, I launched the conversation on a sea of flattery, lauding his intelligence and talent. Then I said sadly, switching to being the "good mother" of Dr. K's evaluation, "What a shame it is that you're missing out on so many opportunities for advancement in your career. Everybody at AT&T thought so much of you! And what about the kids' education, for example? Are you happy that they're going to have . . . like a—a second-class education? I can't resolve these things. I can't understand your thinking. I want to understand you, but I don't. Can you explain?"

"There's nothing to explain," Iraj said. "You know all the"—the tape of this conversation is full of static, but I think he used the word *altercations* here—" that led to this thing. You know everything about everything. Now you are telling me you care about me. Would you have said that if nothing was changed? Now you are telling me that it's better for the kids to live with their real father and mother. Would you have said that if the situation wasn't like it is? For two years I waited; you never did. You never even came close to that. Now it is too late to talk about this. You know exactly what happened and what led to this. So going back through the history of everything in the past two years will change nothing."

"No, I'm not saying that. I'm saying that sometimes we realize things late . . . or later."

There was lots of background noise on the line.

"No," Iraj said. " This is not something that I understand later. I thought about this a lot. It's just that I waited for two years and I was thinking about this. And recently, of course, I couldn't take it any longer, and even there I talked about it a lot. I consulted with many family people, and this was really the only way. You put yourself in my shoes, I mean that was it. That was the only way. Of course you can tell me it's not too late now, but then again it's going to be the same talk, the same conversation every time."

"Well, I don't—"

"I think going back through this thing over and over doesn't make any sense.

"Yes, but I'm—"

"As I told you, if you can think within the same framework that I told you yesterday, within the existing conditions, the existing situation, the way it is now. . . . This is what it *is*. Now I think at this point the best thing, at least for me and the kids, and I suggest you do the same, is to make the best of the situation as it is right now."

"But I don't see that the situation can be very good. I'm not making judgments, Iraj, but I'm concerned about my family having the best, the best of everything, and that's a true concern for all our lives. So that's all I wanted to say, that's a concern of mine."

"Yeah, I'm concerned too, but it doesn't change anything."

Iraj was happy to lead me into a blind alley. I had to change the subject. "What have you guys been doing?" I asked.

"Nothing. We're just hanging around and trying to see what can be done about living conditions, about our business, whatever. Life goes on. Life goes on, believe it or not. Life goes on and nothing changes."

"I guess it depends on the choices you make. . . . And I think we need to consider all of our lives and all of our choices for the good of everybody, not just one person. And there are options, there are definitely available options that are much, much better."

"We have a lot of options right here. And none of those options is to leave Iran, if that is what you mean. And I have done this out of concern and . . . I don't know. We are again around a circle. What you're talking about is around the same circle. . . . Every time, you find a new angle to talk about me and the kids leaving the country—that's what you're really telling me, right?"

"I am saying I think you ought to consider life-style, education, career—all the things that help to define a life. And I believe that is something we could do for all of us. It has a lot to do with personal fulfillment for you—I mean, I can't see you fulfilled in that kind of society. I want my children to be fulfilled. I think this is very important. I don't want them to go twenty-five feet backwards. I don't think you want that for them. I thought education was important to you. And so I think that these options are something we should think about carefully. Very, very carefully. And I think we should discuss them and talk about them with each other, because I think they're extremely important."

The connection was very bad; Iraj and I were having difficulty hearing each other. So I shouted, "Give my love to the kids. Are they there?"

"No they are not. They are not coming to the farm

anymore. The farm was fun for them only in the first few days. They like to play with the kids there better."

"Oh, oh, " I said mournfully. "So they don't come to the farm."

"No. They haven't come for a while. Anyway—"

"Give them my love, please."

"I will. Uh, uh, the only other thing I was thinking last night was that . . . considering everything . . . for whatever it is worth, when I said yesterday or the day before that if you ever consider to come here, you do it for the children, only for the children I said then, I think that's a lie. That should really include me too."

So he was *not* closing the door on discussion about our future and our options. But he was getting back to his major point: I should join the kids *and him* in Iran.

"Okay?" he asked.

I wanted to keep him talking. "Uh-huh, okay," I said.

"It hit me last night. Thinking back. The kids had the picture album out . . . they were looking through all the pictures and everything, all the memories and everything. . . . So, anyway, it's up to you. You know what to do. You are concerned about your career, and your lifestyle or whatever, well, it's up to you. But discussing this over and over, nothing is going to change. As a matter of fact, if you want to have an input into what you refer to as your family now, meaning the children and me, if you want to have an input, you should be close to us. That's where you can have an input. But being there, whatever you do there, is not going to have any input. As a matter of fact, these phone calls are getting on my nerves. Over and over talking about the same things, it really is useless. It's not only useless, it is distracting. I don't know what to say to the kids. They tell me, 'Mommy is going to come' . . . or not come . . . I don't know what to say to them. If you are so concerned and you cannot do anything about it, just let me know."

I said, sweetly, but very forcefully, "Well, I want you to think over what we've talked about. About personal fulfillment, career fulfillment, and economics also. I don't take these things lightly, and I know you don't either. And I don't know what kind of life-style we could expect there, but I know it's not good. And I don't want that for us. And—"

"You are telling me that you don't want that for *yourself*, right?"

"No, I said I don't want it for *us*. I said—"

"Well, it is for the children and me. You cannot change that."

"But I don't think it's good for you or the kids either."

"Okay I heard that. I heard your recommendation. I heard your opinion that this is not good for me and the children. I heard that, okay? In spite of that, I'm saying it *is*—good or bad—it is for me and the children. Now you can either include yourself within that or exclude yourself. And all I was telling you is that, if in long term, you do want to have an input into what direction we are heading, you should be closer. Instead of calling me from Pennsylvania, and telling me that this life-style here in Iran is not good for my children—which is not going to do anything—you have to be part of it, if you want to improve it or give me any direction or something like that. Do you understand what I am saying?"

"Yes. All right." This conversation was not ending the way I wanted it to. I really needed breathing room to marshal my counterarguments. It was time to be sick. "I just wanted to connect with you. I really think that I have to lie down now, because I don't feel well."

"You didn't really solve the thing you called about."

"I don't feel well. So I'm going to lie down, and I'm going to call you later."

He then inquired about my health, somewhat skeptically, ending, "Why don't you just come? You don't feel well. Just come. It is the best for you."

"Good-bye. I must go now. Good-bye."

I hung up. Damn. The call had fit his agenda, not mine. But at the very least, had I made him think about all he had left behind and the possibility he could get it back? I prayed to God that I had.

When we analyzed this last conversation, Sue, Mike, and I decided that we had to switch gears. I had to change my focus to center almost exclusively on Iraj. Asking to speak to the children, inquiring about them and their well-being, and discussing their future only antagonized him. And perhaps it gave away my game. He was responding best when I talked to him about him, his needs, wants, success. The future seemed to matter to him only in terms of *his* life. I had to concentrate on massaging his ego.

We also decided it was time to try to use my dad's importance to Iraj. We invented a story about how my father had been taken sick and how worried we were. We based this tale on a piece of reality that Iraj knew all about. My father had been successfully treated for prostate and bladder cancer quite a few years before and had been in remission all this time. We had the cancer recurring in our story—which caused me quite a lot of worry and guilt. I secretly felt as if God might punish me by making it come true. Iraj surprised me by ignoring this altogether, not giving so much as a cluck of acknowledgment or sympathy. Still, we hoped he was thinking about this and that it would have an impact on him.

We also realized that I couldn't continue to stall him about the money and court orders, so we'd developed a story for me to tell about how proud I was about my progress fulfilling his "requests." I convinced him that I had done all the paperwork for getting the court orders rescinded, that I had packed all the things he wanted sent and was waiting for a time for pickup from the shippers. The major matter, of course, was the money. I claimed I was borrowing the $200,000 from several members of the family and their friends, but the checks were still coming in, so I hadn't been able yet to set up the Bank Melli account. Oh, how he seemed to glory in all this. He thought he'd won, won everything. He was on an ego trip, in control he believed, and loving every minute of it. He was also irrational as hell in lots of ways. His calm, calculating tone of voice as he said these irrational things was chilling.

We came to a turning point, a very low one for me, on May 7. Iraj blew up. He said he was sick and tired of my telephone therapy. He went back to his ravings about what a terrible mother I was, about how awful Mike was, and questioned whether Mike wasn't still in the picture. He made nutty accusations about my conduct and said he wouldn't talk with me until he had tangible proof that I was "reforming." He wanted to see the papers and the money. He said he didn't believe a word I'd said about wanting our little family to be reunited and he wouldn't until he held the court papers and cash in his hands. I stayed calm on the phone, but as soon as I hung up I let out a long string of screams and curses.

Dear God, how could I reach someone this far gone? I felt desperate and terrified about the way he might be treating the children. I had to know what was going on in Iran. Since they'd abandoned the farm, what were the conditions under which the children were living in Tabriz? Did Iraj have plans to take them to Teheran, where it was more likely that he could get a job—if he could get a job, considering the fact that he'd run out on his obligation to do public service? If he did move, it was highly unlikely that the children would go with him. Probably they would remain in Tabriz with his parents and other relatives, just as I had on my first visit to Iran.

I needed to get information about Iraj's plans—and the information was available only from his family and friends. I knew I would have to try to convince them that I sincerely wanted a reconciliation. But it took me a while to force myself to act. Contacting Iraj's friends didn't bother me; just the thought of contacting Jamshid made me wild. More than anyone else, Jamshid, I felt, had betrayed me. We had had a good relationship, a friendship even. He had been my pal in Iran on my first trip, accompanying me sightseeing and befriending me within the family. He had endeared himself to me as a happy young bridegroom whose wedding I attended in Iran on my second trip in 1979, just a few months before my own marriage the following summer. I really got to know Jamshid very well in 1986. By this time the young bridegroom had matured into a family man, a very proud and loving husband and father of three daughters who was facing the dangerous prospect of being drafted into the Ayatollah's army.

I had cared and worried about Nasser and Jamshid. And I'd supported Iraj's efforts to get them out of Iran.

The war with Iraq had been going on since 1980. Since 1984, Iran had been launching one "final offensive" after another. The casualties were astronomical; the tales of how many men the commanders were willing to sacrifice in their jihad, their holy war, were horrifying. Iraj grew more and more frustrated because of his unsuccessful attempts to save his brothers, particularly his beloved Nasser, from military service. Nasser, imprisoned for so-called political crimes against the Khomeini regime, would be drafted the moment he was let out of jail. Undoubtedly because of this background, the teenager would be put into the front lines—a death sentence. And so in 1984, Iraj became a smuggler.

Taking his most important step in a master plan to get his brother Jamshid, Jamshid's wife and daughters, and his brother Nasser to the West, Iraj went to Turkey in March. He stayed there for several weeks—what a joy for me to be free of him!—and set up what he called his "base," making contacts that would end in the creation of a kind of underground railroad.

Once more Iraj proved just how smart and clever he can be. He had absolutely no experience with anything remotely like the smuggling of human beings out of one country and through others to a final destination in a free land, yet he was successful, enormously so. The escape route he developed was complex and fairly safe, starting in Iran and going through Turkey and Eastern Europe, over to the Caribbean, and then up to Canada, the end point. Apparently Iraj did some trial runs to test his scheme and work out the bugs, and then he set up the operation in earnest.

All of this was enormously expensive. Iraj had drained our joint accounts at an alarming rate. He demanded that I help raise money to finance this project, not only by turning over the small amount of money I had in a separate account, but also by getting money from my family. He was a raving maniac on this issue, especially where it concerned my dad. Iraj started to attribute more and more brilliance to my dad, more influence, more of everything until he'd virtually turned him into a mythic figure who could solve any problem. At this time my father was in the hospital recovering from yet another operation for prostate cancer. Iraj made bizarre demands that my father leave the hospital to help him by "pulling strings," and by going with him to Turkey—all this in addition to providing money, of course.

Iraj would scream until he was hoarse that my father was well enough to do something for Nasser, that everyone had to work on getting him out "like it was a full-time job," everyone was responsible for the boy's life. I knew he was absolutely nuts. But I also worried about Nasser and Jamshid, and I didn't feel I could leave Iraj until this crisis was over.

However, I refused to get the money he was demanding, and there was a simple reason why I wouldn't. Other members of the Salimi family, well off now financially, were *volunteering* to help pay the expenses of this operation! I begged Iraj to be prudent, to have a thought for Sara, Cy, and me and our financial security and allow his family to underwrite some of these costs. Every time I voiced that opinion Iraj nearly took my head off. From his reaction you would have thought I'd suggested he humiliate himself by dancing naked in the lobby of the AT&T building or that he sell his mother into white slavery!

From day one of this crisis, Iraj had been crazed on

this issue, but he had quickly grown into the staggeringly demented man who was furious that my father wouldn't get out of a hospital bed to help him. In the beginning of our conflict over my not raising money for the cause, he had punished me by forcing us to live on a household budget so absurdly low we practically starved. I hesitate even to mention the amount! I didn't give in. His response was unremitting abuse. But I held firm.

Iraj's underground railroad cost us $72,000 of our savings in the beginning. Nasser was its first passenger, of course. Iraj had documents forged for him, smuggled him through the mountains into Turkey, and for a month "took care" of him—as if Nasser, then eighteen or nineteen, needed a daddy—in a modern apartment in Istanbul. Iraj came back to the States alone; Nasser traveled the route Iraj had set up through Europe to Barbados. In a couple of weeks Nasser arrived on our doorstep.

This boy was impossible. Conceited, arrogant, a sniveling little punk, he lounged about giving me orders and whining. He was bored; he wasn't having a good time. I tried to ignore him, a difficult goal, and I was really glad when Jamshid arrived. He came out alone along the same route as Nasser. Exhausted at first, Jamshid clearly was delighted to be in a safe, comfortable place. He proved to be as good a guest as Nasser was a rotten one. I appreciated his company and how affectionate he was with the children. He played with them a lot, missing his own daughters very much. And I was touched by his determination to make a good life for his wife and children. Language was a major obstacle to his goals, so I arranged English classes for him and drove him to class each day. He was grateful and a very good student. I also felt sorry for him because Iraj was so uncaring and rude to him, while he fawned on Nasser.

After several months, Jamshid's wife and daughters got through. None of them could stay legally in the United States, so Canada was their destination. However, Iraj got the idea in his head that if we bought a gas station for Jamshid and his wife, they would be permitted to stay in the U.S. Putting down a deposit on a gas station was one of the things that Iraj had wanted $50,000 from refinancing our house for, and to do something special for Nasser.

To get settled Jamshid asked for and got political asylum in Canada, and we helped set him up there with his family. Soon Nasser joined his brother and sister-in-law in Canada.

With both of his brothers safe in the West, Iraj should have been rejoicing, but for some reason all he could think about was buying that gas station for Jamshid, and getting him back into the States. It was then that Iraj put on the pressure to get me to sign the papers to refinance the house, and all hell began to break loose, ending in his horrible nights of terror, and ultimately the divorce.

So Jamshid didn't have a gas station in the U.S., but he owned a restaurant in Canada, which he ran with the help of Lelah and a couple of cousins, and he was doing quite well. (I gathered that Nasser simply lazed around the place "finding himself" and generally being petted and obnoxious.)

Jamshid had betrayed me, but I felt I had to try to see if I could get any help from him, at least try to find out where Iraj was and learn something of his plans. I decided it would be best if I went to Canada. It's too easy to brush someone off on the phone. Face to face, Jamshid might find it much more difficult to go on treating me in such a hard-hearted way.

S·EVEN

SINCE APRIL 12 I HAD SPOKEN TWICE TO JAMSHID AND Lelah. Neither had apologized; neither had shown the slightest remorse over their part in the kidnapping. Immediately after Sara and Cy had begged me to come pick them up, I'd called Jamshid back. In a fit of emotion I'd told him how the children had cried and what they'd said.

"Do you understand what you've done?" I shouted. "You've been part of a conspiracy to hold my children hostage!" He hadn't seemed very concerned about that.

His wife had been more forthright with me when I'd reached her some days later. I'd demanded to know how she could have been part of the plot to kidnap Sara and Cy and take them to the country she had been desperate to leave with her daughters. And I asked her how she thought I must feel. "Who cares?" Lelah had responded gruffly. Obviously I had no illusions about getting sympathy or help from Jamshid and Lelah, but I could try to use them for my purposes.

Jamshid seemed taken aback when I phoned to say that Sue and I were coming to see him and Lelah. He hemmed and hawed, sounding for all the world like a guilty man who didn't want to confront one of the people he'd harmed. But finally, reluctantly, he agreed to see us.

On the plane to Toronto, Sue and I polished the speeches we'd roughed out. And I worked hard to put myself in the mood to play the role of a fallen woman trying to redeem herself, desperately wanting to be part of the Salimi family once again and to be reunited with her husband. I fought so hard against the rage and disgust I felt that I made myself sick to my stomach.

We checked into a hotel and went directly to Jamshid and Lelah's apartment. I steeled myself to cross their threshold and enter the place from which my children had been stolen. I couldn't look into the faces of this treacherous couple for fear my anger would show. The sounds of their children's voices saddened me enough, but when I caught a glimpse of the toys that Sara and Cy had taken from home to play with on their "vacation" here, I was overwhelmed with grief. Bile rose in my throat. I wanted to rip Jamshid's heart out. One of their daughters started to play with a game of Cy's. Suddenly I was crying—out of sadness, yes, but also out of fury that I didn't dare express. Thank God for Sue. She took over, explaining that I was just too distraught about the situation in general, Iraj's refusal to believe me, my apprehension about meeting him in Iran. I rocked myself and nodded. Jamshid promised to speak with Iraj.

I got a grip on my emotions and told him how ill my

father was. Fortunately, we had perfected the story, because Jamshid had a lot of specific questions. We were confident, though, that our account was seamless and would hold up. We couldn't get any information out of Jamshid, but we had delivered our messages and, I hoped, convinced Jamshid my position was genuine. Now we wanted to get out. Fast. As if there was plague in that apartment. But it would seem impolite, so we had to force ourselves to sit there like dummies and try to make pleasant chitchat.

Adrenaline was zinging through my body, and for a long time after we got back to the hotel, I couldn't calm down. I was so angry and so bitter. Seeing the toys had pushed me over the edge.

I knew I might have made a misstep by going to Canada; it proved to be more than that. The repercussions were unexpected and severe.

On May 14 I spoke with Iraj, making short work of asking about him and the kids and quickly mentioning that I had gone to visit his brother the week before. He was not in a good mood, and his first question should have alerted me that something was up.

"Where did you stay?" he asked.

"A hotel in the city. I couldn't be around children."

"Jamshid didn't call me. I assume it was a regular visit," he said in an ominously quiet voice. "What was the purpose? What did you do?"

"I was just telling Jamshid how I feel about you and the kids."

"Did you talk to Nasser?" he asked.

"No," I said, explaining that he'd been away.

The call went on in this apparently innocent vein for a minute or so, but I was getting shaky.

It was almost a relief when Iraj burst out, "It is bothering me that you are spending the kids' money. I want a hundred thousand dollars. The house is two hundred thousand dollars equity; the contents are one hundred thousand. My kids need a bedroom here. You borrowed two hundred thousand, but I see no papers, account, withdrawal options. I won't do communications with you, I have the right to tell you to move the kids' bedrooms here! I have the right to get support from you. You have no motherly love, or you would send the money. I don't care if the State Department says traveling to Iran is dangerous. Get here!"

"You're demanding all this money—"

"You can sell the house and get money from your rich family," he interrupted. "You go around in the same circle. The starting point is my letter."

"I need to talk face to face."

"I'm not going to wait on you long. One week! The money and you here."

"I'm not comfortable going there."

"Is that your answer?"

"No," I said quickly.

"I won't meet you anywhere. You come here. You need to apologize for what you've done. What have you done? You're a bitch."

He hung up. Things went from bad to worse. The next call really threw me. For once I didn't have to call him. He called me, screaming from the first. He said he'd learned that I had gone to Toronto for a "sexual liaison with that boyfriend." What? He told me Jamshid had seen me with a man.

Were all these people on drugs and hallucinating? I was dumbfounded and told him so, firmly saying that Sue was my only companion on the trip.

He shouted that my visit had been for ulterior motives. He issued his ultimatum again: If I didn't arrive in Iran within a week and with papers and cash in hand, he would never speak with me again or allow the children to do so. Further, he would move them out of Tabriz, and I would never, ever know where they were.

He was screaming. And he was throwing everything within reach of the phone. I could hear things breaking and thudding against walls or floors. Iraj was having a tantrum.

I lost control and called him and his family a bunch of criminals.

He hung up.

I pulled myself together, and we worked on organizing a script for the next conversation, praying there would be a next conversation. We *had* to get things back on track.

When I got him on the phone, I quickly explained that I had no boyfriend, and I was perfectly capable of going to Canada by myself but had chosen to have Sue with me. And I apologized to him. It did no good. He blew up again. "Proof!" he shouted. "I want proof of the sincerity of your words."

And that proof was to take the form of money and papers, papers and money, as he kept repeating. He accused me of having an affair in Toronto simply to mock him and his family, then he screamed, "The hell with the kids."

My nerves snapped. I lost it. I threw the script to the wind. I condemned. I cursed. But there was some residual good sense beneath my anger that prompted me not to completely abandon the role I was playing with him. I ended by saying, "If you can take my going to Jamshid's so wrongly and turn it against me, then maybe you're not a person I can love. Right now, I hate your guts." And I slammed down the phone.

It felt good. Great. It was terrific to be the one hanging up for a change.

Then I came down. Hard.

Dear Lord, what had I done? I was scared. And ashamed. For the sake of my children I should have held on. They needed me, and I had lost control. If Iraj made good on his threats, they might be lost to me forever—I wouldn't even know where they were living, or with whom.

He might do anything—anything. I was sure then and I'm sure now that he'd just had a psychotic break.

And I've never felt more guilty or more desperate in my life.

I became despondent in the days after my loss of control with Iraj. I didn't follow my exercise program, and until then I'd been religious about doing it every day; I didn't attend a single class in the graduate education program I was enrolled in. I wasn't eating well and I didn't even think about trying to get to sleep anymore.

Now I began to spend more and more hours in Sara and Cy's rooms, touching their things, curling up on their beds, looking through their books, holding their toys. I would pull out scrapbooks and spend hours pouring over photos of them. Their odors lingered in their blankets and the clothing in their closets. Sometimes I could imagine them so vividly that it was as if I could see them playing or reading or getting ready for bed. I was mourning their loss as if they were dead, and I was joined in this vigil by their cat, Benjamin Franklin, who prowled their rooms restlessly, crying forlornly. But I didn't cry; I was beyond tears, too deep in grief even to cry. I just couldn't stand it. Gone. My children were gone—I hadn't seen them for a month; I hadn't been allowed to speak to them for almost two weeks.

And Jamshid and Lelah had their three little girls at home to care for and love. How I hated them and their treachery—all of it, from their helping in the abduction to the most recent lies they'd told Iraj. I dwelled on them, trying to reconcile what they had done in the last couple of months with my relationship with them in the past.

> Life can only be understood backwards;
> but it must be lived forwards.
> —Soren Kierkegaard

During the months after my visit to Iran, Iraj sent me many letters reaffirming his marriage proposal and begged me to come back. He was sure I would be happy with him and urged me to disregard press accounts of conditions in the country. In the early summer of 1979 he wrote specifically to invite me to Jamshid's wedding. I'd had many good times with Jamshid and was really fond of him; I'd also been doing a lot of agonizing over my relationship with Iraj and knew it was time to make up my mind. I decided to return to Iran.

I felt just as apprehensive on the long flight, but for different reasons. How would things work out between Iraj and me? What was the country really like under the leadership of the puritanical Ayatollah?

It was great to be reunited with Iraj. And it was exciting to be off to Tabriz—but not until I donned a *chador* his mother had sent for me to wear, because women in Western dress were being stoned by the Revolutionary Guard. That news shook me, but still I was really looking forward to the wedding festivities, which Iraj had told me would be so different from any I'd ever known. This wedding wasn't at all like a Western one—except for the bride's gown, which was white satin, encrusted with pearls and beads, and complete with veil and tiara; it would be worn many times for parties, as well as for the religious and civil ceremonies. This was a wedding in the nomadic tradition of the Salimi family, not in the tradition of the bride's urban, middle-class family, which was headed by her father, a policeman. And in nomadic tradition, the wedding lasted about forty days and forty nights, or maybe it was only a month. But it seemed like forever.

I hadn't arrived in time for either marriage ceremony, religious or civil, but I was told the ceremonies were the least of it. The rest of the "wedding" was a procession to homes of family members, where the couple was feted and given gifts—lots and lots of gifts. I thought this custom would have made more sense in olden times when it took many days to travel between family members spread over hundreds of miles of desert; it seemed a little archaic in 1979. However, as there isn't a lot of entertainment in Iranian society, I could see it provided a welcome opportunity for partying and visiting, and that it wasn't a tradition that was going to be abandoned anytime soon.

The Ayatollah had outlawed Western dancing and music at these ceremonies, but this didn't make any difference to the groom, his bride, or either of their families. I attended some rousing good parties for Jamshid and

Lelah. The whole thing fascinated me. Lelah had fetched a very high dowry—Jamshid paid 100,000 *tomans* to her father—because she was considered one of the greatest beauties in Tabriz. Green-eyed, red-haired, and voluptuous at sixteen, Lelah was indeed extremely pretty, and very warm and friendly to me. In addition to the hefty dowry, Jamshid had built a lovely house for her; it was marble-faced and two-storied. He was doing extremely well as a mechanical engineer in the oil refinery, but I suspected that Iraj had helped out financially. One of the things I'll never forget was seeing a little open-backed U-Haul truck, perilously overloaded, come to a halt on the dirt street in front of their brand new house. Jamshid and his brothers set about unloading dozens of rugs, small wooden inlaid tables, samovars, cushions, trays, and vases. But the most impressive item on the truck was a huge wooden bed, its head- and foot-board magnificently carved, which had been made for the couple and was the gift of her parents.

After about a week or so, Iraj and I returned to Teheran, where I stayed with him for almost three months. He had a large, airy five-room apartment in the north of the city, not far from the American embassy. He was excited about the revolution, which he believed was going to turn the country into a real democracy. I was skeptical, more skeptical with each passing day. But all that aside, Iraj and I were getting along very well. We believed we were previewing what marriage between us might be like.

I thoroughly enjoyed playing housewife in Teheran, with its curious mix of the exotic and the modern. On my daily shopping rounds I progressed from the baker to the green grocer to the butcher; so different from supermarket shopping, so much more fun. I bought spices and pistachios in the Grand Bazaar and read in a park just off Takht-E-Jamshid, a major boulevard—until the choking pollution drove me back into the apartment.

Iraj and I had romantic evenings at home with candle-light dinners and music. We got to know lots of couples our age who were well-educated and professionally successful, and we enjoyed dinner parties and outings with them. And I began to see firsthand why Iraj was so important to his family. He had an uncanny ability to cut through miles of the thickest red tape and get something accomplished even when no other Salimi had been able to make any progress, such as getting a phone installed, or the proper permits issued to expand a business. If bureaucracy had made getting things done difficult under the shah, it made them impossible under the Ayatollah, yet somehow Iraj was able to succeed.

We had adventures. We made a hot, dusty, and difficult trip to the vast oil fields of Abadan; we went down to the Persian Gulf; I rode a camel, and improved my Farsi. But there were clouds on this sunny horizon. We weren't the least bit afraid for *my* safety—Iranians would tell me straight out that they hated America, but liked Americans—but we were afraid for *our* safety. Living together without benefit of marriage subjected us to many dangers. We could have been arrested, stoned by our neighbors, or worse.

Soon, though, I did become really afraid. And that was when I became an eyewitness to history. I was there when the Ayatollah denounced the United States as the "Great Satan," when our embassy was stormed and our people taken hostage. Fanatic throngs clogged the streets, demonstrating passionately for the Ayatollah and with mindless fury against the old regime, its supporters at home, and its allies abroad. I was horrified by the violence exhibited by these rabid demonstrators, who burned effigies, flagellated themselves, hurled rocks at things foreign. Night and day jeering mobs surrounded our embassy and overflowed into nearby streets, shouting, "Death to all American devils!" Terror was the new Shah of All Shahs.

I stayed inside as much as possible, a prisoner in Iraj's apartment, which seemed to me to have suddenly been set down in an utterly different country from the Iran I'd been exploring and learning to appreciate. This was strange, barbaric territory now. My family was worried sick—and so was I. And Iraj was as appalled. We talked late into the nights, with him trying to persuade me to stay and marry him and me trying to persuade him to leave. Although he was sickened by the chaos and violence, he felt it would wear itself out sooner rather than later, and that in any event I would be safe married to him. I couldn't go along with it. The fate of my countrymen made me sad, frightened for what might be happening to them, and angry.

Unsuccessful in my last ditch effort to get Iraj to leave with me, I made plans to go home. I won a hard-fought battle to get a reservation on one of the last Pan Am flights out of Iran the week after the siege of the embassy. My good-bye to Iraj was tearful. Yet I have to confess that I was relieved to the point of joy to be headed for that plane. My departure was scary, though. I had about fifty dollars in American currency in my purse for whatever I might need at JFK in case my parents were delayed picking me up, and a female Revolutionary Guard at the airport spotted it when she searched me in the departure lounge. She went wild, screaming, raving. But at last, heaven only knows why, she let me go, bruisingly pushing me through the gate. It was horrible, and I felt fortunate beyond words to get out of her clutches and onto that plane. But I was shaking like a leaf, desperate for the plane to get safely off the ground. The flight was full of jubilant American businessmen celebrating their escape to freedom with Bloody Marys and Scotch on the rocks. I was terrified that the Revolutionary Guard would storm aboard and arrest us all because of the alcohol.

The events from November on regarding the hostages are well documented. Reading about the ugly turmoil and cruel treatment of them every day in the paper disturbed and angered me as it did all Americans. And I feared for Iraj's safety in the midst of people who seemed to have descended on the earth from a long-ago time when brutishness and ignorance held sway. The Iranians were so proud of their great and ancient civilization— how could they deny it by plunging into such a dark night as the mindlessness of mob rule?

Just six months later Iraj fled, calling me from Germany and begging me to join him there. He was ready, he said, to live in the West with me. We toured Germany and had a wonderful time. He proposed, urging me to marry him right away. My head full of romantic dreams, I agreed.

Our wedding was the exact opposite of Jamshid and Lelah's. Not a single family member or friend attended the ceremony in the serene, quaint city of Copenhagen. I was a bit disappointed; nonetheless I thought it was a perfect place to start a perfect marriage. Within days, my beautiful dreams were fading. Iraj was not a happy groom. As soon as his green card was issued, we returned to the

United States, and from the first he acted resentful, as if I had taken something from him, denied him something he yearned to have.

When I discovered I was pregnant, I was overjoyed, and Iraj was too. He adored Sara, though he never lifted a finger to care for her or to help me in any way. He added criticism of me as a mother to his growing list of complaints. I thrived on mothering Sara, but my dreams of a good marriage were now irretrievably shattered. I was gathering courage to find out about getting a divorce when I learned I was pregnant again. No matter how bad the relationship with Iraj was, I was overcome with happiness to be having another child. When Cy was born, healthy and bright-eyed, Iraj surprised me yet again. Here was the male child so much desired by Iranian men, and yet Iraj turned from his son. He paid no attention to the baby. Any time or affection he had for the children was all directed to Sara. His reaction baffled me. What thoughts filled his murky mind about having a son?

Shortly after Cy was born, I developed a friendship with Ellie, another American woman, also a new mother and the wife of an Iranian who worked in the same company as Iraj. As Ellie and I grew closer, we began to confide in each other about our problems with our husbands. Some of those problems were remarkably similar. Both of us were criticized daily by husbands who came home from the office, plunked themselves down on the sofa, and stayed sprawled there, watching us closely, making "suggestions," that were in fact demands.

As far as Iraj was concerned, I didn't know how to do anything—do housework, care for the children, cooking, or analyze world affairs. My opinions were as "stupid" as my way of mopping a floor was "wrong." When I defended one of my comments or observations about news or politics, or explained why I cleaned terrazzo tile as I did, I invited his anger. It simply enraged him that I didn't acknowledge that he knew everything, was absolutely right on all issues, and that I dared try to "explain away" my "inadequacy" and "incompetence." I grew more and more quiet, my bubbly spirits stilled. I felt I was only my true self around my women friends, Ellie in particular. I didn't realize then, however, that even around them I wasn't quite the energetic, enthusiastic, and self-confident person I'd been before.

I did a lot of hard thinking, a lot of analyzing. I tried to figure out what came from a clash of cultures between Iraj and me and what came from his personality problems, and mine. Take for example the business of his sprawling on the sofa and giving directions as he reclined. This, I decided, was cultural, and I should try to disregard how irritating it seemed. This was what he'd been raised to do when he got home from work. It appeared to be more than it was because our house wasn't furnished with rugs and cushions, and I hadn't grown up seeing men come in and lounge around in such a fashion.

The close observation too was something I'd noticed in Iran. People tend to watch each other and comment on what they see. They don't come home and read the newspaper or chat or turn on the evening news. And as they remark on what they see one doing, they relate it to things the person has or has not done before, or what a relative did or did not do in the past; a lot of this, I had thought when I could understand more of the language, was negative, whether comments were made in front of the person in question or behind his back. So, I rationalized, even the comments on everything Iraj watched me do were a cultural difference, one I believed I could handle, since I realized exactly what it was.

But what was I to do about the incessant criticism of my every move and word? I tried many things, all unsuccessfully. I could only deal with it by accepting his harsh judgments of me or by closing my mind to his faultfinding. Sometimes I did far too much of the former; most of the time I shut myself off. This took a heavy toll on my feelings of self-worth and on my pleasure in daily life.

Iraj complained all the time about his coworkers, his boss. He was frustrated and angry that he was being slighted at the office. On several occasions he railed about the fact that he worked with idiots who hadn't the ability to recognize his genius! I realized that what he was *saying* was absurd, but what he was *feeling* was true for him, and painful. I felt meltingly sorry for him. He seemed so homesick and displaced at such moments. I deluded myself into thinking that he only needed time, time to adjust, time to grow comfortable with the ways of work and homelife in the West. At least I'd come far enough to understand that his westernization was a thin veneer; scratch it, and Iraj was still an Iranian without a secure place even in his own society, where his family had moved relatively swiftly from being nomads to being stationary members of a new middle class.

My self-esteem had just about hit rock bottom when, slowly, my conversations with Ellie and other women made me start to wake up. Iraj went far beyond Ellie's husband in being mean and inconsiderate. I was raising the children, keeping house, waiting on Iraj, doing his errands, and being his home secretary. There was more than cultural difference at work. Sometimes I could hardly recognize the frazzled, lonely woman I saw in the mirror. I had known a stormy homelife throughout my childhood, but compared to Iraj I was the picture of stability and happiness in my relationships. Brooding, melancholy, tyrannical, and by turns repentant, kind, and generous, he was a Dr. Jekyll/Mr. Hyde, with Mr. Hyde in the last throes of swallowing Dr. Jekyll as our marriage wore on.

By the time Cy was a toddler, the blinders were completely off my eyes, and I knew that Iraj was a man in deep psychological trouble with whom I could never have a successful marriage. Still, however, he was able to manipulate me. In the true pattern of the abuser, he would come humbly back after a particularly vicious verbal assault, to which I reacted by going to "visit" my sister or parents or threatening to leave for good, and he would beg, plead, cry for forgiveness for what at those moments he would term his "nasty, mean ways." Then came the endless promises of good behavior. He got to me when he broke down. I would be filled with compassion for him, filled with guilt for what I might have done to make him unhappy, and I would accept his apologies, believe in his promises, and make up. But soon, it would start all over again.

All this time. All these dramatic, terrible events. I was heartsick remembering the past, even more heartsick over the loss of my children. Still, I would go on remembering and mooning over Sara and Cy's things—until suddenly I snapped out of it. I can't say exactly why or how this happened. I believe that my anger at Iraj and at Jamshid's treachery, the visions of him and Lelah gloating over my despair and living happily with their three daughters, safe and snug in Canada, had the effect of a hard kick in the rear. And I believe God helped me then to pull myself out of the black hole I was in and regain my will to act.

I blanched in embarrassment when I realized I'd been wallowing in grief, bitterness, self-pity. I would not go on one more minute that way. I had to get up and get busy. I had to go back to class, to prepare for a future that I had to believe in. I had to exercise and eat right so I would be healthy enough to fight. If I collapsed, who could deal with all the disparate elements of the situation and be able to get the kids out of Iran? My family would try, but I was the key.

I stormed back into battle. Iraj had gone berserk in that last interaction; I needed to analyze all this. So, again, I turned to Dr. Kranshawe and to a psychiatrist who had seen both Iraj and me in the past, Dr. Thomas Cipriani. They knew the full history of the family I'd grown up in, the abuse I'd suffered during my marriage to Iraj, and how I'd finally been able to break out of that pattern of abuse and free myself. And they were invaluable in helping me assess the situation.

It was the psychiatrist, Dr. Cipriani, who first labeled Iraj "a tortured soul." Straddling two cultures, belonging to neither, Iraj was living in a psychological no-man's-land where he was always torn and always uncomfortable. Ironically, his problems were deepened and worsened because of his intelligence and drive, and his mother's prodding him to use those qualities to better himself. He had pulled up some of his roots but hadn't successfully transplanted them elsewhere, and those remaining long roots from his homeland kept pulling at him. His psychological problems were a curious blend of things uniquely— and pathologically—his and those universally the product of cultural and social mobility.

Who was Iraj Salimi? Even he couldn't be sure. Something as simple and fundamental as his name wasn't a given, as far as he was concerned. Most of us never consider what our names should or shouldn't be. For Iraj, his name was something he felt he should choose, and I think it is a powerful example of his confusion over his identity and how much of himself he thought he could make and remake. For our purpose here he is "Iraj Salimi." When he applied for U.S. citizenship not long after our marriage, he decided to change his name to something "more American."

He made lists, consulting friends and acquaintances for suggestions. After a lot of going back and forth, he finally chose "Ronald Fars." Fars is an ancient, aristocratic, and powerful name in Iran going back to the origin of the word for their language, Farsi; Ronald sounded elegant and important to him—Ronald Colman, Ronald Reagan. Of course, whenever he went back to Iran, he was Iraj Salimi.

Just as he had no true name, he had no true role models. His father was ill-educated and passive, a man of the "old ways," except that he was unforgivably henpecked. Iraj was crazy about my father, loving his success, his personal charm, his power. Iraj would claim that my father was his "soul mate," that they saw the world identically and were the closest friends. This was far from the way my father saw his son-in-law and their relationship. And at some deep level I believe Iraj knew his claim to closeness with Dad was false, or at least shaky. And even Dad wasn't perfect in his eyes; Iraj was disappointed that my father wasn't a "more firm husband, a more strict disciplinarian." So even my much revered father "failed" him.

Without authority figures in either culture to look up to consistently, Iraj vacillated, following the example of first one, then another, and almost always inappropriately. I think he was trying to find a center, a self that comfortably gathered up all his divergent beliefs, attitudes, and behavior. In virtually every instance, though, there wasn't any real role model, so he was thrown back on his own.

Overwhelmed with this responsibility for his own emotions and actions, he couldn't cope. He'd blame others for his frustrations and failures—primarily me, and when I wouldn't do, his coworkers, boss, the president of the United States, the shah, then the Ayatollah. He destroyed relationship after relationship with people at work, moving from one section to another at AT&T, off to another company, back to AT&T. These stormy professional relationships weren't quite as ugly as our personal relationship, but in some cases they came close. When even blaming others and rationalization didn't help, he would blow up. He'd get so enraged, he'd strike out at everyone and everything around him. This included traditions and institutions—and me, his favorite and best scapegoat.

The traditions he most frequently and violently attacked or embraced were Iranian and Islamic. Iraj was extremely ambivalent about Islam in general and his

Shiite heritage in particular. He often told me and our circle that he was an atheist. At other times, though, he would seem to observe some Islamic traditions. I recall a time when he was about to get Nasser out of Iran that he decided I should have the "modesty of a good Muslim woman" and wear a scarf over my hair whenever I ventured out of the house. This was only one of many such edicts I would not follow, though I rebelled too quietly perhaps.

I've read a lot over the last few years about Iran, about the Muslim world, and about psychology, to try to increase my understanding. A number of things written by Middle East scholar George Fuller have been helpful. He tells us that Sunni, the majority Islamic sect in the Muslim world, has a less apocalyptic theology than the Shiite sect.

Iraj's family, like almost everyone in Iran, is Shiite. About 93 percent of the people in Iran are Shiites; some of the tribal minorities are Sunnites; the rest are Zoroastrians, Jews, and Christians. Fuller characterizes the Shiites as being noted for "extravagant rhetoric, xenophobia and [the] embrace of martyrdom." Iraj might deny his Shiite heritage, but it was there for all to see. What was his language if not extravagant? Certainly he went to extremes in his threats, accusations, professions of love and hate. Was he xenophobic? Yes and no. Out of control, in the grip of his obsession with smuggling his brothers out of Iran, he would often crow about their superiority, his superiority, the superiority of "most thinking Iranians" to the mullahs and Americans ruining everyone's destiny. (He'd been a big supporter of the Ayatollah's regime in the early days, but when his brother was put in prison, he became so angry that he ordered me to put away—not throw away, put away—all of the Persian pieces in our house.)

And he definitely was given to martyrdom, in his megalomaniacal family "leadership," particularly. He really did see himself as a saint and was only too happy to point this out to me; in sharp contrast I was a devil. And maintaining all these contradictory and wildly emotional images of himself often led to rash, destructive acts. What could have been more destructive than kidnapping his own children and leaving behind the wreckage of lives, a career, property?

America, progressive and rich, enchanted Iraj. He admired the can-do philosophy of most Americans, and our national emphasis on invention and innovation. Most of all he was a sucker for things. How he loved the availability of things in America. He couldn't get enough—stereos, cars, Walkmans, books, CDs, personal computers, cable television. Truly, Iraj Salimi could shop till he dropped. On the other side of the coin, though, he also hated America, the land of power over other countries in the world, the "young upstart" nation with no tradition and virtually no history. How he must have yearned for a country that had only all the things he liked most about Iran and America. But that was a country he could not make.

And I could not make a life with Iraj. I have learned and I am learning so much about myself, particularly why I married Iraj and why I stayed in a dreadful marriage so long. As I write this, my sisters and I are in therapy together, trying to learn to appreciate the positives in our early family life and overcome the negatives. This job may take a very long time for the three of us. We are superconscious of Tolstoy's observation, "All happy families resemble one another, but each unhappy family is unhappy in its own way," and we're committed to plumbing the depths of how we were unhappy in our own way.

One of the questions I'm asked most frequently is why I stayed married to Iraj for so long. The short answer is that I was the perfect victim, prepared to do the bidding of those close to me and to expect little for myself. But I expected a lot for my children. When Iraj started to make life so difficult that it amounted to abuse of the children, I had to act. I had had the support of my women friends, my sisters, then a therapist. Every step I'd taken had empowered me to take another. I'd gone back to college to get the credits I needed for a teaching certificate; I'd started working part time, and the salary I was earning, about fifty dollars a week, was so beautiful because of all it represented to me it might as well have been a million. When Iraj threatened my life, I was able at long last to realize that the temperature was at the boiling point, and that I had to stop "adapting" and jump out of the pail.

This is the background with which Dr. K, Dr. Cipriani, and I were working. What was the best course of action?

First, both doctors felt that my outburst with Iraj might not have been as damaging as I thought it was. Submerged once again in his paternalistic, anti-American society, Iraj was isolated from Western influence. While it might seem that the family and the culture gave him a kind of airtight reinforcement of his position, the doctors emphasized that this was not necessarily the case. It was simplistic to assume he was now a thoroughly paternalistic, completely authoritarian Iranian male. They felt it was crucial to remember he was that man "straddling two cultures and belonging to neither." He had been out of Iran for a very long time, more than a decade. He'd been Americanized in too many ways to find life hunky-dory in a country governed by fundamentalist Islamic laws. No more Scotch and Marlboros for him late at night when he was stressed out. No more of a lot of things Iraj was accustomed to. Moreover, he didn't seem to have a job there to give him income and much needed distraction of some type, so he was focused on this crisis and conditions in his parents' traditional Iranian home. His readjustment had to be difficult and painful.

The doctors pointed out that my voice, while important in Iraj's ear, wasn't the only one. There were two other voices making a huge impact on him—the children's. Not only was Iraj unaccustomed to being responsible for them, he was also unaccustomed to being with them. Sara and Cy were unhappy. If they were their usual vocal selves, or even if they'd been cowed into being quiet, as I desperately feared, they would display this unhappiness. It couldn't fail to have some effect on him, no matter how much he tried to ignore or discount it. So in this fight, I had two strong allies inside the enemy camp, and even at that very moment, Sara and Cy's homesickness and their longing for their mother were probably eating at Iraj. His level of stress, Drs. Kranshawe and Cipriani pointed out, had to equal if not to exceed mine. They thought there was every possibility I could get him to begin talking to me in earnest very soon. And, they suggested, I should press hard for that visit with the children, who were undoubtedly pressing hard, too, to see their mother!

I redoubled my efforts to reach Iraj. I called him at the farm, in Tabriz, at every number in every place he could be. Whenever a phone was answered I was told he was "away on a trip." I tried to reach his cousin in Chicago; I telephoned some of Iraj's old friends and colleagues. All of them said they had no news of him. I was tearing my hair out in frustration. But then I started to hear that he would be back, and I became certain that I'd be able to get a call through to him.

Now I was sure about our next steps. It was time to call in the marines!

EIGHT

DURING THAT LAST MISERABLE TANTRUM IRAJ HAD THROWN following his fantastic accusation that I'd stashed a man in my hotel room in Toronto, mocking his family with the "affair," I had scribbled a note on the top of my script for that day: *We need Rambo!* And did I ever mean it. As Iraj shouted and smashed things against the wall, it seemed our prospects for dealing successfully with this maniac had dwindled until they seemed nonexistent. And the prospects still seemed poor after my conversations with the good doctors and with my family.

We were feeling that everything we'd done to date might have been utterly futile. Time might be running out. Iraj might be hiding the children right now or be on the verge of doing so. I couldn't afford to be squeamish any longer about recovering the kids. We had to turn to the one alternative we'd been avoiding. In fact, we *did* need Rambo, and we had to find him fast.

We started to search for competent professionals who were able to undertake a commando-type operation to recover Sara and Cy inside Iran. The U.S. military's best special forces units had been marshaled into a super task force to go into Iran and get out our hostages, only to fail and lose everything in the desert, so what was I thinking?

It was not so irrational or impossible as it might seem at first. This wasn't a large-scale government-against-government action, where we might go in and be detected by radar or have our helicopters conk out on us. I'd thought about going into Iran, fantasized about it enough to have a few ideas that made sense. First of all, a well-trained covert group could enter the country with papers from another country or sneak in without Iranian papers through Russia or Turkey. Tabriz is close to the Turkish border, and as I'd learned from Iraj, several roads through the mountains offered good escape routes. If Iraj could smuggle people out of Iran, so could I with a little help—make that a *lot* of help—from real professionals. The odds were definitely not in our favor, but they weren't insurmountable. And I was going to find either the bravest people on the planet or the looniest to help me.

Sue, Mike, and I devoted all our energies now to locating a recovery group. We used the phone at my house, the phone at Sue's, while going through all the magazine and newspaper stories we had collected, looking for names of recoverers in the success stories about children retrieved from abroad, from the Middle East especially. The first hurdle was just getting names and numbers. The yellow pages does not have a listing for the kinds of guys we were trying to locate. It was a slow, plodding process. We spent hour upon hour contacting someone who knew someone who knew someone. . . The first names had come from that short list given to me a couple of weeks before by Holly Planels. (It was this list that had included Patrick Buckman's name.) This was a great starting point.

I even called Ross Perot's office, since he had rescued people in his company when they were in jeopardy in Iran. While I didn't get to speak directly with Mr. Perot, I did get a message back through his assistant that he was very sorry he couldn't give me any advice as he no longer had dealings in Iran or contacts there.

The majority of the people we first contacted refused right off the bat to try anything in Iran. We began to get really discouraged when almost everyone we talked to said that the area in which the kids were being held was strictly hands-off and added that such a job was impossible, or too dangerous, or otherwise out of the question. It made me frantic. And I had no sense of humor. If things had been different I actually might have gotten a good laugh from listening to one tough-talking fellow who advised me, "Just tell that ex-husband of yours to take a hike. He doesn't want to be saddled with the kids, and when he finds out you're not going to give him a dime, he'll throw 'em back to you like they're hot potatoes." Maybe. But that gambit was just too risky for me. Under the circumstances I was not impressed with his advice. And I was not amused.

We reached a few people who didn't treat us like fruitcakes that they wanted to hang up on. These guys put up no objection to trying a rescue in such a high-risk area, but most of them sent shivers down our spines because they seemed to be toughs and braggarts, and a few even sounded like real nuts. How I wished I were dealing with Patrick Buckman! But he would undertake such a recovery anywhere—*except* Iran.

I thought a lot about the advice Patrick had given me about the charlatans I was bound to encounter if I went this route. Many of them, he'd warned, would be after a fat fee, not a successful operation. They'd demand most of the money in advance, and with it snug in their pockets, they wouldn't pay much attention to the actual recovery, only going through the motions of planning and executing it, perhaps even aborting it at the last minute. Then there were the wild and reckless guys with glory on their minds and a death wish in their hearts. We were on guard to screen out these sorts of people. Among other things, we insisted on references and recommendations from people they'd accomplished successful recoveries for. And we checked and double-checked those references.

We were aware at all times that there was no glamour in this, only a very real danger to Sara and Cy. And, I think, we were able to make the good decisions we had to make because we were so conscious of how unprepared we were to deal with these people! It was crucial in this unfamiliar situation, I understood, for me not to get swept away by someone's words, or to be overwhelmed by how little I knew. I decided right at the beginning to approach these people as if I were interviewing them to repair my car or fix a leaky roof. If I kept thinking about how I was trying to recruit 007 or hire a real-life Chuck Norris, I'd be in trouble!

I'd say that the people we interviewed fell roughly into two groups: the paramilitary types and the covert operators. The first were primarily ex–military men, some of whom seemed to be involved with the survivalist movement and periodically went off to the wilderness to prepare for the invasion of—well, God knows who or what. The types I call covert operators were private investigators, ex-spies, former policemen, and so-called recovery specialists. Many of the recovery specialists had started out as reabductors of people, usually teenagers, who'd been in thrall to the leader of a religious or political cult. These specialists often told me of their extensive experience in deprogramming—that is, unbrainwashing— those they'd been able to get out. Some of the private detectives had gotten into recovery work through divorce cases they'd handled.

The language of the two groups differed. The military types would say things about the mission and the grab and reconnaissance; the second talked about safe houses and passports and surveillance. Sometimes I felt as if I'd been dropped into a Sam Spade or Spenser novel, and I'd have to shake my head and try to get them to talk to me like real people.

Of course I had tried immediately to enlist the men whose success in getting a child out of the Middle East was reported in an article I read, entitled "The Search for Lauren." This was a group called Corporate Training Unlimited, which had been organized to provide security for individuals and businesses, primarily against terrorists. And that was certainly the appropriate objective for them, as they were all former members of the First Ranger Battalion of the Seventy-fifth Airborne and Special Forces, more commonly called Delta Force, the army's antiterrorist unit. I spoke with one of the co-heads of the group, Don Feeney, a man in his mid thirties who was originally from Brooklyn, New York. He was very polite and apologetic in explaining that the recovery of Lauren had been a "one-time corporate event" for CTU, and they were definitely not going to undertake another such operation. Another strikeout!

Then our luck began to turn, and we were finding likely candidates, men who weren't averse to a mission in Iran and didn't seem completely crazy, who spoke in a measured way about the hazards of an operation there, without dismissing or minimizing the difficulty but seeming to have confidence that they could pull it off. A few asked me to send them any information I had that might help them evaluate whether or not such an action was feasible. They wanted maps of the cities where the Salimi family had residences; they wanted photos of Iraj, his relatives, the children. I sent along some of these items to a couple of the people who sounded most competent and had the best references.

One serious contender in the early round of calls was a contingent of former Green Berets with offices in the Deep South. Most of these men had served together in Vietnam and were highly trained and experienced. Their leader was impressive, forceful, confident. But as soon as I got off the phone with him, I started to worry. On reflection I decided that the accounts he'd given me of "jobs" he'd successfully concluded were too full of dangers and violence. It seemed to me that he and his men had a chilling predisposition to use force in a situation where delicacy and finesse might work better. I nixed them.

To tell the truth, I was hating this whole process, because of what it meant ultimately. I really was afraid of using force because the children might get hurt;

physically, obviously, but also psychologically. To lessen the possibility of their being harmed in any way, I was looking for people who had some sensitivity, born of a real awareness of all the ramifications of recovery.

At last, though, it seemed all our interviews and references checks paid off. Through connections that friends of my brother and sister-in-law had, we got in touch with a security group headquartered in Manhattan; it was composed entirely of Israelis. Telephone interviews were reassuring; meeting with them in person clinched it: this was the group to go with.

I've given my word not to reveal the real names of the Israelis, their organization, or the nature of the private security work they do in the United States. They are well known in some upper echelons of business and government and had an excellent set of recommendations. I chose the group for a number of reasons, one of the most important of which was their ability to operate within Iran. People in Iran with whom they had close ties did freelance jobs for them, they said. Among other things, those inside the country would be able to make direct observations in Tabriz and give me independent, first-hand information about how Sara and Cy looked, what they were doing each day, and so forth.

Although it was never said outright, I got the impression that the Israeli contacts in Iran had helped in the successful "evacuation" of Jews when the Ayatollah had announced his intention of making what was tantamount to a holy war against them. The threatened large-scale persecution forced many Jews to flee along a secret route; almost all of them got safely out of Iran.

I felt the hush-hush nature of the work of this group the second I entered their Manhattan office. The place looked as if it might be occupied by bankers or ordinary businessmen, which is exactly what the "employees" seemed to be. They dressed conservatively, very button-downed Brooks Brothers. The security of the operation was the best. A number of the assistants in the office were spouses or close relatives of the executives and field men in the group. No leaks there. A very tight, closed outfit. And this was important to me. At the risk of sounding paranoid, I have to say I worried about who knew what. It's that small-world thing. As far away as Iraj was physically, as remote as he seemed professionally and socially, still he had acquaintances, friends, relatives all over the place. You can never tell who might say what to whom. A few loose words, an official document, an inquiry—anything that might come to his attention and alert him to what I was trying to do—could mean disaster.

One of the people recommending the Israeli group, which I shall refer to as the I Group, told us that he had a strong suspicion that the key members had formerly served in the vaunted Mossad, the Israeli secret service. No one in the Israeli group ever mentioned such an association, but they didn't have to. After working with them for only a few days, it seemed clear that they were highly trained, very clever, and completely familiar with how to operate across international borders and against dangerous people. If they hadn't been in the Mossad, I had no doubt that they had been in one of their country's security agencies.

I was really impressed with the three men I dealt with. My primary contacts were two agents, whom I shall call Aaron and Isaac, and the head of the organization, Joshua. Aaron was a rather small man, about five feet six, who had a sweet and reassuring manner. Balding and tall, Isaac was much more reserved and stiff. And no one could have had any doubt that Joshua was the boss; tall and distinguished-looking with iron gray hair, he had a forceful personality and was impressively articulate.

Right off, Joshua directed the organization's contacts in Iran to start keeping tabs on Iraj, emphasizing that while they were monitoring his movements initially, they were to give the highest priority to getting as much information as possible about the children. This was the first of many illustrations of how softhearted and kind these Israeli men were; at every turn they showed deep concern about the welfare of the children and a great understanding of how I felt. They seemed to put themselves in my shoes and tried to track down everything current about Sara and Cy for a very worried mother.

We started with only the most general discussion, deferring serious planning until we had more information and I'd had some additional time to try to get through to Iraj. Persuading him to bring Sara and Cy out of Iran was still the goal—but for a very different reason now.

The I Group was not keen on a recovery in Iran, but they thought that if it became necessary they could pull it off, using one of their ace operatives. This man would enter Iran posing as a German businessman who was exploring the possibility of establishing a new plant in Tabriz. Why German? Because the I Group's man had legitimate German papers and because the Germans have a long and friendly history with Iranians. (When I was in Iran I often heard favorable things about the Germans; the nationality the Iranians had seemed to me to most dislike were the British.) Backed up by their people already doing surveillance on Iraj, the "German businessman" would wait in Tabriz for the moment when the children were out of the house and could safely be taken. He would escape via a route the I Group would not disclose, but which I presumed was one that had been used successfully in the flight of Iranian Jews. The in-country operative would handle Iraj—"detain him" was what Joshua said, and wouldn't I give almost anything to see them do that?—until they'd had ample time to get over the border to safety.

I was not casual about this. I was fully aware of how dangerous it was. Yet it made me rest easier to know that we had this plan in our back pockets in case Iraj could not be persuaded to bring the children out of Iran to meet with me in a third country.

Rob had given the I Group a modest retainer to get them started on their work. Now he and they negotiated a fee, especially for all the work to be done within Iran. The initial charge was $40,000.00.

When the phone rang on May 21 I was hoping it was Isaac or Aaron with some news for me. I was totally unprepared to hear the voice of the caller who greeted me: Iraj. And, trust me, it took a full minute for me to compose myself.

Very quickly it became clear that Drs. K and Cipriani, Sue, and Mike had been right. My outburst hadn't been the tragedy I feared; it had shaken Iraj. It also had convinced him that I wasn't acting, that I was being real with him, though he said he wasn't yet convinced of my sincerity. In other words, he'd faced the consequences of pushing me too far—the most serious of which for him, I'm sure, was the possibility he might not get any money from me.

Now he said that our last conversation had "troubled" him, and he realized "your outburst was honest, at least." So he had reconsidered his position and was willing to meet with me in Turkey. However, he would *not* bring the children, as this trip was to be a test of my sincerity, which would include my bringing cash with me to turn over to him.

I didn't have to pretend to be very interested in his proposal; I was ecstatic. And then he confirmed our suspicion that he was scared that he'd pushed me too hard before, because he put the children on the phone. Oh, God, how sweet their voices sounded. I hadn't spoken to them in weeks, and at first I could barely talk because I was so choked up. Cy and Sara were excited to hear my voice and told me how much they loved me and missed me and wanted to see me. And both said they wanted me to come and get them right away. When Sara whispered about how badly she wanted to come home, Iraj stopped her. He said if she spoke that way again he would not let her talk with me. Both children wanted to know if I was coming to Iran. As before, I explained to them that because I was an American it was very difficult for me to travel there. When Sara asked why, Iraj snatched the receiver from her.

To my relief he ignored what had passed between the children and me, emphasizing that he was quite agreeable to meeting me in another country. He said he'd given this some thought and decided Turkey would be the most convenient place for him.

I took a deep breath, pretending I hadn't even heard him talk about his convenience, and told him how happy, how thrilled, I was. I made my voice breathy, seductive, and played up to the sexual innuendo in comments he'd made earlier about seeing "if it is possible for us to reconcile," and "to have what we once had." This was really hard for me, because Iraj had said all this in the saccharine voice that I had come to hate in the last months of our marriage, when he'd been the most abusive. This syrupy tone was one he adopted when he was wheedling for money or sex, mostly sex, and I knew how easily it could slide down the scale into low, growling sounds of rage. It literally made me nauseous. But nothing, nothing was going to stop me now. He'd swallowed my baited hook—and this was one fish I was determined to reel in.

I told him again how happy I was, weaving into the conversation that since I'd been ill I was a little bit afraid of traveling all that distance alone. Perhaps my sister should come with me, I murmured.

To my surprise, he agreed, even saying he would enjoy seeing Sue.

There was one other thing he wanted, he added slyly. He wanted me to get a visa to travel into Iran "just in case," he said, "I can convince you that it is safe and wonderful here."

I gulped and merely said that I would certainly look into getting a visa, but with relations between the two governments the way they were, I had my doubts. In fact, it was out of the question because of the State Department ban on travel to Iran. So as to divert him from arguing this point, I tried to move to another subject, but he wasn't finished. There was going to be a conference on computer technology in Teheran in the middle of July. This might be an excellent time and place for our ultimate reconciliation, he said. A friend of his from the Philadelphia area was planning to attend, and

Iraj thought it might be very pleasant for me to have him as a traveling companion.

What the hell was this all about?

The conversation closed with my promise to call the following week to talk about arrangements for our meeting.

I hung up and started whooping and hollering with glee. A breakthrough! A giant step forward!

Sue was overjoyed. Mike was overjoyed. So were Beth and Rob and the Israeli group. Then those of us who really knew Iraj calmed down, and pretty fast. He was a cunning man, devious as the devil himself. He'd designated Turkey as the meeting place, arrogantly saying it would be most convenient for him. It was close, but Rome or Cairo wasn't a much longer trip by air. Why Turkey? He'd said he wanted me to get a visa to travel on with him from Turkey to Iran, if he could persuade me to do so. Persuade? I'd been subjected to his sort of persuasion in the past—screaming, threats, force causing bodily injury, sleep deprivation, attempted rape—and I hated to think what he might be planning for me now. Whatever it was, *persuade* would not be the word that any normal human being would use to describe his tactics, that was for sure.

All we could do was be vigilant, try to pick up on any clues he might drop inadvertently, and be prepared to counter any threatening move he might make.

Worried about his changeability, we decided I shouldn't wait a week to call him again but instead contact him on May 23. As we feared, he was a different man than he'd been on the twenty-first. He insisted that I agree to travel on with him from Istanbul to Tabriz. I acted surprised, insisting that it was dangerous for me to do that.

Iraj was having none of it. "If you really want to reconcile for my sake and the sake of the children," he said, "you would be willing to travel anywhere!"

I argued sweetly but to no avail. He was clearly furious that he wasn't controlling me; he was mad to exercise power over me. I wasn't sure how to handle him at this point and kept quiet.

And he made a significant demand: he wanted the children's American passports and his own American passport that he'd left with Jamshid. I was to bring them with me—along with the cash, of course.

What in heaven's name was he up to?

My father was in perfect health, thank God, and I was keeping in close touch with him and my mother. They were very supportive, and they were well coached in the roles they were to play if Iraj made a direct call to them. My sisters, brother, and I were concerned about this possibility—or should I say probability?—because of the past relationship that Iraj had constructed with Gloria and Ralph. He seemed to drop out of his memory the ugly scenes that had involved them, choosing to remember only good times, when they had treated him with the warmth and affection due their son-in-law. Oddly enough, he believed they were on his side against me in the divorce. This absolutely was not the case. My father had completely turned on him as soon as we'd moved back to the same town and he'd had the opportunity to see for himself how Iraj treated me and the children. My mother had been a force in trying to keep us together for a much longer time, but then her eyes too had been opened. Actually, for quite a while my mom had put a lot of pressure on me to stay married. Everything in her experience dictated that she would advise me that marriage was hell and one simply had to endure it. But, after a particularly awful evening one Halloween at our house, she had completely reversed her position.

All the grandchildren, costumed, made up and adorable, Sue and her husband, Beth and her boyfriend, and my brother and his wife, as well as our parents, had joined us for a little family party and early supper on Halloween in 1987. The children were quite young, so trick-or-treating was going to be only a few visits to our closest neighbors, and the family fun was the major event of the evening. At first Iraj joined in. Then something happened to him. He snapped. He strode out of the family room into the living room. The next hour and a half was hell. The men in the family each took a turn trying to find out what was the matter and coax him back to the party. Iraj glowered at them, wouldn't say a word. He turned on the television to a horror film, with the volume knob all the way up. Eerie sound effects, dialogue, and music boomed out at an earsplitting level. He was trying to drive my family out of the house, he began slamming doors. Beth took the children out for their tour. My parents left in disgust—after my father had taken me aside and told me in no uncertain terms that he was very upset and concerned and wanted to talk with me later about what was going on in my house with the lunatic I was married to. Sue's husband took their children home, but she stayed, afraid for my safety. Finally, I sent her away and desperately tried to make peace with Iraj, only to end up sleeping in Sara's room.

Iraj never called my parents while he held the children in Iran, or at any time after. I think his not calling is testimony to the fact that he really did know, deeply, that he had done an unforgivable and criminal thing.

We were in touch often with the I Group, who were now putting together ideas for a plan to rescue the children. And I was working with my attorney and law enforcement people to make sure I did everything I should, followed every law, every procedure, filed every paper. I no longer thought in terms of *if* we recovered the kids, but *when* we recovered them, and on the wonderful day that came to pass, I wanted everything in order. I wanted all the paperwork in place so the law would be in position to protect me and my children. As this case was unique in the township where we lived, the local police detective had a big job to do. I helped him dig for the information he needed.

Mike and I pored over the State Department brochure on what to do in cases of abduction, created a simple distilled version of the steps they recommended, and distributed our paper to everyone involved in the case.

We checked the papers the lawyer had prepared to get a warrant for Iraj's arrest, which had to be held until the right time. Once the warrant was issued, we immediately would have to apply for another warrant, a so-called UFAP, unlawful-flight-to-avoid-prosecution order. We got the forms we needed. When we got the kids back, we would have to make a formal request for revocation of Iraj's passport; there were more forms to get and fill out for the passport revocation. I felt relieved that we were getting all this squared away in ample time. Little did I know that this was not going to be the straightforward process we'd been led to believe it was.

My next phone conversation with Iraj was much the same as the last. Now, however, he reversed himself on having Sue travel with me. He insisted that I come alone to Istanbul. I was jumping out of my skin, grateful that Sue and Mike were at my side trying to help me come up with things to say to steer him away from such a treacherous topic. Partly to change the subject, partly to make him wonder if I might be considering coming to Iran, I asked about his job opportunities. He wasn't forthcoming. I was sure I could sidetrack him by praising his talent in general and his accomplishments in the computer field in particular. To my amazement, he only listened to a bit of this, then interrupted me to press me to agree to come to Iran.

I brought up the subject of schools and opportunities for the kids, as I had in a conversation some weeks before. He dismissed the subject. Sounding to me like the abuser I'd known during our marriage, he pounded home the point that he wanted me in Tabriz, insisting that if I cared for him, if I loved the children, he would not have to tell me the obvious, for I would be running to their side. He harped on this. And harped. He pushed the point from every angle. He simply would not let up.

I had to get off the phone! My nerves were shot. I couldn't stand another minute of his assault. I claimed I was too distracted and disturbed by my father's illness to talk about this any more, murmured what I hoped sounded like the sweet good-bye of a helpless woman, and hung up.

Changing his mind. Blowing up. Sticking to a point no matter how illogical. Jerking me around. These qualities in Iraj were all too familiar to me, and obviously I didn't have the world's best track record in dealing with them.

But I was getting lots of good guidance, following our well-thought-out strategy, thinking before I spoke a single word. However, I was extremely eager to enhance my skills at manipulating Iraj. I believe that a lot of his behavior was out of his control, but some was not. As a matter of fact, many of the qualities he was displaying were quite deliberately affected. Just like the playground bully, Iraj knew that being bellicose and erratic inspired fear and enormous frustration. This was exactly what he was aiming at. It was very much to his advantage to keep me off balance while wearing me down. He was counting on my giving up and giving in and agreeing to come to Iran with American passports and American greenbacks in hand.

To counter Iraj's strategy with equally clever verbal assaults, I turned for help to law enforcement handbooks on negotiating in hostage situations and with terrorists. In these authoritative sources I got good news and bad news. The good news was that I already was following the basic advice; the bad news was there wasn't much more I could learn from these books. I was staying calm, feigning being on Iraj's side, pretending that any objections I had to giving him what he wanted were based on things outside my control, like the State Department ban on travel to Iran. My tone was right, I was sure. What it all boiled down to was keeping my nerve, staying the course.

I had to believe Iraj *would* meet me in Turkey. I had to prepare for the trip. Sue and I turned ourselves into scholars, trying to learn everything we could about the geography, history, and culture of the country. We spent hours studying Turkey in the atlas, and the streets of Istanbul on the map that we'd purchased.

The first week of June ended. I could not reach Iraj

until the twelfth as he had gone away with the children on another of those mysterious trips. How this tormented me. What was he doing with my children? Where was he taking them? They couldn't communicate much with anyone but him, though in Tabriz they did have grandparents, aunts, and an uncle to depend on. Alone with Iraj, though, God only knew what they were eating, wearing, thinking. I was desperately afraid that they felt abandoned by me, since they had been with their father for two long months and had been allowed only a few short conversations with me. I prayed they could hold on a little longer without thinking I was failing them. Just a little longer.

At last the day arrived when I could speak again to Iraj. I was determined to follow Dave Christian's dictum and be on the offensive, be the one in control in this conversation. I started with the complete fabrication that my father had had surgery while Iraj was out of touch, but he was stabilizing, so I felt free to travel the following week on Thursday, Friday, or Saturday.

He threw me for a loop.

He wanted to meet in Erzurum, a Turkish town only an hour's drive from the Iranian border. My skin prickled.

"Erzurum," he continued, "will only involve another three hour's flying time for you, so it isn't much bother to you, Jess."

Of course not, I thought sarcastically. I was flying halfway around the world to meet this criminal, what difference did a few more hours make? One hell of a lot. He had the gall to try to get me to a remote location an hour away by car from Iran. Red warning flags were flying. I had to think fast.

"Ah, but Istanbul would be so much more romantic. I've always wanted to see 'the window to the West.' And a lovely hotel on the Bosphorus, so comfortable and modern, would be heavenly. Please, Iraj, make it Istanbul."

He wouldn't budge. He talked up Erzurum, but his only real argument was that it caused him less inconvenience to make the shorter trip. Truly the man was a megalomaniac.

I mentioned my father again, and Iraj interrupted to instruct me to send dad a beautiful bouquet from him with a note. The note was to read *Hang in there. I don't want you to die, but anyone else in the family is welcome to though.*

I kept a straight face through the rest of the call, which blessedly lasted only a few more seconds. But the moment I hung up I threw my head back and laughed.

It was the only laugh of the day, especially because the demand to meet in Erzurum instead of Istanbul was ominous. It looked as if Iraj was seriously plotting my kidnapping. And if he somehow got around the protection we could arrange for me and dragged me inside Iran, I would never get out.

My stress level rose a notch, something I wouldn't have believed possible before the call, since I thought I was as stressed as I could be. The warm and loving support of my parents and especially of my sisters and brother kept me going. But it was Mike who kept me sane. He was there for me every minute—tender, kind, concerned, working with demon energy. And I knew without a shadow of doubt that he loved me and my children.

A truth expressed fourteen centuries before by the Chinese philosopher Lao-tzu came home to me with force:

To love deeply makes you strong;
to be loved deeply makes you courageous.

NINE

WE WERE WORKING LIKE MAD. THE PAPERWORK FOR THE court order and bank account—all phony of course—was finished now. We had it checked and rechecked, and everyone who reviewed it agreed that it looked authentic. However, the bank account really worried me; we'd pretended that I hadn't quite gone along with Iraj's wishes and instead had set up trust accounts in the children's names, but not for the full amount he had demanded. My story was to be that I'd had a hard time collecting on the promised loans. If I hadn't been worried that it would be too easy to find out the bank account was fake, I'd have sent the papers to Jamshid to make the charade seem even more convincing. As it was, though, it seemed like a better idea to take the "paperwork" with me to Turkey to show to Iraj, sort of like flash cards, and try to keep all of it in my possession. My hope was that I could use the papers as a bargaining tool; after all, if they'd been genuine, that's what I would have done.

We'd collected and fed information on Iraj to the I Group. The idea was to create two reasonable sets of plans, one to recover the children in Iran, the other to recover them in a third country—which, of course, was what all of us preferred. I'd gone through picture albums and gathered dozens of loose photographs of Iraj and members of his family, so the I Group could identify the players in the Salimis' terrible game. In the eventuality that we might have to accept the more risky alternative of going into Iran to get Sara and Cy out, I'd also located snapshots that included views of the family's houses, neighborhoods, and places of business. Each photo had been carefully labeled, and I'd written long memos detailing every single thing I could remember about the family and their routines. I was doing everything I could to help the I Group help Sara and Cy and me.

We'd been working with Aaron and Isaac by phone and mail; now it was time for us all to meet, so we headed into Manhattan for a session with them. We had a dual agenda: to review progress on recovery plans and to address the more immediate problems associated with meeting Iraj in Istanbul—or wherever His Majesty would agree to join me.

The ideas for recovery were still sketchy, since we were all sort of holding our collective breath to see if Iraj really was going to agree to make the trip, and if he might change his mind and bring the kids with him. So there wasn't much progress in that area. But there was exciting news. The surveillance team inside Iran had made its first report. Sara and Cy were in Tabriz under the general care of Iraj's parents, and they'd been spotted playing with neighborhood children. They looked normal and healthy. This was most encouraging, though little more than we already knew. My heart sang, because for the first time we were getting outside confirmation from people on our team that the children looked okay.

I'd been thinking long and hard about the recovery, and as the I Group finished talking about a couple of preliminary ideas on the subject and informed us about the surveillance report, I realized it was time to tell them what I'd decided: whatever plan we came up with, I was going to be part of it. An important, central part of it. No one was going to snatch the kids away from Iraj without me being right there. Sara and Cy had to be able to see me, hug me, and know that I—not a stranger—was reclaiming them. The I Group freaked.

"Out of the question. A very bad idea," Isaac the laconic said immediately, while little Aaron was shaking his head and repeatedly saying, "No."

I wouldn't back down. They argued with me, finally admitting that in such a tricky mission they simply didn't want to be encumbered with an amateur, and an amateur who was a nervous mother to boot. I wouldn't accept that. I felt strongly that I could protect my children when no one else could. Call that foolish, and perhaps it was, but it was too strong a conviction to deny. It was also based on a lot more than emotion.

The first in-depth account of a recovery I'd read was the one in *Parenting* magazine about Patrick Buckman's exploits on behalf of a woman whose young son had been abducted by his father and taken to Europe. Patrick and his associates tracked them to Milan, where the boy's father was performing at the local opera house. En route to that city, Patrick stopped in London, Bern, and

Innsbruck to meet with contacts and prepare escape routes, which included setting up safe houses and obtaining false passports in case they were needed. Once in Milan, Patrick learned that the father had moved; Patrick located the new apartment, staked it out, and waited. Soon a pattern emerged. The father dropped off the boy each morning at a day care center where the children had a long noon recess. Patrick planned to take the boy from the playground and was about to act—when the father suddenly showed up. Trailing father and son to Genoa, Patrick started all over again, watching and waiting. The father had a role in an opera and often took the boy with him to rehearsals during the day. When a stranger appeared with the child outside the theater, Patrick acted. He drove past the pair and parked, leaving the engine of his car running. He walked toward the child and the stranger, an older man. As he passed, he wheeled and struck the man, leaving him temporarily stunned, grabbed the boy, and ran to the car. The child was hysterical and struggling. . . .

But the boy's mother had been waiting in the car. What if she hadn't been there? The child might have been so traumatized that he wouldn't have gotten over the recovery for months, years, maybe ever. I wouldn't have Sara and Cy shocked and frightened by being "stolen" by some stranger who would try to explain what was happening to them—after the damage had been done. No. I was going to be right there to protect and comfort my children. As I've said, the Israelis were family men and sensitive to these kinds of issues. Still, they objected to my participation. I dug in my heels. I said I'd take full responsibility for any amateur blunders I might make, and that was that. What could they do but shrug?

It was, after all, my show. That point settled, we moved on to the matter of my meeting with Iraj.

The I Group was terribly worried about my safety during any confrontation with Iraj. From listening to the tapes of his phone calls and doing a general analysis of his letters and actions, they believed he intended to harm me. They presented their case.

Convinced he'd been duped in the divorce, suffering from loss of face, Iraj was a violently jealous and angry man, bent on revenge. He had resisted having my sister accompany me to a meeting with him. He wanted me to join him in a small town that was far less modern and sophisticated than Istanbul, and Istanbul was bad enough. Kidnapping was a distinct possibility, but the Israelis suggested another danger, something that hadn't occurred to my sisters, brother, Mike, or me. They said they wouldn't be the least bit surprised if Iraj intended to behave reasonably in Turkey only up until the minute he had the recision of the court orders, money, and passports in hand, at which point he'd do anything he chose to me, including physical assault. They also believed it was quite likely that "the boys" Iraj had recruited to help him smuggle his brothers out of Iran would be working with him during my trip to Istanbul. I was astonished for a moment, then it sank in that everything they were suggesting was plausible. And it became more plausible as they went into greater detail.

Fellow Middle Easterners, the Israelis deeply understood the culture from which Iraj had emerged. They explained some of the origins of the code of honor that grew out of a nomadic tribal way of life. They felt that the ancient tradition of seeking retribution for any wrong done to a member of the family, clan, or tribe was motivating Iraj. Since he'd lost face, kidnapping me or punishing me by assaulting me—or worse—might seem to him the "correct" thing to do. Some of his family probably was supporting him, pushing him to punish me. I nodded vigorously, visualizing Homa.

No matter how we analyzed the prospective meeting, we ended up convinced it was fraught with danger for me, even in Istanbul. Erzurum, we agreed, was really perilous. I had to charm Iraj into coming to Istanbul, or bribe him with an offer to pay all his expenses. Both, we decided. To counter the threat to me that Iraj posed, Aaron and Isaac wanted to accompany Sue and me and use two to four local agents as backup. In effect, I would be watched over, if not actually guarded, every minute of the day and night. Then too, if by any remote chance Iraj brought the children with him, there'd be people on hand for a recovery.

I glanced at Rob, who was nodding in agreement. He was footing the already astronomical bill for the services of these men, and I could only wonder how much more costly this was going to be with the addition of travel expenses and pay for two men, working full time, and the hiring of some four locals. My brother looked my way, and as if reading my mind, he smiled and nodded, telling me without words that I was not to give a moment's thought to the cost of the operation. If it wouldn't have embarrassed us both, I'd have run right over and given him a big hug.

We talked about how I might overcome the danger inherent in the encounter with Iraj and manipulate the situation to our advantage. An idea I threw out—and withdrew in almost the same breath—was to use force on Iraj, have the operatives literally wrestle him to his knees and order him to have someone in his family bring the children to the place we were meeting. I could just see it.

Jessica Doyle, age sixteen. She won a statewide contest for "Outstanding High School Junior" in 1972. *From the author's personal collection.*

Jessica in front of a mosque in Teheran, Iran, at age 22.
From the author's personal collection.

During the same trip, in Ahwaz (southern Iran).
From the author's personal collection.

Sara's first birthday.
From the author's personal collection.

Jessica with Sara (age two) and Cy (two weeks old).
From the author's personal collection.

Sara and Cy at Niagara Falls in 1988.
From the author's personal collection.

Halloween marked a turning point in Jessica's
relationship with her husband.
From the author's personal collection.

Tabriz, Iran, 1990. These two photographs were taken during the time that the children were being kept in Iran by their father. *From the author's personal collection.*

Cy during recovery in Alexandroupolis, Greece.
From the author's personal collection.

Sara and Cy in their safe refuge in Florida.
From the author's personal collection.

In Florida, together at last.
From the author's personal collection.

And boy oh boy, how the image satisfied my yearning for revenge. Unfortunately, though, I knew it wouldn't work. Iraj's mean, stubborn streak would keep him from giving in even if a gun was at his head and he had every reason to believe he'd be shot.

The goal being to convince Iraj to bring the children to a second meeting, the I Group had no doubts about what I should do: seduce Iraj. Sex was the way to get to him. They weren't the least bit shy about their opinions or expressing them bluntly. Through sex I could control him. Get him to bed and then twist him around my finger. I'd argued this point with so many people, I was sick of it. Privately, I still felt everyone was overestimating my appeal and how much Iraj was at the mercy of his hormones, but I decided to keep my doubts to myself. What if they were right? It was worth a try, and besides, I didn't have any suggestions that might put new weapons in our arsenal. So we focused on Iraj's greedy desire for money and passports and his need to humble me—and for sex. I left the meeting feeling like I'd been miscast as a siren in a bad movie.

Within a few days I was feeling less like the Vamp than like a couple of characters from mythology rolled into one: Atlas carrying the weight of the world on his shoulders, and Sisyphus pushing the rock up the hill, watching it roll back to the bottom, and having to climb down and push it up again. Iraj was maddeningly changeable, irrational, forcing me in every conversation to start all over on the subject of the trip.

On June 21 I started feeling like a very different character, a Biblical one: Job. I had made hotel and airline reservations for Iraj and for Sue and me and had informed him of all the "wonderful arrangements" that were set for the trip just three days hence. I waxed eloquent, describing the four-star accommodations of the Hilton on the Bosphorus and its romantic ambiance. He didn't comment on any of it, jumping right into an interrogation of me about the objectives of the meeting. He wanted me to come directly to Teheran, "much better," he said, "more productive and economical."

Dear Lord, we were supposed to be meeting in a little over seventy-two hours and here he was spinning me on his merry-go-round again. I prayed for patience and repeated my reasons for not traveling into Iran.

"This meeting is probably a waste of time," he said with infuriating nonchalance, "since the issue of where the kids will live is closed. They live with me. In Iran. That's it."

I took a deep breath. Something wasn't right here in his tone, in his words. I knew that he desperately wanted to get at least $100,000 from me, and he wasn't a bit nonchalant about that. He'd overacted. He was pretending to be casual and bullheaded to keep control over me. I had him.

"Well," I said, "I really am sorry that you don't want to talk about a true reconciliation based on what's best for all of us." Then I switched to the most alluring and seductive tone of voice I could muster. "I've been feeling so sure that our getting together at the Hilton in Istanbul could be productive. Fruitful. I thought a nice dinner, perhaps a drink on the terrace overlooking the Bosphorus, then we'd be relaxed enough to have a really good talk. But, well, if you really think there's nothing to talk about, no options . . ." I let my voice trail off, and in the pause I could almost hear Iraj panting for a Scotch on the rocks and some sex on a soft bed.

I wasn't wrong. In a moment he said grumpily, "Well, I

don't think there are any options to discuss, but I'll meet you in Istanbul anyway."

Hooray. I hung up the phone feeling like the victor. Oh, I knew I had many, many days ahead of battling through Iraj's objections, reversals, and threats, but I also knew I was going to win.

June 21 was the summer solstice. This first day of summer made me feel especially bitter toward the Salimis. The kids ought to have gotten out of school last week; we should be looking forward to long, hot days of tending our vegetable and flower garden, an activity the children were very enthusiastic about, and day trips to the beach, picnics, and baseball games. Damn it, next year we *would* be doing all those things—together!

What a tough customer Iraj was! During a conversation on the very last afternoon before the trip, when I was simply supposed to confirm all the plans for him, he dared to try to get me to change the location to Erzurum, and agree to travel on to Iran, as well as to promise to wire him money before I traveled, and on and on. Being tough with him had worked; I wasn't going to go soft at this point. I held firm. He crumbled, saying that he would see me at the Hilton.

Waking and sleeping, doubts crowded my mind. I worried that I didn't really have what it took to manipulate Iraj, who might just not show up in Istanbul. God, there were no guarantees of any kind. Except that Iraj wanted money. But what if he suspected I wasn't really bringing any cash or access to a bank account with me? He wouldn't show up, that's what. And I was spending so much money. Iraj would come; I had to believe that. The money would draw him. Or he would come to kidnap me, beat me up. The I Group would protect me, and my own wits, and Sue's careful eye and quick intelligence. Bruises and cuts held no fear for me; abduction did. When I imagined even a day as my ex-husband's prisoner inside Iran, I quaked. And this fear debilitated me. The only way for me to deal with it was to discipline myself to put it out of my mind, savagely crushing thoughts of such a thing. But I couldn't afford to handle the anxieties of playing seductress by repressing them. I *had* to deal with them, because my success in getting the kids back home depended on how well I could act the part.

The best way out of trouble is *through* it, or so the adage goes, and I determined to deal with this head on. I imagined Iraj touching me and my skin crawled; at the thought of him kissing me, I felt like vomiting. Actual intercourse with him? Repulsion, utter repulsion that caused my muscles to contract and rage to fill me. Even the idea was a violation. Memories would come flooding back of his brutal attempt to rape me, and they made me long to kick him, hit him, strangle him. I *had* to get over this. If I didn't convince Iraj that I was sincere about wanting to reconcile with him in every way, all was lost.

I wasted time thinking up ways to put him off if he was determined to get me into bed. I couldn't be coy and I couldn't be rejecting or he'd see right through my pretense. I had to be prepared to go through with it. The only way I could manage, I decided, was by totally turning myself off to thoughts and feelings during sex with him. What had the married ladies in Victorian England, made frigid by their culture and insensitive lovers, advised their engaged women friends and daughters? Something like, "Close your eyes tight, spread your legs wide, and think of England." That's what I'd do, but with one huge difference: I wouldn't think of England, but of

Sara and Cy and how my failure with their father in bed could condemn them to years of misery.

Aaron and Isaac pointed out what Sue and I were feeling keenly: we needed some training and practical advice for handling unforeseeable events in Turkey. They started teaching us what we needed to know to help them in their surveillance of us. I'd told the I Group everything I'd ever learned about Iraj's smuggling ring and the "base" he'd set up in Istanbul, which wasn't much. Unfortunately, I didn't have the names of his contacts in Turkey or any descriptions of them. Iraj might have many people lined up to help him in Istanbul. We had to be extremely vigilant at every moment during our trip.

Unfortunately, we were told, novices like me and my sister were prone to give away the fact that they were being protected. We had to practice going right by Aaron and Isaac without so much as flicking a lash, walking along without glancing back to see where they were. It was a lot harder than we'd thought it would be. We made up a simple name code to use in calls and contacts to let them know if we were in trouble or Iraj was with us or we were about to move to a new location with him. For example, "No, this isn't Mr. Johnson's room; the operator must have made a mistake," meant everything was fine. But mentioning Mr. Thomas meant we were worried about Iraj getting violent; using the name Williams indicated we were about to leave the hotel with Iraj.

We practiced taking phone calls and using the code and learned about unobtrusively passing written messages. Sue and I were beginning to feel like real 007s, and privately we enjoyed a lot of laughs over the whole thing.

But we were all business in our training sessions, which were scheduled to continue on site in Istanbul.

It probably goes without saying that I was most alert during the sessions on kidnapping, and most appreciative of them. The first thing we were to do if we thought we were about to be dragged off was to make a huge fuss; scream, yell, struggle. Aaron and Isaac believed that Iraj and his accomplices would use a car to abduct us. If we were blindfolded, they advised us to employ our senses, all of them, to try to judge from sounds, from anything we heard the men say to one another, and from bumps and odors what we might be driving over, through, or around. If we were able to see and we weren't tied up, they suggested we make sure the car door was unlocked, surreptitiously slide a hand onto the handle, and be prepared when the car slowed to open the door, jump out, and run. I found these lessons particularly sobering.

We worked hard enough to have made M, 007's boss, proud of us. Joshua reminded us, though, that what we needed most was horse sense, good old common horse sense.

During all of this we were also tackling the very tough problem of what action to take if Iraj did an about-face and brought Sara and Cy with him. How should we go about recovering them?

We went over the very tentative ideas we'd been tossing out from the beginning. Actually separating the kids from Iraj would be relatively simple; he could be overpowered and tied up, if necessary. Then under escort of Isaac, we'd race out of the hotel to a car or taxi that Aaron would have waiting and rush off to another hotel or guesthouse where we would be registered under assumed names. All this, we were told by the I Group, was easy enough for them to arrange in Turkey. The hard part was figuring out how we should leave the country. In such a situation, it isn't simply a matter of racing to the airport and getting on a plane. Iraj might set those henchmen of his on our tails; he might lodge a false complaint with the police and get us in hot water. A delay of that kind could enable him to pull off a reabduction of the children. We had to account for these pitfalls, though we realized that we weren't going to be able to put together a sensible, precise plan with so many unknowns and imponderables. If Iraj brought the kids, we'd have to play it by ear.

Suddenly we had a new and thorny problem on our hands. The children's passports had expired, and the State Department would not permit me to renew or extend them unless the children were with me. I explained until I was blue in the face to successively higher officials what the situation was, all to no avail. We fought to cut through bureaucratic thinking and red tape—and little did we know we would go on fighting for weeks to come. We pulled strings; we used every important contact we had. State was intransigent. Everyone from the department said the same thing: all would be well, not to worry. Once I got the kids, I should just take them straight to the closest embassy or consulate and the passport extensions would be immediately forthcoming. I explained that we might be in danger, on the run, far from an embassy. Didn't matter to them.

I couldn't believe it. No help from State before, now this. Were these people morons? Or just so stupidly devoted to their procedures that they were made deaf, dumb, and blind to reality? I really was beginning to hate this government agency.

How did Mike feel about all this? Worried. He was my

constant support, involved in every aspect of the problem and its solution. Yet now, with action on the horizon at last, his hands were tied. He couldn't do a thing except feel very, very worried about my safety. I tried to reassure him even as he tried to hide his apprehension from me. And deep inside, I think what we shared was a strange, completely unwarranted, absolutely illogical certainty that we were going to triumph, that we would get the kids back.

We dashed around taking care of last minute details, Sue and I packed our bags, eager to tackle this task and succeed.

Mike and I spent the day before departure alone together. It was one of the most beautiful times of sharing we've ever known, and we clung to each other through the night. His murmured encouragement meant the world to me. And when he said, tears in his eyes, that he supported *anything* and *everything* I would do in Turkey, I cried. I'll never forget him saying, "There's only one thing that matters now, Jess—getting Sara and Cy back home. You know that, don't you? Nothing else matters." I love Mike very much, and forever.

We were holding each other while we slept, when the shrill ringing of the phone woke us up. I groggily reached for the receiver, noting that it was very early morning. Of course my first thought was that Iraj was calling to curse me and yell at me and tell me the trip was off. But it was a friend warning me about what was on all the news programs: overnight a massive earthquake, measuring at least 6.2 on the Richter scale, had struck in Turkey and a huge section of northwestern Iran. We turned on the television. Every channel was in the midst of a news special on the terrible devastation in the region. British, German, and Italian film and television crews had rushed into the area, and their first reports were dribbling out. The little film footage and videotape that was being transmitted revealed almost unbelievable destruction. Enormous fissures had opened, swallowing people, buildings, cars. Violent shock waves had caused buildings to crumble. Rubble and bodies filled frame after frame of film. My mouth was bone dry, my pulse racing. Tabriz had been rocked by this quake, but the area where the family farm was located was very close to the epicenter and had sustained the greatest damage.

I grabbed the phone and called the farm. All phone lines were down. Oh, God, please, please let my babies be safe, I kept praying as I placed call after call to Tabriz without getting through. I phoned Jamshid, hoping against hope that he might have received word from Iraj or someone else in his family about their fate. But Jamshid hadn't heard from any of them—as a matter of fact, he didn't even know there had been a quake. He seemed annoyed that I'd bothered him so early in the morning and quite unconcerned about this cataclysm. I was just amazed at his reaction, because over ninety percent of his family lived within the circle of the quake's most destructive force.

A hasty round of phone calls followed. All of us bound for Turkey agreed that we should go ahead as planned. Still, I didn't let up trying to reach Iraj, and finally, about two hours before our flight was to take off, I got through to him.

I was panicky. All I'd seen on television was death and destruction.

"Are the children all right?" I shouted.

"They're fine," Iraj shouted back. "They're safe in Tabriz. The city was pretty much spared. Very little damage there, and the kids only felt some tremors. Everything's okay."

"Thank God, oh thank God." I was too shaken to give a thought to playacting. "Iraj, I swear, you better make sure those kids are safe and they stay safe. You're responsible for them. You alone. You took them to that godforsaken place with all these dangers, and you have to make damn sure you're keeping them somewhere that's not dangerous. There are always aftershocks in these big quakes, and second quakes. Are you positive—"

"Jess," he screamed, "shut up! The kids are fine. You're overreacting. Like you always do. I told you, most of the damage was way up near the border. Everything's fine here."

"Bring the children to Istanbul. It's too dangerous for them in Iran. Please, Iraj, it's only for two days, but we'll have them with us and we'll know they're safe."

"They're safe right here. I'm not bringing them with me. It's just you and me on this visit, understand?"

"Well, let me speak to them."

"No. They're busy now. I'll see you in Istanbul, Jess. As planned."

The bastard hung up.

I could only shake my head—and hurry. It was time for my last good-bye to Mike. I made a lot of promises about keeping myself safe and winning this battle in the war. He was crying, I was crying, and it was much harder to tear myself out of his arms even than I'd anticipated. I've never known a man as compassionate, self-confident, and loving as Mike, and it broke my heart that he couldn't go to Turkey with me and be a key player at this stage in our unfolding drama with Iraj.

Sue and I flew from Philadelphia to New York, then boarded our flight to Turkey, which stopped over in

Frankfurt. There we met up with Isaac and Aaron and reviewed our first steps in Turkey. After a flight delay, we were finally able to climb back aboard the plane to Istanbul.

Neither of us was able to rest much on the plane. We were too wired. There had been a vague air of unreality to all our planning and practice sessions until these last hours when we were about to set foot on foreign soil. Now we were acutely aware of the challenges facing both of us, but I was particularly nervous about how much was riding on my performance. As we'd just been reminded by Aaron and Isaac, the success of this first meeting with Iraj hinged on my acting ability. I was so nervous.

And I had the most peculiar and disturbing feeling that I'd left something terribly important at home. I checked my purse, the bag of gifts I'd brought for the children, my carry-on luggage. I had everything I'd planned to bring, including a diaphragm that I'd tucked into my suitcase, hoping against hope that I wouldn't have to use it. It didn't seem I'd forgotten anything on the list I'd carefully put together of things to pack for the trip. But the haunting sensation wouldn't be banished; could it simply be the echo of the sense of loss I felt at being separated from Mike?

Istanbul was just ahead, and the ancient city seemed to me a profound symbol, as well as a dreaded reality. It is the only city in the world that stands on two continents. Its main section is located at the southeastern tip of Europe; its suburbs are in Asia. Between the two sections flows the Bosphorus, the beautiful and historic strait that cuts through from the Black Sea to empty into the Sea of Marmara. The Golden Horn bisects the European part of the city, with Stamboul standing on its right bank, the port quarter of Galata on its left. The whole forms a roughly triangular promontory, and at its point the Bosphorus and the Golden Horn meet and flow together into the Marmara, forming what a Byzantine poet called the city's "garland of waters."

I could imagine Iraj standing in the Asian section, myself on the European side. And in this vision I viewed my job in a slightly different way. I saw myself not as an actress but as an architect and builder. I had to construct a bridge across a treacherous strait so my children could cross safely. But the bridge wouldn't be made of anything substantial; it would be built from pretenses, mortared with lies. Oddly enough, that didn't make me feel a single twinge of guilt. The only person in this whole miserable mess who ought to feel guilty was Iraj. And suddenly I just couldn't wait to face him. It was time the tables were turned, time for me to manipulate him successfully. Nervous as I was, still I was eager, primed for the fight.

Pressing brochures into our hands, talking a mile a minute in broken English, scarcely watching the road, our taxi driver was such a likable hustler that he kept us smiling and laughing on the drive to the Hilton. He urged us to change to a cheaper hotel—"too much money that Hilton, too much money. Much better I take you to first-class hotel, half price of Hilton." He wanted us to take the tours that he and his brothers and cousins offered, have lunch at his uncle's restaurant, see his sister's clothing store, and on and on.

"Tourists," he declared, pounding his chest, "Ahmed's big specialty."

Sue and I broke into gales of laughter. We were anything but the typical tourists poor old Ahmed believed us to be. He took us from the airport to the hotel by a very long route, shamelessly running up the meter as much as he dared. We didn't mind. Suffering already from a bit of jet lag and keyed up, we appreciated the scenic but expensive drive after we got off the drab stretch of road from the airport into the city. Ahmed cruised the narrow, hilly streets, pointing out historical landmarks. The closely built houses gave way occasionally to permit us a dazzling view of sparkling water on which sleek yachts and squat freighters were sailing.

We actually were a little sorry to have to say good-bye to our avaricious, jolly taxi driver.

The grandiose lobby of the Hilton was impressive indeed. Its magnificent marble floor was dotted with oriental carpets, on which were grouped comfortable furniture, huge copper pots, and plants. Our room, large, clean, and well-furnished, as one expects in a first-class hotel, differed from its clones throughout the world in one respect; its balcony overlooked a courtyard and the Bosphorus beyond. Shaded from the hot June sun, the balcony was the perfect spot to relax before we unpacked and started to work, and by unspoken agreement each of us collapsed onto one of the comfortable chaise longues there. Cypresses, horse chestnuts, and Judas trees grew along the not too distant hillsides of the Bosphorus. The last of the pink blossoms of the flowering Judases and the fading red and white candles of the chestnut trees colored the otherwise dark green clusters of leaves on the stands of these trees that stood between and below the buildings. The serenity of the gentle breeze and the water view worked on me, and I drifted off to sleep, to awake in a couple of hours to the room service tea and snacks that Sue had ordered for us.

Refreshed, our energy returning in full, we were ready to get going. We made contact with Isaac and Aaron, who hadn't acknowledged our existence since boarding the plane with us in Frankfurt, and set up a meeting for later in the afternoon. They had been busy contacting the four locals they'd employed to help out. They were deploying a couple of them immediately and would meet with all of these operatives very soon to give them instructions. We had a little over twenty-four hours to prepare ourselves for Iraj's arrival.

Sue and I set out to explore the hotel. The public areas were enormous. There was an arcade off the lobby that featured half a dozen shops selling everything from incredibly expensive jewelry and designer clothes and leather goods to books and maps, crafts and exotic Turkish tobaccos. We wandered through the cocktail lounge and bar, which had voluminous gold drapes at the windows and several gigantic copper cauldrons standing in corners and by columns.

Sue wiggled her eyebrows. "All the better for us clandestine operatives to hide in, my dear," she commented. And we laughed.

There was a casino on the lowest level of the hotel; a magnificent marble terrace, partially covered by awnings, let out onto the courtyard, which was beautifully landscaped and featured a sculpture garden. People enjoyed drinks and meals on the terrace in this lovely environment. Feeling very much as if we were on a movie set, we continued to explore, finding an Olympic-size pool surrounded by lush greenery and beds of brilliantly colored flowers. Chief among the flowers were tulips, which originated and were cultivated to their present form in Turkey, not Holland, as most people think.

RESCUED

The Hilton was everything the pictures in its promotional brochure had promised, and more. The I Group hated it. Not because of its accommodations and amenities, which were outstanding, but because it was a very difficult place for them to do their jobs. As soon as they joined us they outlined some of the problems: the possibility of "losing" us and Iraj in such a place, of being spotted in the huge and airy public areas, which offered them no cover. They had met with their associates and checked out the hotel, watching us at the end of our tour around the place, and they were sure no one was keeping tabs on us, so they felt it was okay for us to talk in the lounge.

We had a brief chat about what we had learned so far, and we identified the spots within the Hilton where we could "bump into each other" as if by accident to pass emergency messages after Iraj arrived. Then we adjourned for a "training session." All of us trooped up to Sue's and my room and practiced a few hand signals and giving our code-name messages over the phone. We developed one very important signal then, a way to alert the team if a serious, dangerous emergency arose. One of us was to unfasten her handbag and drop it so that she'd have to kneel to scoop up and replace the contents. This would take time, and it would be quite conspicuous. The person tailing us couldn't fail to spot it, and it would give him the opportunity to catch up with us and act. Very reassuring. Aaron and Isaac really put us through our paces, and by the time we were satisfied with the results it was getting late. We parted for dinner, Sue and I opting for the Chinese restaurant on the ground level of the Hilton, and an early lights-out.

The next morning there was still no evidence that we were under surveillance, so the Israelis suggested they take us to a few key places in the city. We drove through Taksim Square, with its colorful array of shops along the streets and vendors along the curbs, and we saw the outside of the Topkapi Sarayi, which for four centuries was the imperial residence of the sultan and his court during the Ottoman Empire. Today it's a renowned museum.

The place we really wanted to visit on a trip that otherwise had only a solemn purpose was Haghia Sophia, the extraordinary place of worship that is a monument to the golden age of the Byzantine Empire. Almost all visitors are as overwhelmed as we were by the fabled dome of Haghia Sophia, which soars to a height greater than that of a fifteen-story building. Huge chandeliers hang from incredibly long, thin chains. Unfortunately, much of the mystery and sacred nature of the place was lost on us because of the large numbers of tourists moving through the nave. Then too, I was saddened by the general air of neglect about this great treasure; the grounds were littered, the gardens untended.

Our next destination was Kapali Carsi, the covered bazaar, which is really like a small city, with something on the order of five thousand shops of all kinds and a dozen mosques along with gardens and fountains. It fascinated Sue, as this was her first visit to the Middle East; I was not as impressed because I'd seen many older, more authentically oriental bazaars in Iran.

Obviously Aaron and Isaac knew Istanbul very well. They took us to a small restaurant on a side street near Kapali Carsi for an early lunch. It was the best meal we had in Turkey, starting with *dolmasi*, various cold stuffed pepper and grape, cabbage, and other leaves, proceeding to a main course of *Doner kebab*, pressed lamb cooked on a rotating spit over a charcoal fire and carved off in thin slices. It was served with cooked vegetables, and we washed down the meal with *ayran*, a liquid yogurt that goes very well with this type of food and is similar to the yogurt beverage served in Iran. We finished with thick, sweet Turkish coffee. Sue relished every morsel. I could eat only a small amount; I was too anxious.

This was a pleasant interlude, serving the important purpose of orienting us somewhat to the city. The Israelis had constantly pointed out strategic locations where we could meet up with them if there was trouble. Now we listened in a much more grave manner; Iraj would arrive in just a couple of hours.

The place of protection for a U.S. citizen in any foreign country is the American embassy or consulate. Promising myself I would not rave about my grievances against the State Department, I learned the best route from the hotel to the consulate. Then we checked out local restaurants and shops, and the Israelis demonstrated some pointers that would help them to follow us.

Tailing someone, I learned, is easy only in the movies. How many times have we seen the TV or movie hero follow the villain with only minor hitches? But in real life Istanbul, with its narrow streets clogged with traffic, tailing someone required a level of skill that filled me with admiration. Sue and I walked far behind Aaron as he followed Isaac. As people pushed and shoved us, often obscuring our view, we could see for ourselves how important it was not to turn a corner too fast or cross the street too quickly.

Then it was back to the Hilton to freshen up—and to wait for Iraj.

TEN

It was five o'clock. Isaac called our room to let us know that their associate stationed at the airport to watch for Iraj had spotted him. He was wearing dark glasses and carrying a newspaper. I chuckled. Were the glasses an accessory Iraj had chosen to make himself look cool—he always did like looking cool—or were they a disguise? I knew he was scared to death of the long arm of the American law, and I hoped he was worried about being picked up on an international arrest warrant for kidnapping. Let him squirm as he thought about it; let him suffer as he contemplated what punishment he might face. I only wished that I had the kids safe so I could enjoy the sight of Iraj being arrested.

Sue and I decided to meet him in the lobby. We positioned ourselves in wonderfully comfortable overstuffed chairs near the main entrance. After we'd talked ourselves out, we glanced through magazines. This was really phony on my part. I couldn't get interested in anything; I was going over and over things I'd say, the looks I'd give Iraj. And secretly I was hoping and praying that he would walk through the door with Cy holding one hand and Sara the other.

Almost an hour passed. We started to get really nervous. One second I was sure he'd stood us up; the next I was positive he was on his way and was just delayed by the problems that had developed because of the earthquake. Sue said my fidgeting was making her crazy, so I decided to take the long hike to the one ladies' room we'd found that had a pay phone inside the vestibule, where we could make calls unobserved by any of Iraj's cronies who might be spying on us. I called Aaron and Isaac. They hadn't had Iraj followed from the airport, so the man might not have been he. Suddenly I remembered the newspaper that the fellow seen leaving the plane had carried. Iraj didn't read the paper very often, and he would never bother to tote one. My heart sank. I was sure the man at the airport hadn't been Iraj. I paced, wringing my hands. Finally I was able to reconcile myself to the fact that there was nothing I could do but wait and returned to the lobby.

Sue went to the arcade and bought some small presents to take home to her husband and children. We speculated about what could be holding up Iraj, and at six-thirty P.M., we took ourselves off to the terrace for tea. We distracted ourselves by watching a wedding party nearby. The bride and groom certainly had chosen a lovely spot with an excellent view over the courtyard for their reception. We commented on the clothes and makeup of the women, the beauty and expense of table decorations, food, the excellent service they were getting. We speculated about the occupations and status of the men. The party ended and still no Iraj.

Sue and I hung around the lobby until about eight, surprised the house dick didn't come over to have a little talk with us. What kind of women spent three hours in a hotel lobby? Finally we decided to have dinner; we left a message at the desk as to where we were going and went to the coffee shop for a light meal.

We resigned ourselves to the idea that Iraj wasn't coming that evening, perhaps not at all. Had he ever reached Istanbul? Perhaps he had but had gotten cold feet and scooted back to Iran. Worse, we speculated, he could have canceled out because he'd gotten wind somehow of what we were up to.

Back in our room, we checked with the airline and confirmed that Iraj hadn't picked up his prepaid ticket at the airport in Erzurum. We called the Israelis to give them this information and discussed what Iraj's failure to show up might mean. All of us feared the worst: Iraj had never intended to meet me; he merely wanted me to incur the big expense of the trip and experience the anticipation of it, then endure the agony of being hugely disappointed. On the other hand, the damage done by the earthquake might have delayed him. If he didn't show up the following day, we'd have to give up on this trip. We were scheduled to leave the day after that, so there wasn't much time left, only about forty or so hours. What a waste. What a loss.

Sue commiserated with me. Then we had an idea that wiped away our sadness. There might be a bright side. In one of my last conversations with Iraj, I'd learned that again the children were suffering from stomach problems and he was having trouble getting liquids down them to prevent dehydration. He was getting weary of the role and responsibilities of a single parent. That was clear. Then there was the earthquake. It had been so severe that even Iraj might worry about the kids' safety. What if he'd been delayed because he'd decided to bring Sara and Cy to Istanbul? It would take extra time to pack some things for them, get airline reservations, and get them organized. And why hadn't I heard from him about the delay? Because he was a man so careless of others' feelings and comfort that it might not even occur to him to phone the Hilton and leave a message for me.

I felt an almost delirious joy at the prospect that he might be traveling with the children even as Sue and I sat cross-legged on the bed wondering about what was going on. We decided to call Canada and see if Jamshid had heard from Iraj. Unfortunately, he'd heard nothing, but he did suggest that there seemed to be so much disruption from the quake that the border check between Iran and Turkey, which took a very long time under the best of circumstances, might be causing great delays.

We turned in early, perplexed, wondering what the next day might bring.

The phone woke us up at eleven A.M.; Sue and I were disoriented and still operating on Stateside time. I was shocked to hear Iraj's voice. He had just checked in and had been shown to his room. He wanted to clean up and asked me to meet him in the lobby in one hour. We notified the Israelis and hurried to get dressed.

I was shaking. At last I was going to face this kidnapper, and I couldn't even guess what my reaction to him was going to be. Whatever it was, I wouldn't let it prevent me from convincing him that I wanted a reconciliation more than life itself. I psyched myself to play my role, squeezing my eyes shut and remembering my long-lost feelings for Iraj.

We went down early, stationing ourselves beside an extravagantly oversize vase across from the elevators. Out of the corner of my eyes I caught glimpses of Aaron, Isaac, and one of the locals he'd introduced to Sue and me. All systems go. This was it.

In about fifteen minutes, Iraj emerged from the elevator. I forced a big smile as he walked across the lobby to us and hugged Sue and then me. Practically his first words to us were, "I really need a drink. What's the best place around here to get one?"

We ushered him out to the terrace, where he called for service even before we were seated at a table. He quickly ordered a round of drinks and lit a cigarette.

I murmured things like how good it was to see him and how well he looked. Waiting until he'd taken a long drink of his beer, I asked what had delayed him.

He had missed the flight we'd booked for him because of a twenty-three-hour delay at the border. Nothing special, he added swiftly, just routine, but everything was fouled up and taking longer than usual because of the numbers of relief workers and press flooding into the area where the earthquake had struck. He described some of the devastation, but having seen the CNN coverage, we obviously knew more details about the tragedy than Iraj did. Unable to get another flight from Erzurum that would get him to Istanbul in time to meet us before our scheduled departure, he'd had to take a bus.

I nodded and said all the polite things, but I was finding it impossible to make eye contact with Iraj. The reaction I'd wondered about just half an hour before was all negative: I hated this thug, this criminal, this terrorist. I was frozen, almost paralyzed by my feelings. Fortunately, Sue was carrying on like a champ. I worked at shaking off my feelings and getting back into my role while I listened to her tell of our travels and brief tour of Istanbul. I began to get control of myself and was able to add a few comments to hers.

So far not a word had been spoken about Sara and Cy or the abduction. All three of us were treading lightly and trying to feel our way into interaction with each other. We discussed other members of the family, and Iraj wanted to know about my father's condition. Sue and I provided an account replete with medical details, which we'd scrupulously invented for him. After a bit more chitchat about mutual acquaintances, he started talking about the children. He spoke roughly about them and the problems they'd been having.

My eyes burned with tears of sympathy for the kids, and my hands shook with anger at their rotten father. I kept my gaze riveted to the foam on the beer I'd ordered.

Iraj told us that the children turned up their noses at Iranian food. Sara wanted to subsist exclusively on Snickers bars because, she said, they were made in America. Iraj recounted this without any apparent awareness of all the longing and rebelliousness it signified. He didn't mention Cy specifically, and I could tell that Sara was giving him a very hard time. Apparently he'd ordered her on numerous occasions to swallow the food he put in front of her and she'd refused. So, my girl wouldn't swallow his food anymore than she'd swallow his line. I wanted to cheer for her, but at the same time I was terribly worried. Was she starving herself, jeopardizing her health?

I knew I had to look at Iraj, to make conversation, but I didn't feel I dared. He appeared not to find anything odd about my behavior, my silence, or about the fact that Sue was carrying the conversation. I attributed this not only to his insensitivity, but also to the beer. He'd been chugging it down and was on his third or fourth while Sue and I were nursing our first. I liked that. I wanted him fuzzy-minded and out of it. But unfortunately the alcohol was about to make him mean, which at first I didn't catch on to, as he described how much the children missed me and begged to be with me. Then he explained that he'd told them I was dead and that they'd never see me again.

How could he do such a thing to them? I wanted to rip out his damned heart, pound his face to pulp. Now tears were pouring down my cheeks. My God, his craziness could make neurotics out of my beautiful, healthy children. I had to get a grip on myself, overcome my feelings, and start playing this jerk like he was a Stradivarius and I was Itzhak Perlman.

I cleared my throat and asked how Sara and Cy were spending their days.

Rather than answer immediately, he signaled a waiter, ordered another beer for himself, and lit his next cigarette off the one burning in the ashtray. He was glancing around constantly, chain-smoking, pouring beer down his throat.

I suggested that he should relax after his exhausting trip.

Then he blurted out the cause of his apprehensiveness: he'd thought we might have a squad of marines waiting for him, or even worse.

Sue and I laughed, exchanging glances over his head. Didn't we just wish. But we rushed to reassure him that there was no ulterior motive at play here.

He elaborated on his suspicions. We listened.

I'd realized a couple of weeks before that Iraj was most pleased when I seemed to be utterly naive, a kind of Rebecca of Sunnybrook Farm he felt infinitely superior to. I adapted that persona and asked him how he could even think for a minute that a woman like me could dream up such a thing. Setting a trap for him? We let him know that a scheme like that was far beyond our abilities. This naturally led into a little lecture that Sue and I had rehearsed.

I had asked for this meeting, I reminded him, only to explore the possibility of a reconciliation. I regretted my past mistakes. I wanted my family back, especially him. I finally had realized he was a man of great complexity, and I'd probably misunderstood him for quite a few years, but now having grasped this, I desperately wanted to show him that I could get on the right track and put the pieces of our lives back together. I paused, waiting for Iraj to comment. He had a brooding look on his face and stayed silent.

Sue jumped in to back me up. Speaking as a caring sister, she told him how much she wanted to see us reunited, a happy little family again.

At last Iraj spoke. If I didn't return to Iran with him tomorrow, he would consider the trip a waste, fruitless. If I didn't go back with him it would be proof that I was not sincere about what I was saying. He didn't wait for a response to this, however; obviously wound up tight, he lectured loudly on why and how he had abducted the children. Dumbfounded, Sue and I listened as he bragged about how clever his scheme had been, how well planned. He illustrated lavishly, telling us, for example, how devious he had been in getting the pictures of the children he needed for their travel documents. Pretending he'd forgotten his camera when he'd visited the children about two months before the kidnapping, he had borrowed mine—here he paused and cocked an eyebrow, as if waiting for one of us to comment on how wonderful, how smart, how preciously devious he'd been—and had taken photos of Sara and Cy against a sheet-covered wall in his hotel room. "With your own camera, Jess," he chortled, "with *your* camera."

I could have strangled him.

He explained that his brothers were all too eager to pretend that they were so concerned and loving toward me. His cousin Bobek, too, he said, had been enthusiastic about deceiving me into believing that he would be along on the Canadian trip to watch over the children, their protective escort. He snickered, actually snickered over this.

Iraj's long recital of the details of his treachery included one that delighted me. He'd assigned the job of safeguarding his assets in Chicago—that silver Audi, his household possessions—to Bobek, who was now fleecing him! I could barely keep the grin off my face.

He ordered his fourth beer, or was it the fifth? Alcohol was talking now, nonstop. He couldn't keep himself from crowing about how he'd whisked Sara and Cy away from a Nintendo game and to the airport in Toronto. He flew them to Paris, because he believed both airports there were the easiest ones to get into and out of with the kind of Iranian travel documents he had for the children. He was never questioned about their citizenship or why they were traveling on his passport or anything else, so it seems he was correct in his assessment of Orly and DeGaulle. All along, Sara and Cy were upset, making a fuss and asking questions. He said he just told them over and over that they were going to make a little visit to their relatives. He said the kids were exhausted from the straight-through flights and slept a lot on the ten-hour bus trip from Mehrabad Airport to Tabriz.

Dear God, no wonder the kids were sick. He'd put them through a grueling ordeal and seemed to have no awareness of the fact, but talked instead about his own discomfort during the trip. The bastard. The rotten, no-good bastard.

He looked slyly at Sue and then at me. My muscles tightened in anticipation of what he was about to say. I had a fair idea that he was about to lower the boom on the matter of the money.

I knew that Iraj's brother, the one who farmed in Iran, had converted a third-floor attic supply area in their parents' home into an apartment for Iraj and the children. His father had been bedridden for the past few months and his mother was sick. Sara and Cy were unhappy there, and Iraj was planning to buy a place for them. He stared hard at me.

Money. He wanted me to flourish a bankbook and say, "Here, all yours." Danger. I had to ignore it, smooth things over.

"Gosh," I said, "this must be so hard on you. It must take a lot out of you to have to care for the kids *and* your parents."

He continued to stare at me. Then suddenly, he broke into a lecture. The subject? How urgent a matter it had been for him to protect the kids from me. Both Sue and I were shocked. "What?" we demanded simultaneously.

Iraj's response was so irrational that we couldn't really follow what he was saying. But I vividly recall that in the midst of calling me names, he said that the children were wonderful only because of the years of my loving attention and care for them! Then he leapt to my affair with "the Lumber Guy," demanding details. Sue tried to turn him from this subject by talking about how pointless it was to go over the past when there was a future to build.

"No," he screamed. "I want to know all about it. Everything. Everything, you hear?"

I swallowed hard and glanced left and right. People were staring, as I thought they'd be. Had Iraj lost all self-awareness? I was speechless. Sue was trying valiantly to get him to relent, saying it wasn't an important relationship anyway; it had been too casual a thing for him to get this upset over. Meanwhile, although I was trying, I simply couldn't dream up a response to his bizarre demand to "know everything" about my relationship with Mike. Instead I abjectly apologized, calling myself a fool, telling him I knew I'd caused him pain, saying I really wanted to make it up to him. He looked absolutely furious.

"You can go to hell," he said. "The children and I will live our lives—without you!—in Iran, even if they don't like it. One day they will thank me for this." I remember these words perfectly; what followed was a garbled diatribe. He attacked me, he described how homesick the children were, how much they missed me. One illustration upset me so much I thought my heart would break. Both Sara and Cy had a small photograph of me, which he'd forbidden them to look at. He told us he knew they were hiding the photos and tried to sneak peeks of them, holding them cupped in their little palms. He called me a bitch, an unworthy mother, but at the same time I was a woman who'd given everything to her children!

Flabbergasted, I took a sip of beer to give me a moment to collect my thoughts. What kind of point was he trying to make? Was he listening to himself? He made no sense at all, condemning me on one hand and giving me credit on the other. How on earth was I supposed to deal with this deranged man? Sue looked troubled; I'm sure she was as concerned as I was about redirecting the conversation into a channel that could be productive.

The terrace restaurant offered a lavish midday buffet, and the place was packed with the late lunch crowd. Sue declared that she was starving and suggested we eat. Acquiescing, Iraj ordered more beer and another pack of cigarettes, and I suggested that it might be a good idea for us to take a walk after lunch.

Fortunately, my suggestion got Iraj to take a different tack—he began telling tales of Istanbul's sights and prattling about his exploits in the city—and soon he was feeling so good about himself as he boasted of his adventures that he invited us to enjoy dinner at one of his favorite restaurants, the Galek.

The adventures Iraj had been relating had to do primarily with Nasser and getting him through Istanbul and to the West. Abruptly, he switched from the past to the present. Sue and I lingered over after-lunch tea, while Iraj gulped yet another beer and began to recount his current activity. Iraj was continuing to smuggle young men—and God knows what else—out of Iran. He was quite proficient at arranging the forgery of birth certificates and other documents and getting people across borders, he said. The smuggling had resumed with his nephew, who was twenty-two, and could have been drafted at any moment; it had continued with the sons of cousins, then friends of the family. His circle of prospects was rapidly extending outward.

I could afford to let my mind wander a bit, I believed, for I had lived so long and unhappily with his obsession with smuggling his brothers out and his bragging about how he'd done it that I was pretty sure I knew everything he'd say. He'd do anything, break any law, run any risk, to be a hero in the eyes of his family. I was sitting there, thoughts drifting, when it suddenly occurred to me how crazy it was that he could speak so insultingly about Iran when he'd taken the children there and just before lunch had declared he'd make them live in Tabriz forever. And then it hit me—my God, he could be using Sara and Cy in his wildly dangerous smuggling activities! All those mysterious trips. Were they being dragged along on the rides through the mountains and across the border into Turkey? It would be just like Iraj to realize that with Sara and Cy in the car, he'd appear less suspicious, more like an ordinary daddy taking the kids to visit relatives.

I looked at the cocky bastard. He was glowing with pride and excitement, utterly fearless about breaking Iranian and Turkish law. Did he think he'd never get caught? Or, if caught, that somehow he could avoid punishment? Well, I knew, even if he didn't in his blind state of delusion and egotism, that punishment for him would be as swift and harsh as it would be for any other Iranian.

Now I was listening closely, trying to remember every word, and wishing I had a notebook in my lap. It seemed to me that he was confirming that he had used the children on at least one such smuggling junket. I had to summon every ounce of my willpower to keep silent and maintain a poker face while inside I was shaking with anger and fear for the children's safety. They could be shot by border guards, blown up in one of the unpatrolled but heavily mined mountain passes. If they were captured with their father and his cohorts, they wouldn't get easy treatment because they were children. God only knew what terrible dangers Sara and Cy were being subjected to by Iraj. The bastard. The unforgivable bastard.

Iraj stopped swilling beer long enough to order dessert for himself and us. His habit of commanding what others, me in particular, would eat annoyed the hell out of me and always had, but he refused to give it up! He chose an attention-getting confection, raspberries flambé, and a large chocolate mousse.

Now I was fired by fury determined to get to him, to manipulate him so I could take my kids out of harm's way. I would have tried to seduce the devil himself if it would have helped get Sara and Cy out of the danger of being used by this vicious opportunist of a father. So it wasn't hard at that point to come on to Iraj. Shamelessly, I murmured sweet things to him about how I'd missed him, how long it had been since we'd been alone together. We *really* needed to have some intimate communication, I said, so that we could understand each other's deepest needs and wants.

Mellow now from so much beer and good food and all the ego massaging that Sue and I had done, Iraj must have felt noble and generous, because he conceded that he had taken so much on his shoulders in so many areas that he had shut me out years ago. I'll always remember how he drawled, "You are not one hundred percent to blame for the troubles, Jess."

Abruptly he pushed himself away from the table and stood up. Obviously he'd decided it was time for our walk.

We ambled along nearby streets. As we got farther away from the Hilton, Iraj would stop occasionally to ask for directions. I noted that the Turkish dialect he spoke was not well understood by the locals. He was more relaxed, and I thought it was time to bring up "our future." I was feeling much more confident and gave him a pretty little speech about how eager I was to travel through Europe, perhaps even live there. I asked about his most recent thinking about the children's education and his career. He said he intended to enroll Sara and Cy in the English-language school for the fall session.

I mentioned that I'd read in the paper—actually Betty Mahmoody had told me—that the revolutionary government wouldn't permit children with an Iranian parent to attend any school except a traditional one. He shrugged, indicating that it didn't matter because the kids would be speaking Farsi very well in a couple of months. Obviously he hadn't given a thought to Sara and Cy's education, which strengthened my belief that his ferocious declarations about staying in Iran were calculated, empty threats. He told us about his experience applying for a teaching position at Tabriz University. He'd been accepted immediately—and offered a starting salary of $100.00 a month! He actually said that they had a lot of nerve to offer him such a pathetic salary for his brilliant mind!

Now I was cooking. He'd confirmed our guesses about how he was finding life back home: the terrible economy in Iran, no plans for the children's school; dissatisfaction with living with his parents; no American cigarettes, no alcohol at all; no sex. Iraj Salimi really was crazy if he thought I bought his story. No way he wanted to stay in Iran. The man probably was fervently wishing to get back to the West. I had a lot to work with now. All I had to do was get him drooling over all the dreamy little material things he was missing, and over personal liberty and professional opportunities and television and movies and night life and on and on. I was going to have this man missing the good life back in America so much that he'd wet his pillow with tears every night that he had to spend in Tabriz. And so I took every opportunity to insert into our conversations a tidbit about something or other I knew he loved and didn't have anymore.

We returned to our hotel to change for dinner. Once we were alone in our room, Sue threw her arms around me and congratulated me on a sterling performance. She even thought my initial lapse seemed natural.

Before we could settle down for a good rehashing of the day with Iraj, we had to get in touch with Aaron or Isaac to tell them where we were having dinner. There was something new on their end. They were keeping an eye on a couple of characters hanging around outside the Hilton, just in case they were working for Iraj. We noted that but didn't get particularly upset about it. We'd expected as much.

Both Sue and I were impressed with how wild-eyed and wild-tongued Iraj had been all afternoon—and how devious. His attacks on my character, motives, and actions and his threats were designed to intimidate me; his irrationality, whether inadvertent or planned, would normally make me defensive and vulnerable. I did fine—

no, better than fine; I did a masterful job of handling him—when I kept in mind that nothing he was saying could be trusted and went full speed ahead with my own agenda. We decided to keep conversation as light as possible at dinner. When we returned to the hotel, Sue would leave me alone with Iraj, and what happened after that was anyone's guess.

The ride to the restaurant over twisting, potholed roads in a taxi with no springs in the seats was very uncomfortable. But I was just glad to get to our destination, because the minute I'd slid into the back seat of that taxi I'd been reminded that this could be the vehicle Iraj intended to have take me to the prison of Iran.

There was a picturesque café on the riverbank just a few yards from the restaurant. We decided to stop there for a drink. Iraj ordered more beer for us all, and after we admired the view, he turned to Sue. At first he inquired in a very polite tone as to what she thought of my affair with the "low-life Lumber Guy." Keep the conversation light at dinner? Hah.

Sue got no chance to respond to Iraj, because he was off on another diatribe about me. I sat back in my chair, figuratively buckling my seat belt for another ride on his emotional rollercoaster. He started from the beginning. Again. There were my crimes and character flaws to rage about; there was the blame to be placed entirely on me for the failure of our marriage and for putting him in a position where he *had* to abduct the kids. This was preparation for hysterical ranting about Mike. And so it went, on and on. While Sue and I waited for him to wear himself out, I wondered if there was anything within my ex-husband for us to work with, to appeal to except avarice and a desire for revenge.

Enraged, he went over and over the same ground. Then he started all over again. His compulsion, his sickness reminded me of those trick candles on birthday cakes. The flame flared and burned out—for a moment. Then it sprang to life again, the cycle repeating until the candle was exhausted. The only difference was that Iraj seemed never to *get* exhausted. The axiom that anger is cleansing must apply only to those who are basically healthy, because Iraj's anger only led to more anger, with frequent escalations of rhetoric as he worked himself into a blinding rage.

Whenever there was a pause in his fiery attack against me, Sue would talk soothingly to him about understanding and forgiveness. Often she would defend me by telling anecdotes to illustrate what a wonderful mother I was, what a caring sister and devoted daughter. She talked about how fun-loving I am and what a great sense of humor I have. (I love to tease her about this in happy times today, reminding Sue that I am an absolute paragon of virtue. I have it on the best authority—hers!) She laced her defense of me with reminiscences, often introducing one by turning to me and saying, "Jess, remember when . . . " She even managed to get a hint of a smile from Iraj with a story about me as a child, when I was called "little clown" by everyone in the family.

These recollections helped quiet Iraj and improve the overall mood so that I could talk once more of hopes for a happy future as a reunited family. Astonishingly, Iraj did not once mention the money, passports, or court orders. I began to get very suspicious. What was he up to?

We finished our drink and headed for the restaurant along a path on the riverbank, driven to walk as fast as we could by the gagging stench of sewage coming from the water. The inlet here was nothing more than a huge septic tank, not a very good promotion for the pretty little restaurant that sat on a knoll a few yards from its edge. Naturally, we decided against sitting in the outdoor section of the restaurant, which was festively decorated with hanging lights. Iraj's conversation at dinner—we did *not* order seafood—was at first pleasant enough. When the delicious lamb dish he'd requested was served, he talked interestingly about Middle Eastern cuisine, then about art and architecture. But soon he was haranguing us about American attitudes and government policy toward Iran. He demanded that both Sue and I cancel our return reservations for the next morning and go back with him. Did it surprise him that we found his nasty, arrogant, threatening invitation easy to resist?

At last dinner was over. I was pleased with myself because I hadn't let Iraj beat me down or wear me out, and I felt I had handled my rebuttals to his attacks and replies to his questions very well. I was not looking forward to the rest of the evening, however, as Sue and I had agreed that she should leave me alone with Iraj when we got back to the Hilton.

When we reached the curb, a car with *dolmus* the word for taxi, painted on it started its engine and eased along, stopping in front of us. Iraj gave directions in Turkish, but not hearing the word "Hilton," I peeped at Sue. She was scowling. I tensed, and my heart started to beat harder; it began to race when I saw the grin on Iraj's face as he leaned back in the seat. Sue and I were flanking him; the I Group had recommended we try to get Iraj to sit between us in a vehicle, and we'd managed it rather smoothly on both taxi rides. We scooted closer to the doors when I made a fuss over Iraj's comfort and said we had to give him a bit more room.

The driver was taking the dark road very fast, I thought. But despite the speed, it seemed to me after several minutes that it was taking longer than the ride to the restaurant had, and I did not see any familiar landmarks. I was scared. I inched my hand onto the door handle, after noting that the lock buttons were up. I was ready. I glanced surreptitiously at Sue. Her hand also was resting lightly on the handle of her door.

I caught myself chewing my lower lip and stopped, hoping I hadn't betrayed my suspicions to Iraj. I sensed excitement and satisfaction in his manner and started to worry even more. Throughout the evening I hadn't spotted Isaac and Aaron or the men working for them, whom we'd met. I urgently wanted to crane my head and look out the back window to see if there were car lights behind us on this lonely, narrow road. But I had learned my lesson on this score and resisted the temptation.

The windows were rolled up. That was odd on such a hot June night in a car that wasn't air-conditioned. A bad sign. I looked at the back of the driver's head, caught him staring at me in the rearview mirror, and quickly turned away. I decided to find out what Iraj would do if I rolled down the window, and I cranked the handle.

"Put that up," he said. "I don't want dust blowing on me."

"But it's so hot," I protested. "We need the breeze."

He grunted in annoyance but didn't force the issue.

I peered out into the dark. We were in a remote area and there were few lights. More light was coming from the houses along the way than from the widely spaced, dim lights along the road. Where the hell were we? We were not going back the way we had come. The Hilton is on the Asian side of Istanbul—Iraj always referred to it as the Islamic side and to the European section as the Christian side—and near a huge park. But we weren't passing any buildings that looked familiar—we weren't passing many buildings at all. And Iraj, who hadn't shut up since he'd arrived, was silent as a stone.

My nerves were about to snap. I kept watching the road, trying to gauge the speed at which we were moving. I was ready to shout "Jump!" to Sue the minute the driver slowed down, but he seemed only to go faster and faster. Oh, God, was I being a fool and imagining things, or were we hurtling toward the mean destiny Iraj wanted for us? He had made that demand that Sue and I go back to Iran with him. Was it his last test, and had we failed it?

I was about to do something drastic when the driver veered onto a large street bathed in sodium light. The Cumhuriyet Caddesi, the road that led to the turnoff to the Hilton. Ahead was the French consulate, just beyond that Taksim Square. I slumped against the seat, just barely repressing a sigh of relief.

·ELEVEN·

In the glare of lights under the awning of the Hilton I could see the evil, amused sparkle in Iraj's eyes. The snake. He'd been toying with us. That had undoubtedly been a legitimate *dolmus*, but Iraj had told its driver to take us for a ride, a long ride through a dark, lonely area. He'd wanted to see our reactions, and after all, he wasn't paying the bills on this trip, so the hell with cost. Since he looked so pleased, I guessed that we hadn't done very well at hiding our nervousness from him.

Oozing what he must have believed was charm, he escorted Sue and me into the lobby and invited us to his room for a nightcap. This was Sue's cue to decline, which she promptly did. I accepted of course but said I couldn't bear to sit still one more minute and asked him to walk with me through the courtyard garden. He agreed, and both of us went to freshen up.

Once in our room, Sue put her arms around me and gave me a big hug. She reminded me how much I'd rehearsed for this encounter with Iraj, how smart I was, how critical these next hours were in getting the children back. There were so many *hows* in her pep talk that we started to laugh, and some of my nervousness dissipated. I splashed cold water on my face, ran a comb through my hair, and gathered my things. Sue reminded me that she and the I Group would be watching me every minute, so I shouldn't worry about my safety.

I took a few minutes alone on the balcony of our room to compose myself, mentally ticking off the roles that I wanted to draw on to shape the way I behaved with Iraj in the next several hours. There was the good mother— Homa without the nagging and demands; the fallen woman—repentant and eager to reconcile; the naive soul, somewhat helpless. But one very important, almost contradictory persona was the woman who could and would stand up to the bully, because twice lately being tough with Iraj had worked when nothing else might have.

I gave Sue, already on the telephone with either Aaron or Isaac, a peck on the cheek. I was wearing a good-luck bracelet which I began to twist on my wrist. I took a deep breath and went out to the hall. Iraj was waiting for me, and, silent, we rode down in the empty elevator. Soft rock music drifted from the bar-lounge and it inspired me to change course. I suggested to Iraj that it might be fun, just like old times in Princeton, to try this nightspot. His face lit up. I'd made the right move.

Business wasn't good, though the band was, so we were seated at a table on the edge of the dance floor, which was bathed in blue light and hazy with cigarette smoke.

My bottom had scarcely touched the seat of the chair when Iraj was imperiously snapping his fingers for a waiter. My Lord, the man had put away gallons of beer during the day and evening; it was a wonder he was still ambulatory. I'm not much of a drinker and the three glasses of beer I'd had during the day had been about two too many, so I ordered a white wine spritzer, but Iraj was now on Scotch—his favorite, naturally, Johnnie Walker Black Label, as I was picking up the tab.

Either the alcohol or self-satisfaction, perhaps both, had made Iraj much more placid than at any time since he'd arrived. This was a good sign, and I launched into some reminiscences about pleasant evenings we'd spent in places that were so similar to this Hilton nightspot. He chimed in agreeably, recalling one nightclub he'd particularly liked. I was pleased with this chatter, as it was establishing a warm, nostalgic tone. Within a few minutes I thought it was time to start emphasizing the glories of the West, which at lunch he'd confirmed he was missing so much. But now I steered away from areas I felt I'd exhausted, like his job opportunities. I mentioned the two new stores in the shopping center near our house, an upscale men's clothing shop and a electronics store. I talked about the elite wine-tasting club some friends had joined, and the elegant new car my brother-in-law had purchased. I chattered about anything and everything I could think of that had to do with luxury, elegance, comfort, and fun—all unavailable or outlawed in Iran. I returned to the idea I'd mentioned earlier in the day, that I was eager to travel in Europe, perhaps even to live in Holland or one of the Scandinavian countries. He had scarcely taken note of this before, but now it piqued his interest, and he talked at length about the merits and drawbacks of several countries. He thought it might be great to settle in Copenhagen, where we'd been married, or in Stockholm, where we'd stayed for several weeks after our wedding, trying to get Iraj's green card for his entry into the U.S.

I kept smiling, not even betraying by a blink the awful memories that were flashing through my mind. It was in Sweden, where, a bride of only a couple of weeks, I think I got my first real introduction to the seething well of anger in Iraj. Getting the green card had been a nightmare. He'd made scenes in public and thrown tantrums in private. He'd raged at embassy personnel about the numbers of forms he had to fill out and pitched fits over the time it took to get the paperwork processed. It was a wonder to me that he was allowed into the States, even though they really couldn't deny him entry, since he was married to a citizen. But in Iraj's recollections, none of this had happened: Stockholm had been beautiful and our stay there had been blissful.

Things were definitely going my way. Now my smiles were genuine, my chuckles unforced.

"You know, it might not be a bad idea if I sold the house, got the equity out of it, so we wouldn't have to worry about money for a long time," I mused. Iraj looked surprised. I pressed on. "I remember how much you wanted to get your Ph.D., but your duty to your family dragged you away from Princeton. Maybe you could start working on it again soon."

He loved the idea and started to amplify on it, talking about the high-tech future of the world. I backed every outlandish idea he advanced, including his boasts about the brilliant work he could accomplish if he owned the latest computers, the genius of the papers he could then write. I encouraged him to dream of setting up a house full of all the most advanced technical equipment, which would enhance his creativity and allow him to establish his commanding preeminence in computer technology. What hogwash, but he behaved as though he believed every word of it. How could I have married this vainglorious, spoiled, cruel man? I felt the deepest sense of estrangement from myself, as if another person had gotten involved with the smug, egotistical stranger across the table and left me to bear the burden of dealing with him.

The band slipped into a slow tune, and Iraj pulled me out onto the dance floor. I steeled myself for this big test, tamping down my feelings of revulsion, and walked into his arms. He was panting in my ear, his clammy hand roving over my back, and I squeezed my eyes shut and thought of . . . well, England, but the England of Koo Stark and Prince Andrew, not Queen Victoria and Prince Albert. I buried my embarrassment and disgust and shamelessly played the tart to this half-drunk creep who was imprisoning my children. A cheap prostitute couldn't have pulled this scene off better than I did, and I'm only surprised that the management didn't encourage us to leave.

The set ended, the band announced a break, and Iraj led me back to the table. He was obviously turned on, but instead of suggesting we go back to his room as I expected, he blew up.

His face an ugly red, the veins in his neck and forehead bulging, he demanded to know how I could have divorced him, driving home the point that no one had a *right* to reject him, least of all me. I was so startled and dismayed that I just sat there with my mouth open. He looked like a snarling ferret during this tirade on my duty as a wife to accept his behavior, no matter how much I disliked it. He jabbed his finger at my chest, saying, "Do you understand that? Do you understand?" I nodded, my muscles tightening.

He sat back, struck his fist on the table so hard that the fresh Scotch and water in front of him slopped over the sides of the cocktail glass. "Now," he said, "I let you off the hook before when Sue was here, but you are not going to get off it now. You are going to tell me all about your Lumber Guy. Everything. How good was he in bed? What did he do to you? You are going to tell me everything, you slut, everything about you and your lowlife bum."

I shrank back in my chair. My God, Iraj truly was the Hydra. Every time I thought one head had been cut off, the monster grew two in its place. These two heads of the monster were really grotesque; one was jealousy, and as nasty as the emotion was in him, I could handle it; but the other—his prurient interest in my sex life with Mike—was too revolting for me to deal with.

Bowing my head as if I was ashamed, but actually to hide the horrified expression on my face, I apologized once more to him for the "awful mistake" I had made in divorcing him. Okay, everyone had told me to use feminine wiles to the hilt, so I tried to look especially appealing and seductively wet my lips. Then I told him I'd realized almost at once that I'd done a terrible thing and was sorry, but at last I knew the truth—that I wanted to be back with him and have our little family reunited.

This was not what he wanted to hear. He ordered me to give him details, and he said that if I didn't give them to him, he was going to leave instantly.

Deliberately misunderstanding, I told him that Mike was a person who had been appealing and smooth at first. I'd been too inexperienced to see beyond the facade to the real man beneath, who was shallow, not very kind, and a little bit boring. I'd been blinded by my loneliness and needs in the beginning, and by my naiveté, so I'd made a horrible blunder and gotten involved with him. I said I'd been thinking of breaking off the relationship at least a week before the abduction.

I hadn't managed to satisfy Iraj with this explanation. Even with its implied favorable comparison of him to Mike, it didn't fit the bill. He made that clear. In graphic detail he suggested what Mike might have done to me in bed, what I might have done to him. He demanded to know if his vivid sexual descriptions were accurate, and, if so, what more "perversions" we'd engaged in.

"Iraj," I remember saying, aghast, "you have gone over the line. I am not going to sit here and make up lurid stories to appeal to some kind of a sick need in you to hear racy stuff!" In a more conciliatory tone, I reminded him that the relationship with Mike was a thing of the past, a big mistake I had admitted to, apologized for, and that it had taught me a lesson. I wanted to move on.

He jumped to his feet, shouting "American whore" at the top of his lungs and throwing the F word around.

I, too, got to my feet, and leaning across the table, I said low and adamantly, "You are making a fool of yourself. Just look around. Everyone is watching you, thinking you're crazy or drunk."

This stopped him long enough for me to move around to his side. I grasped him by the elbow. "Come on, let's go out to the courtyard. If you want to yell, yell outside where you won't get so much attention, okay?"

He seemed to have some understanding of where he was and how much negative attention he was drawing to himself. His vanity must have taken over. He shook my hand off his arm and stalked away, tossing over his shoulder a peremptory, "Come with me."

I got some strange and disapproving looks, some sympathetic glances from the patrons and waiters as I followed Iraj out of the bar. He was taking long, angry strides through the lobby toward the terrace and garden beyond. I didn't dawdle, but I certainly didn't trot after him. I took my time and considered my best moves to turn this negative to a positive. I looked at my watch. It was almost 3:00 A.M. Sue and I had to check in at the international counter at the airport at seven, and we'd have to leave the hotel an hour before. My muscles tightened. I had only three hours left to accomplish something here. The pressure was really on now.

Iraj had stopped at the railing on the terrace, his back to me. When I reached him, he whirled on me.

"God damn it, I'm sick and tired of this," he bellowed. "If you were sincere, you would have given me that money by this time. All you're giving me is bullshit, bullshit, bullshit! You are doing nothing to prove yourself. Nothing. And you must prove yourself if you want to see Sara and Cy again—ever!"

I reached out to touch his arm. "Iraj, please, calm down. Look, I know you must have been angry and jealous and that you are blowing up now because you love the children so much—and also maybe because you still love me a little. All this has been too much for you, since you adore the kids, and you're such a sensitive man, right?"

He didn't answer, but he looked at me as if I were an

imbecile who'd amazed him by at last succeeding in adding together three numbers. Encouraged, I went on, imploring him to forgive me and begging him to understand my position. I was speaking softly but firmly. It would be foolish of me—in fact he'd be ashamed of me, I said—if I were so stupid that I'd turn over all the items he wanted when I didn't have any guarantee that anything was in it for me. This was a risky statement, but the right one, because I saw the gleam of respect in his eyes and knew I'd appealed to the "bazaar mentality" that was so much a part of him and his culture. Bargain. Give away something for nothing and earn the contempt of the person you are dealing with. Demand that you get as much—or even better, more—than you give, and you're respected.

Okay, I'd been the good mother and the repentant. Now it was time to be a tough bargainer, a role that was real and that I relished.

"Listen," I said, "bring the children to meet me here in Istanbul and give me a promise that you'll at least try to work out a reconciliation with me, and I'll give you what you want. But not until I see the kids."

"You bitch," he countered. "You have no power here. None. You have to prove yourself by giving me the money, at least a hundred thousand, because I have all the power and I make all the rules. You don't seem to be understanding that."

"I understand you have most of the bargaining chips, Iraj, but not all of them. Most of all, though, I understand that you are making it very hard for me ever to love you again. Is that what you want, to kill every good feeling I've ever had for you? To kill the possibility of my loving you again? Is that what you want, to turn me away?" I didn't wait for his answer. I flounced over to a wrought iron staircase that wound down to the garden.

There were only a few people around at this early morning hour, mostly staff, two or three guests. Fog covered the Bosphorus, but I could see the wavering lights of ships on the water and, closer by, the minaret of a mosque. I walked slowly along the path. I was very worried. A conversation I'd had in late April flashed through my mind. I'd talked with a woman named Mandy Randall who'd bargained with her ex-husband for seventeen months while he held their son in Egypt. She'd gone through just this kind of hell during two trips to Egypt and thousands of phone calls. But in the end, she'd bargained successfully for the return of her son. I was exasperated and fearing failure after only a little over three months, and that would not do. Damn it, I'd hang in here, and I too would be successful in bargaining to get my children back.

Glancing back over my shoulder at the glass-enclosed elevator, I glimpsed tall, thin Isaac riding down to the casino level and breathed a sigh of relief. I wondered what Sue was doing and where she was, and if little Aaron was nearby. I had protection against my maniac ex-husband for myself, but none yet for the children.

All Iraj wanted was money. He hadn't even mentioned the papers overturning the custody and support orders or—and this surprised me—Sara's and Cy's passports. Cold cash was what he really wanted me to fork over.

Iraj caught up and stopped me by putting his hand on my shoulder. "Maybe we can settle all this in bed better than any other place," he purred. "Come up to my room, Jess."

So cold cash wasn't the only thing he wanted from me.

I stared wide-eyed at him. "With all this pressure on me? With all the cruel things you've said? You turn my every word against me and won't even talk seriously about a future. No way." I turned my back and walked on, finally stopping at a low stone wall. Iraj was on my heels. He spun me around.

"Don't turn your back on me, you whore. You think you can just walk away. You think you can behave like an immoral slut with that Lumber Guy and I'm just going to forget it, but I'm not." He flailed his arms and started all over again with his lewd summary about "the affair with the Lumber Guy."

The trick candle on the birthday cake . . . the Hydra. I exploded.

"You idiot," I wailed. "I traveled thousands of miles to talk with you and all you do is act like Torquemada during the Spanish Inquisition! You think you really are the Grand Inquisitor, don't you? You act like you want to torture me, put me on the rack or burn me at the stake or something. Well, I am not going to be broken by you, you kidnapper. You are keeping my children hostage and you're attacking me every other second. I won't stand for it! I want to see my children. You bring them here to Istanbul and I will give you money and those documents you want."

I opened my handbag and took out the paperwork for the phony bank account and the fake court orders. I flourished them, shook them under his nose, then said, "I deserve to be able to visit with Sara and Cy because I am their mother, and I won't take any more jerking around from you." I shoved the papers into his hands. "See these papers? You bring the kids to visit with me and you'll get your money. That's the deal. Got it?"

He was absolutely stunned. And I was breathless after my outburst. I moved away from him and sat down on the stone wall. The silence was heavy. I looked out on the water. I reminded myself that I had to get a grip on my anger and be prepared to bring this all around to a conciliatory phase—if I could. But I knew I hadn't lost anything, because Iraj, the Hydra, didn't seem to have come to Istanbul for any other purposes than to bully me and extort money from me. Oh, yes, and for sex. In the puritanical Iran of the fundamentalists, prostitutes had been stoned and all the brothels closed, some burned— and a man didn't dare touch a "good woman." So celibacy was the rule of the day for single men. Obviously Iraj was not living happily in his brave new sexless world. I sneaked a peek at him. He was absorbed in looking at the papers.

Long minutes passed. I was breathing normally by then and lost in sad thoughts about what Sara and Cy had been and continued to be subjected to. My innocent babies were being victimized; they were the knives their heartless father plunged into my heart and gut and twisted. I wondered if they were hoping against hope that I would return to Tabriz with Iraj and get them out of that horrible house presided over by their old, sick, cranky grandparents, who didn't understand them or appreciate how they'd been raised. I felt as if I was trapped in one of those terrible dreams, paralyzed, unable to move, with danger closing in from every side.

I made no effort to check or wipe away the tears that rolled down my face and dripped off my chin. Iraj came to me and started to stroke my hair with his free hand. I was proud that I could keep myself from flinching at his touch.

The Don Juan Hydra head was dominant, I realized, as he said, "Don't cry, Jess. Come on up to my room. I'll make it all right."

I could have thrown up. "Iraj, I just can't be a good lover, or any kind of a lover now." I snatched the papers from his hand and thrust them into my bag, got a tissue, and dried my eyes. "I feel crushed. My children are lost to me, my father is dying of cancer, I'm alone without my dreams. I wanted a good life for Sara and Cy and for you and me, but I think that's all hopeless now."

He sat down next to me and sighed heavily. "I might be able to love you again, Jess, but you've got to prove yourself. I do not trust you."

Devious, cunning, he probably felt he'd pushed me too far, so now he was adopting an agreeable manner. Nonetheless, I thought this might be progress. I was convinced of it as he went on, saying he would agree to a second meeting, to which he'd bring Sara and Cy. I pressed for a date, pointing out that it was June 25—actually, the twenty-sixth already—and the children had to go back to school in early September, so we had to settle things between us. He dismissed this point as minor, and one he couldn't address at the moment anyway because he had to arrange to get nephews, cousins, and others out of Iran. This led to the suggestion that yet another good way for me to prove myself to him was by helping the young men he was smuggling to the West. Just what kind of help he wanted me to give them, he didn't say—money and a place to stay, probably—but I knew I'd be hearing the particulars on the telephone soon enough.

I'd been fed up with this whole business of these escapees for a long time now. At first, and especially during the worst of the Iran-Iraq war, I was a wholehearted supporter of getting as many boys out of that insanity as possible. But the 1988 cease-fire and the attitudes and behavior of the Salimi brothers really had opened my eyes. I'd come to the conclusion that there was no ethical or moral justification whatsoever for this illegal activity. These men wanted to run out on their own country and benefit from everything that the West had to offer them personally. They gave nothing back to the countries that hosted them or to the land where they'd been born and raised. In my view they were opportunists of the worst kind. And Jamshid, Nasser, and Bobek had been major players in the criminal conspiracy to kidnap Sara and Cy. They deserved to be thrown out of Canada and the U.S., hurled right back into the Iran that they'd fled from, and to which they were condemning my children.

I couldn't help but make a comparison between these men and my grandparents on both sides, who were all immigrants. They had worked hard to earn the money for their passage, waited their turns for papers, and fulfilled all the tough requirements for acceptance into America. Then, appreciating all the advantages America offered, they had been constructive citizens. But Iraj and his pals didn't want to play by the rules, Iranian or American, and they had contempt for anyone who did. None of them had a moral compass that pointed anywhere near true north.

Iraj was babbling on about how much he loved his family, how important family was. He almost worked himself into another fit of sermonizing about how superior he was to me in this regard. The expression on my face must have stopped him, though.

This was such hypocrisy on his part. He cared about

his family, all right, but the general concept of family, and my family in particular, certainly wasn't much of a concern of his during our marriage. I remember when Sue was getting married, I had decided to give a bridal shower for her. Iraj got into a snit. His brothers needed to escape from Iran and I was giving this frivolous party! I'd had to change the location of the party from our house to my parents'. And on the day of the wedding he had refused to go—and refused to "allow" me to go. Sullen, brooding, he'd been venomous about my family being "vile lowlifes" for going ahead with a wedding when his brothers were in such jeopardy. I had gone to the wedding, without Mr. Salimi.

Of course, Iraj had to try to push me again on the matter of his bringing the children with him to Istanbul, so he returned to his tiresome and ridiculous demand that I meet for the visit with him and Sara and Cy in Teheran. I honestly thought I might lose it and start screaming in frustration. I felt as if I was hanging on to my temper by a thread. This maddening technique of going back time and time again to a sticking point was not only typical of Iraj and his sickness, but also of bargaining techniques in the Middle East. A bazaari would go back to his original high price just when the customer thought he was about to agree to a lower one. In Iran they were accustomed to playing this game over long periods of time. One simply had to refuse to be worn down. And I did. I insisted on Istanbul. We had a long argument on the subject, but finally he backed down.

He began to get amorous again, and I put him off by explaining that I just couldn't express the affection I felt when everything was still up in the air and my children were so far away from me. He had started stroking my hair and face again, his pants bulging. Good. I did manage a few hugs and kisses. He urged me to go to bed with him. Next time, I promised, whispering things like "Oh, let's make it soon, very soon," and "We won't start making love at four in the morning next time, sweetheart." I used the early morning hour and our obvious weariness several more times, and he confessed he was very tired, almost done in.

We wandered back into the hotel. Everything was closed, the place deserted except for one or two people on the front desk. We sat on a big, cushy leather sofa and continued to talk. I was terribly afraid Iraj was going to fall asleep on me, and I didn't want that to happen until I could extract a date from him for our meeting with the children. He promised that he'd try for "as soon as possible," but I couldn't get anything more specific out of him. To reinforce a sense of urgency, I brought up my father's illness. I repeated that the doctors were not giving us good news; Dad was dying, and he was begging to see Sara and Cy. Iraj regarded me through heavy lids and only shrugged. I found this very odd and couldn't come up with an explanation.

Dawn light began to seep through the windows; telephones started to ring, and people appeared in the lobby. It was 5:30 A.M. I popped over to the desk and called Sue, then asked Iraj to join us for breakfast. He agreed but asked me first to go with him to his room to pick up some drawings and cards the children had made for me. I stopped by my room to get the bag of presents I'd brought for Sara and Cy. In addition to toys and games, there were quite a few books, one of which had been chosen with great care by my sister Beth. It was a story about an owl and its offspring and undying maternal love. We were pretty sure Iraj wouldn't get it but the kids would.

Sara and Cy had worked hard on their cards for me, and I thought they were the most beautiful ones I'd ever received. I missed them so terribly, and I felt so desperate and helpless and exhausted that I began to cry. I couldn't stop and was soon sobbing. Iraj asked me to lie down with him on the bed. I felt I had no choice if I was to carry off my charade, so I joined him, wetting the pillow and his shoulder with my tears. His fondling turned sexual. I clenched my teeth and endured his touch. Unbidden, the memories of his attempted rape came vividly to mind. I was having more difficulty carrying this off than I had anticipated, and I'd anticipated a lot. When it was getting unbearable, I heard Sue's sweet voice calling through the door I'd left ajar on entering. I bolted off the bed.

Weariness and violent emotion and alcohol had taken their toll on Iraj. He lay there, his arm shielding his eyes. I'd been saved by Khomeini's fundamentalist regime, which prohibited alcohol and Western music— who would have thought I'd be grateful to the Ayatollah for anything? I was almost bubbling over with happy relief that I was getting free of Iraj. I reined myself in just enough to play out the scene properly. I gave him a kiss on the forehead in the most tender and compassionate way I could manage and told him to skip breakfast with Sue and me, as I was very worried about his health after his hard trip and lack of sleep. Then I swallowed the bile of my loathing for him, leaned over, murmured that I loved him, and gave him a passionate kiss on the mouth. He smiled ecstatically, triumphantly. I backed to the door, waving, smiling, and blowing kisses as I said good-bye.

I raced to my room, grabbed Sue, and danced her around in a circle, crying softly, "We did it, we did it." We picked up the bags Sue had packed and almost skipped out of the room. No sooner had we checked out and gotten our passports from our safe deposit box than we were joined at reception by Aaron and Isaac. We handled it like pros, not even batting a lash in acknowledgment.

We decided to go straight to the airport and get some breakfast there. As we were waiting outside for a taxi to pull up, an old woman approached us. She was legless, scooting around on a carpeted dolly like a large skateboard and selling cobalt blue heart-shaped glass ornaments. Sue and I choked up at the sight of her, and we each purchased a heart, not as a memento of this trip, but for good luck in the future.

We collapsed in the taxi. We were worn out, but so relieved and happy that we were high. We giggled like kids while we filled each other in on what had happened when we were apart during the night, and I almost couldn't stop laughing as Sue recounted what she had done. She had kept me in sight as much as possible, even stretching out on her stomach on our balcony to peer over the edge and watch Iraj and me in the courtyard. She'd been on the phone with Isaac or Aaron throughout all those hours, reporting and speculating about what was going on. Now she and I felt free, giddy with the success of our venture. We were silly on that last ride in a broken-down *dolmus*, but both of us were aware of the seriousness beneath that surface frivolity. So much hard work had led to this moment—so much hard work lay ahead of us.

We left Istanbul in an exultant mood. We had as strong a commitment to a second meeting, which would include the children, as it was possible to get from a man like Iraj. We had new information, and we'd avoided falling into any of Iraj's traps. Sue thought I had done a great job of acting and had convinced Iraj I wanted him back. I thought Sue had been the most constructive, and the driving force behind my charade, and I knew I couldn't have pulled off any of it without her. Aaron and Isaac met up with us at the airport and also applauded my performance. They were effusive in praising my handling of the whole late night scene, during which I'd taken Iraj from screaming hysteria in the bar, when he'd been shouting "American whore," to the wistfully romantic hugs and kisses in the courtyard. When they heard about the farewell in his bedroom, they were ecstatic. They felt that sex, or as close to it as they could make me get, was the weapon that would seal Iraj's fate.

Euphoric, I saw smooth sailing to our next meeting, at which Iraj had promised to bring Sara and Cy. Thank heaven I was no Cassandra. If I'd had the power to see the future, it might have flattened me. The sailing would be anything but smooth. And it would take me forty-five more exhausting, nerve-wracking days and nights, some of them pure torture to get through, until I could get Iraj back to Istanbul, forty-five more days and nights until once again I would set eyes on my children.

TWELVE

WE WERE SCHEDULED TO GO STRAIGHT FROM JFK TO Manhattan for a debriefing at the I Group offices. I knew it was vital for all of us to meet and report while everything was still fresh in our minds, but oh, how I wanted to get home. It took longer than Sue and I anticipated to share all the information we'd gathered from Iraj and begin to sort it out. While pleased with what we'd accomplished in Istanbul, Joshua emphasized that Sue and I should not be overly optimistic. Isaac and Aaron's firsthand and objective reports had given him a real understanding of how deranged Iraj was. The I Group was as sure as Sue and I that Iraj already was putting together a whole new set of conditions for a meeting with the children, conditions that focused on passports and money. We agreed that I should wait for him to call me, and meanwhile I should come up with a strong set of recommendations about the time and place of our next meeting. Their guess was that Iraj was going to be more impossible than ever to deal with, a thought I'd repressed on the trip home because I didn't want to burst my bubble of happiness. Joshua was absolutely right, I knew, but like Scarlett O'Hara, I was going to think about that tomorrow. Today I only wanted to think about Mike.

I couldn't wait to see him. The hour and a half trip from Manhattan seemed to take longer than the flight back from Istanbul. I rushed into my house just dying to get my arms around Mike and tell him how much I loved him. The house was empty. I felt bereft, as if I'd run out of a dark place expecting sunlight and there was only more darkness. I called mutual friends and learned that Mike had been so anxious about me that he hadn't been able to tolerate being alone in the house, so he had stayed with friends. He was on his way to meet me. As soon as he walked in the door and I took one look at him, I knew I never wanted to be without him again as long as I lived. I filled him in on what had gone on in Istanbul, and he was very proud of me for carrying off my role so well. We had a wonderful reunion.

Three full days had passed since I'd gotten back from Istanbul. It was July first, a bright, not too hot morning, and Mike and I went off for a long hike through a beautiful wooded area a few miles away. We felt great physically and spiritually when we got back to the house. There was a message on the machine from a peevish Iraj who said he was ticked off that I was not there to receive his call.

I laughed; it was so typical of that man! But Mike was scowling, uncharacteristically angry.

"Who in hell does he think he is?" Mike muttered.

"He needs to learn he's not the center of the damned universe."

That's about as rough as Mike has ever sounded, but I guessed that secretly he would have liked to have been the one to teach Iraj some manners!

I composed myself, deciding to tell Iraj that I had been away from the house because I had been taking my father to and from a doctor's appointment. Should I have been surprised that this explanation annoyed Iraj as much as if I'd said I'd been out frolicking? He curtly said that someone else should have done that "errand." That came from the man who professed to love and admire my father.

I ignored his remark and went directly into a little speech of thanks for his coming to Istanbul, telling us about the city, and taking us to the Galek. I said that I had stirring memories of our visit.

Iraj chose not to acknowledge any of what I said and merely told me that he would be taking the children to the mountains for a while, how long he wasn't certain.

I couldn't believe it! So he was going to put me through hoops, test me hard, was he? He knew that I could do very little except say "Fine, dear," and "Let me know the moment you're back, dear." Which I did. In a sweet voice, and with murder in my heart. Then I asked to speak with Sara and Cy, to find out if they liked their presents. He said they weren't there. I asked when I could speak with them. He wasn't sure. The conversation limped to a close, with him repeating that he'd called originally only to let me know that he and the kids would be away for a while.

"Taking the children to the mountains" meant to me that Iraj was endangering them by hauling them along with him on one of his hazardous operations. I was a bundle of nerves, angry and worried. I hashed this out with Mike and Sue, and telephoned the I Group to let them know that once again Iraj was moving the kids, and I was scared we'd lose track of them. We agreed unanimously that I should call Iraj right back, which I did. The call was a nightmare.

"We left so much up in the air just a little while ago," I began. "I thought you agreed to let me know right away when I should plan our family vacation."

"Jess," he said angrily, "I am exhausted from this trip I took to see you, and I can't even think about another."

Then he dropped his little bomb.

"Besides, something Sue said really bothers me. Thinking it over, what she said, I don't know if there will be a visit."

"What on earth are you talking about?"

"She said . . . well, I am really bothered by a word she used. She said your affair with that Lumber Guy was 'casual.' I cannot believe you would pick someone up in a casual way. I do not like that."

Oh, no, not again! The lunatic. Was he bringing up Mike again to drive me crazy? I forced myself to speak reasonably, to tell him that Sue meant that the relationship had not be serious in terms of a deep love; she'd been trying to explain it was only a brief infatuation. "I simply was starved for attention and friendship back then, vulnerable, so it was easy for me to believe Mike was the person I wanted him to be rather than who he really was. Can't you understand?"

He angled for me to apologize yet again, to grovel, and I sensed that he was about to work himself into a sweet frenzy and deliver another screaming tirade on this subject. Very, very quickly, I changed the subject.

"Look, I really want to see the kids and you. I am going to just go right ahead and make arrangements for all of us to meet in Istanbul in three weeks, then fly off to some city in Europe for a really wonderful vacation. And after I make myself sick rushing around making all these arrangements for flights and hotels and everything, I expect you to have the decency to bring the kids and go through with the visit."

"We'll see, we'll see," he muttered.

We had to get cracking on our plan for recovering the kids. The I Group agreed. And so we had our first big meeting to develop it.

How did the I Group go about planning what all the professionals call a "mission"? Well, it certainly wasn't what I would have expected—the creation of a step-by-step, highly specific blueprint. I'd thought these people would start right off putting together a formal plan, the sort of thing one might imagine was developed for the Desert Storm campaign. The reality was more along the lines of the planning that the Earp brothers might have done before the shootout at the OK Corral—the creative script conferences for the movie of the shootout. It required a lot of imagination in the beginning; a lot of detail work at every other stage.

Ideally, Joshua said, we would have started out with an explicit statement of the basics, the "givens," of the situation so everyone understood them in the same way. Unfortunately, the givens weren't as fixed as one might hope, except of course if we were to do the recovery in Iran. So we would have to build several scenarios to account for the uncertainties.

We began building around the most probable event: Iraj would bring the children to Istanbul for the promised visit. We felt there was an excellent chance that he had responded positively to my forceful, take-charge manner during the phone call and would come. He'd feel more comfortable in Istanbul than in any other city except Tabriz or Teheran. However, the I Group did not want to recover the children in Turkey, which they thought was too risky a place for the operation. They much preferred to make "the grab" in a European city, which we'd discussed prior to my meeting with Iraj; this was why I had proposed a European vacation at our meeting in Istanbul. I'd extended the vacation notion to suggest that when we reconciled we even might want to relocate to Europe.

Actually all of us believed that Iraj ultimately wanted to come back to live in the United States, but that he was relieved by the talk about Europe because of his fear of arrest. No matter his rationalizations, he knew he had broken U.S. law big time in terms of the court order on custody, and until he was sure that the marriage really was cemented again, he couldn't be certain I wouldn't have him arrested the minute he landed in America. The matter of an international arrest warrant seemed not to bother him so much as the threat an American warrant represented.

But what if we had to recover the children in Istanbul? Could we do it? Yes, but it was far riskier. Turkey is an Islamic country, and if anything went wrong, we would have to expect the court system to favor a Muslim father. Also, getting out of Turkey might be extremely difficult, because, though it is making a lot of progress in modernization, it is still a Middle Eastern country so a woman traveling alone with two children gets more attention than in the West. It was imperative that Istanbul only be a meeting place, a takeoff point for a city in Europe. But which city?

Whereas Iraj had loved the Paris airports, the I Group was only lukewarm on them. They preferred Rome's Leonardo da Vinci Airport to all others. I thought Paris, the City of Light, the city of lovers, would be an easier sell. There were two other strong reasons for choosing Paris. First, what I'd considered a negative about France initially, that the country had been very sympathetic to the Islamic fundamentalists in the past and still might be sticking to that policy, seemed a positive in light of allaying Iraj's apprehensions. The second strong reason for choosing Paris was that I'd never been there, and Iraj would remember the many, many times I'd said I was dying to visit the city. But I always had to think of the possibility of something going wrong and of my having to deal with the local court. In Paris I might be at a severe disadvantage, though not as great a one as in a Muslim city like Istanbul; the court might honor any Persian papers Iraj had had drawn up indicating that he had custody of the children. This was a risk I decided I had to take.

And I would have to go alone on this trip; it would seem suspicious to Iraj if Sue came along on this honeymoon and family vacation. I regretted that this was true, for my sister's loving support was as important to me as breathing. But I felt strong, able to do this on my own.

What about the timing? We felt it was vital for me to follow through and have itineraries and the accompanying hotel and flight reservations all in place as soon as possible. Confronting Iraj with more or less a fait accompli was the way to go.

We broke off at this point. There were dozens of things to do. On the phone and in our next meetings, though, I was told we would be developing the scenario about the actual recovery of the children. That process would consist mostly of asking a lot of questions that started with "What if," and going from there. We would work through the things that might happen and try to figure out ways to act and react to them. Acting was more important than reacting, because we wanted to be in control of events, not at the mercy of them.

Only in the middle of the night, as I lay sleepless, did I allow my anxiety to rise to the surface; during all the waking hours I kept that demon at bay by working as hard as I possibly could. I was the center of an operation that involved a lot of people. And at every turn they were asking me to decide a point, make a judgment, call the shots. Everyone, including my sisters and brother and Mike, emphasized that it was my children who were at risk, so only I could make the tough decisions.

Selling the house. Iraj had loved the idea of getting all those nice greenbacks in addition to all the borrowed cash he thought was already in an account. I could add to my pretense and tell him that not all the people who had promised to loan money had come through, so I really had to sell the house. This make-believe move really might convince Iraj I was going through with the plan to burn my bridges as he had burned his, give up altogether on my life in America, and throw in my lot with him in Europe. To lend credence to this story, I contacted two or three real estate agents and had them tour the house and help me set a price on it. I actually listed it with one woman, so I could give her name and her company telephone number to Iraj. He could check her out, if he wished. This was a powerful bit of backup, we believed.

But now the fabrication about my father being at death's door might be coming back to haunt us. Iraj knew that I absolutely adored my father, and he would not believe I'd abandon him when he was critically ill. What to do? Could I possibly convince Iraj that I would choose him and my children over my dying father? We weren't at all sure that story would fly. My best course might be to lay this dilemma tearfully before Iraj, playing to his ego by begging for his wise counsel in this painful matter. That approach would certainly appeal to his colossal vanity.

We were growing so close to our travel agent, Tom, that he was getting to be like family to us. What a guy. We never confided in him what was going on, but Tom never seemed the least bit surprised when I asked for information on flights to and from the most obscure of the world's cities—how many travel agents are asked to give a client a list of all the scheduled flights from Tabriz, Iran, to Erzurum, Turkey? And he never got the least bit impatient with all the inquiries about hotels in myriad cities, nor the least bit perturbed about the changes in reservations I would begin to make each day. Now we were working cheek-by-jowl with Tom on setting up the trip from Tabriz for Iraj and the children, the trip over for me, and the trip to Paris for all of us. Tom was so cool that he didn't even falter when he repeated my instructions that the children and I were then to be booked from Paris to New York, and that I would not be making any continuing flight arrangements for Mr. Salimi.

RESCUED

Oh, God, the problem of the children's expired passports! This was just terrible. I'd kept mum on this to Iraj. We weren't sure how we would use the passports or what impact their expiration might have on him. I couldn't show up in Istanbul with expired passports and drag the children off to the American consulate to have the documents extended without expecting Iraj to have a fit. He would be sure then that I was up to something, and it could blow the whole mission.

My stomach was in knots for days over the matter of the passports. I couldn't stand the tension. As soon as I got tickets from the travel agent for Sara and Cy and for me, I did something that was against all reason. And for the first time, I did not discuss my actions with anyone.

Boldly, I marched into the passport office in Philadelphia, went to the counter, and filled out all the forms for extending the passports of Sara and Cy Salimi. Acting calm and collected, I slapped the forms, the expired passports, and the airline tickets on the desk before the official, who was pleasant and started processing the application right away. I took a seat as instructed and waited. And waited. An hour passed and then my name was called. Instead of getting my reward of extended passports, I was ushered into a back office.

The computer had turned up the fact that the children had been kidnapped. My application wasn't simply rejected, I was grilled. A long, tricky interview followed, until I was able to convince the officials to check the computer again. They would see that the report must be flagged with my name as the parent who had legal custody of the children and who had reported the kidnapping. In fact that was the case, so I wasn't going to be held for trying to get passports for kids I'd abducted. Unfortunately, it completely blew my game. They cited the rule that applicants for passports must be in the country at the time of the filing of the application. They would not violate that rule, no matter the predicament. Though personally sympathetic, they were unbending. I went crazy.

I explained. I pleaded. I told them every single thing about the recovery operation, going into great detail about the time pressures that made it very dangerous in a foreign country not to have up-to-date passports for the children. I begged them to contact their superiors and get an exception made in this case, this life-and-death case.

They turned rude. Clearly they wanted me to get out and stop wasting their time. Tearful and angry, I did something I knew I shouldn't: I let my terrible frustration bubble over into anger. I shouted then at their inhumanity, their petty bureaucracy. They instructed me to see my lawyer, using his name.

That made me paranoid. How did they know my lawyer's name? I stormed out; then I went home and stormed into my house. And called my lawyer.

The State Department people in Philadelphia had already been in touch with him. They were inflexible on their rule, and they told him firmly that he had to warn me not to try again at some other office to get passports for the kids. But, he said, they had been conciliatory, perhaps even somewhat baffled by why all of us were so worried when it was such a simple matter to get the passports extended in a foreign country. I was back to hating the State Department passionately, for not only failing to help me but actually erecting a huge roadblock to my success in saving my children.

After fuming about this situation, we decided to find another way. Still, the only thing we could come up with was that I would act dumb in front of Iraj, pretending I'd just quickly gathered up the passports without looking at them and hadn't a clue that they'd expired. But what would he do? He was mortally terrified of the U.S. Marines. I couldn't see him accompanying me to the consulate. And, unfortunately, I couldn't see him letting me out of his sight with the children, let alone allowing me to disappear into the consulate with them to get the paperwork done. The whole thing might make him freak and run—with Sara and Cy. I gnashed my teeth. What about having the passports forged? Impractical. Sure to be detected. I couldn't go that illegal route. No, I'd just have to wing it in Istanbul with Iraj.

Wing it. . . .

I was hearing that phrase too often from the I Group when I called to discuss what I thought was a thorny problem in getting the kids or escaping with them. We'd have to wing it, fly by the seat of our pants. I buried the apprehension that these words caused and forged ahead.

It was July 10. I tried Iraj. Lo and behold, he was back from the mountains. I told him about all the arrangements I'd been making, speaking glowingly of Paris, and waited.

He liked it! He paused, mulling it over, then told me that he believed Paris would be a fine place for us to vacation.

I suggested that we meet exactly one month from then, on August 10. That stopped his lovely, agreeable tone. He would have to think about the date, he said.

The call concluded in a very friendly way. How cooperative Iraj was being. I could just see him salivating over getting his hands on all that money.

Five days after that call, though, I became concerned that I hadn't heard back from him. And I was growing even more concerned that I hadn't heard back from the I Group on detailed plans for recovering the kids. I called Joshua, insisting that we not only have a plan for Paris or some other major European city, but also a backup in case Iraj would not come out and we had to take the children from Tabriz.

In the very beginning of our association, the I Group had plotted a recovery in Iran, centered on a "German businessman," which was later changed to a German diplomat so that I might go with him to Tabriz as his Italian wife. Their chief operative would be the diplomat and the plan was to make a clandestine and highly dangerous "grab," then race the kids across the border. Now they had some fresh information from their contacts in the country; Sara and Cy seemed to be fine; there were increased patrols on the Turkish border; and they had up-to-date street maps of Tabriz and of the area around it. I did not ask and they did not tell me where they had gotten these maps.

But I felt uncomfortable with the I Group now. They seemed so resistant to nailing down the elements of the plans, to actually developing an exact method for getting us out of Istanbul if we were forced to recover the children there, for example. I didn't understand them. I had come to like these people enormously, and I didn't have a doubt in the world about the sincerity of their concern for Sara and Cy, but I was full of doubt about their strategy for conducting our operation.

We had only one chance to get the kids back. I wasn't suffering from some sort of free floating anxiety on this matter. I could see it all quite clearly. And I knew that if we botched the recovery, we would never, ever get another chance. Faced with Iraj disappearing with Sara and Cy and my never seeing them again, I believe I was justifiably concerned that every detail of the recovery be scrupulously planned. Certainly we'd have to play it by ear, be flexible and able to "wing it," as they continued to say over and over, but there was also a great deal that could and should be put firmly in place right away.

I couldn't reach Iraj by phone, but I wasn't too worried. I knew what he was up to. As I pondered his illegal activities, I felt a growing sense of strength. He'd made a monumental mistake in bragging to Sue and me about what he was doing. He should never have given us so much information, so much detail. There might be a dozen ways I could use this information against him in Iran, as well as in the U.S. and Canada. I'd have to consult with my lawyer and the I Group on this to see if something could be done along these lines that wouldn't jeopardize the children any more than they were already being jeopardized. If the going got really tough, this newly-tough lady was going to get herself going. Two could play at this game.

I had to count on a successful recovery of the children. And with that as a given, I had to make some decisions about our life afterward. Security was paramount; I asked the I Group to get information for me on how the Witness Protection Program worked, so I could use it as a model for pulling together some ideas. Meanwhile, I was exploring the requirements for living underground through a couple of organizations set up for parents who were hiding themselves and/or their children from abusive spouses. And what I was learning was shocking and frightening, because a successful life in hiding seemed to depend on a kind of suicide: the complete destruction of one's past. First, I would have to change our names—not legally, of course, because that would leave a trail through the courts. I'd have to secure new birth certificates and social security numbers, and a new driver's license. A new social security number is absolutely critical to hiding out successfully; I had no idea before how one could be tracked down through that number alone. I would have to invent a new history for us, moving two or three times before settling in to a new community in order to do so. The children would have to be taught to never, ever mention the past or anything about our situation, and I would have to break off all contact with my family, communicating with them through a third party. I found it impossible to accept any of this at first.

It seemed like forever since I'd talked with Iraj, away again on one of those "trips." I hoped all this activity meant he was wrapping up his smuggling operation in preparation for coming out of Iran with the kids. Actually, I wasn't so blasé about these trips. It was unlike Iraj to be working hard in the summers; the temperature reached 100 degrees by midday in Iran at this time of year. From what he'd told us in Istanbul, I began to understand that he did have a lot to do in order to manage what he'd led me to believe was a large operation. That could mean he had a lot of allies, people who could give him protection in Turkey and Europe. We might be facing a large contingent when we met him. I made a note to reemphasize this to the I Group.

I telephoned Tabriz—and Sara answered the phone! I was surprised and delighted to hear her lovely voice. It seemed a gift from God that she'd picked up the call so naturally. Before anyone could censor her, she told me that she missed me so much she couldn't stand it, and she couldn't wait to see me again. My heart soared. We were able to talk briefly about school, which she was worried about because her father had pulled her out before the end of the year. I assured her I'd spoken with her teacher and the principal and it was okay. I talked with her about what she was doing during the day in Iran. "Playing," she answered a bit forlornly. Her only complaint to me at that moment was that both she and Cy were having a "lot of stomach pains again, Mommy." Then she quickly put on Cy, who'd been anxious to talk to me. He said almost all the things Sara had said about how he felt and how much he wanted to come see me.

I'd suspected that Sara had been nudging Iraj about seeing me or going home—she could be an incredibly pushy little girl when she wanted something. In fact I had been hoping she was driving him to distraction on this score. As I'd guessed, she *had* been unrelenting on the issue. Reading between the lines, I found out that Iraj got her to stop bothering him by telling her about the impending family vacation. So Sara and Cy were hopping with excitement about this prospect.

Iraj got on the phone. He sounded courteous, since, I supposed, he knew the children were hanging on his every word. As he was signing off, he said ominously that in addition to making sure the reservations were flexible in case he had to "change everything" he wanted me to be sure I would "bring the goods." Money, of course. I hung up feeling excited, but bewildered by Iraj's behavior. Only that warning about how he might have to "change everything" had been said in his typically weary, brusque way, and, oddly, it put me at ease.

I tried to imagine myself in Istanbul and go step by step through what might occur. I would get there early. The I Group people would be in place. I would meet Iraj and the children at the airport with gifts and flowers and we'd go back to the Hilton. Would I have to sleep with Iraj that very night? Undoubtedly. If I didn't, we wouldn't be a reunited little family, would we? Okay, I could do that . . . some way, somehow I'd get through it. But what about the passports, without which the children couldn't depart from Istanbul for Paris? There was no getting around that, and I reviewed once more the responses Iraj might have. No matter what, it didn't look good. I took this problem once again to the I Group.

Jacob said he "knew people who might be able to help." He decided to go in person to Washington to see them, and if necessary, plead for their assistance.

I was nervous as a cat the day he went on this trip, so I was a little annoyed that he didn't call me the moment he got back instead but waited until the next day. When he gave me his message, though, I understood why he hadn't been eager to be in touch: he'd struck out. The problem of the passports would haunt me every hour of every day for the next three weeks.

My lawyer had been working hard. He was diligently getting all the papers in place for judgments and liens against Iraj's property in Chicago because of delinquent alimony and child support payments. The little bit of information that Iraj had given Sue and me in Istanbul about his suspicion that Bobek was trying to fleece him had actually given us reason to prompt my lawyer to work on the liens and judgments more quickly. (My lawyer, bright man, had already thought of doing this.) At the bitter end, we wanted to make sure that if any "fleecing" was done, we would be doing it. Actually, despite the down payment on the house in Chicago and the ownership of the silver Audi and a few other things, I suspected that Iraj's assets wouldn't even begin to cover the cost of the trip to Istanbul and the I Group's expenses and their fees for the work they did there. He must have emptied his bank account to go to Iran and set himself up.

Iraj called. Now he wanted me to get a plane ticket and hotel reservation for his older brother, who would be joining us in Istanbul. I agreed. Anything, *anything* to make this work. Iraj said his brother was sorry not to have seen me in so many years and was eager to visit with me. Did he really think I would believe such a thing?

Dear Tom took down the spelling of the foreign-sounding name and said he'd have a ticket and hotel reservations confirmed for him as soon as possible. I called the I Group with the news that Iraj was bringing someone with him and asked if their surveillance group had any new information on the size or composition of his smuggling organization in Iran. They seemed unconcerned about the addition to the party; they said they hadn't contacted their people in Tabriz in the last few days. I felt let down, a little bit condescended to, a little bit lonely in the planning of the operation.

Iraj called. Trouble. He had an idea. He wanted to have a honeymoon with me in Rome for about two to three weeks, after which he would send for the children. I was shocked by this suggestion, and it took me several moments to gather my wits. There was no point, I decided, in trying to hide my disappointment. I'd simply have to work with it. I just insisted that he had to bring the children with him. No if, ands, or buts. I did rush to add, though, that I would bring everything—absolutely everything—he wanted, maybe even a lot more. I emphasized that I had a lot of money borrowed and already in an account, and if the house sold quickly, there would be a great deal of money for me to bring over. He wavered, not giving me much of a commitment that he'd bring the children and stick to the plan to meet first in Istanbul. But about Rome instead of Paris he was quite firm.

I said I thought Rome was a dandy idea, brilliant of him really. With my Italian heritage and the city's great restaurants, wonderful art and shopping, and religious and historic landmarks it would be a marvelous place for all four of us. And the kids would learn so much there. He quickly ended the call, saying he would be off to the mountains and would call in a few days, but in the meantime I was to change all the reservations to Rome.

Rome? What was it with that city? The I Group, too, preferred it—well, they preferred the airport there. It wasn't until almost two years later, reading the account of the abduction of an Israeli defector through the Leonardo da Vinci Airport, that I got some clue as to the "special relationship" that might exist between the I Group and some person or group of persons there. But at that time I was just curious. My father had made a trip to Rome long ago, back when the airport was still named the Fumicino and told me of the terrible damage that had been done there when terrorists shot up the place. I'd had a brief stopover in Rome on a flight once and had gone out of the reception area to look around the airport. There had been armed militia everywhere, the plaster was pitted with bullet holes where some of the walls still hadn't been repaired, and there were odd rubber mats covering the floors. The mats, I was told, were to keep people—terrorists, I assumed—from running fast through the airport. I had a strange foreboding about Rome, and about being anywhere near the Leonardo da Vinci Airport.

Tom. I called Tom and asked him to change all our flights, cancel the hotel reservations in Paris, and line up a list of recommended places to stay in Rome.

"Sure thing," he said cheerfully. "I'll get back to you with confirmations and the names of hotels first thing tomorrow."

Without ever knowing it this man named Tom, whom I'd never set eyes on, was becoming one of my biggest heroes.

But as he grew in my esteem, the I Group shrank. They were delighted, of course, to hear that Iraj had opted for Rome, their very favorite city in which to operate. But when I asked exactly how they were planning now to separate the kids from my ex-husband and if they were anticipating getting any estimates on how many "boys" worked for him and might be available to support or bodyguard him and the children in Rome, they had nothing to tell me. I asked if they had any new thoughts about how I should handle the passport business with Iraj. No, they didn't, but they believed he would go along to the embassy in Rome with me to get the documents extended. After all, Rome wasn't so threatening to Iraj, they said. But what were they doing about plans to get us out of the country after we got the children out of Iraj's clutches? That was still open-ended, they answered. After all the time that had gone by? I was almost in tears.

And it was July 21. The clock was ticking; the meeting with Iraj was still on for August 10, just twenty days away.

THIRTEEN

IT WAS TIME FOR A FAMILY CONFERENCE—MAYBE IT WAS way past time for a family conference. I was scared, because so much seemed to me to be up in the air, time was running out, and still I was getting "we'll wing that" from the I Group on every point I raised with them. It seemed to me that winging it should only apply to those problems or events we couldn't foresee. What we foresaw as a difficulty should be dealt with right away, not left dangling. What was happening here?

Rob, Sue, Beth, Mike, and I got together late on the night of July 21. We reviewed exactly where we were with all our planning. I reported on my last conversation with the I Group as dispassionately and accurately as I could.

I was relieved when they all assured me that I wasn't

overreacting. Rob, our calm jurist, lost his cool almost before I'd finished filling everyone in.

"What the hell are they doing?" he demanded. And for the first time he mentioned their very high fee. "These guys sound like they're piddling around. Damn it, we can't put up with them dragging their heels or being vague. Not now. Not when we're getting so close."

"You know," Sue said, "I just thought of something. Remember that night in Istanbul when Iraj hadn't shown up and we were on pins and needles?"

I nodded.

"It didn't occur to me until this minute, but we shouldn't have been the ones who came up with the idea to call the airline and check on whether or not Iraj had boarded the plane in Erzurum. Aaron or Isaac should have thought of that right away. They're the pros and we're the amateurs, right? But who was acting like pros then? I don't know, maybe these guys just aren't on top of everything the way we want them to be."

She frowned. "I never told you this, Jess, but you recall that you spotted Isaac riding the elevator down to the casino in the Hilton? That was while you were in the garden with Iraj. Well, hon, I really hadn't wanted to say anything before because I thought it might bother you, but Isaac had given up on you getting anywhere with Iraj. He wasn't going downstairs to guard you or anything. He thought it was over, and he was going down to the casino to try his hand at the tables."

I think I gasped at that information. I looked around. From the expressions on every face, I could tell we were in agreement. We needed to have a definitive meeting with the I Group as soon as possible. Rob said he wanted to make the call to set it up. I agreed. He was, after all, footing the bill.

Rob, my sisters, Mike, and I attended the afternoon meeting with the I Group at their office in Manhattan.

I can't remember exactly why the warrant for Iraj's arrest was the first item on the agenda, but it was, and we discussed the tricky timing that had to be observed when it was filed. It had to be issued at the moment that Iraj set foot on Turkish soil so that it would not be recorded through the National Crime Information Center computer link in the Middle East and Europe. Secrecy and surprise were vital. If the warrant was issued too soon and he was stopped at the airport in Istanbul, he'd run with the children, if possible retreating back into Iran. If he was detained by Turkish customs, the children might be held too, which had to be avoided at all costs.

I maintained a professional manner while the I Group went over all this, but I was dismayed. The discussion about the warrant was simply a rehashing of information I'd provided them. I had been the person who'd grown impatient with their lack of response and had called the FBI to get some facts, and I'd enlisted the help of our local policeman when the I Group hadn't been forthcoming. I'd learned that a warrant simply could not float around but had to be issued at the critical moment. I'd already passed this information on to them. What we needed from Isaac and Aaron but wasn't being provided was a recommendation as to who would get the warrant issued from the U.S. and at what exact moment. Would there be someone watching in Istanbul who would telephone my lawyer or our local police to tell us that Iraj had come through customs and the warrant could be issued? What were the specifics of the plan? Isaac and Aaron were the experts, and I wanted them to give us precise recommendations.

At about this point in the meeting Isaac and Aaron got into a quirky little dispute with me. They wanted Sue to be added to the party on the second trip. I just couldn't go along with that; it would look too suspicious. I'd had lots of justification for insisting to Iraj that Sue accompany me on the first trip: I was so weary, I had told him, and so depressed; I'd been ill. But I doubted he would accept such a story the second time.

The I Group wanted to have Sue along for communications and to act as a go-between. I could understand that but wondered why they couldn't come up with an alternative. We had discussed Sue's participation when we'd been debriefed after the first Istanbul trip, and I'd vetoed it then, asking them to give us ideas about how we could transmit messages if I were on my own. When they sketched their recovery scenario later, this became a critical issue, and they returned to argue the point that Sue had to be included in the party. Her participation could be made to seem appropriate to Iraj, they said, because he was bringing his brother. I did not think I could get him to accept her tagging along. His brother was scheduled to stay in Istanbul only until we left; then he'd return to Iran. The ticket was a courtesy, "for family," as Iraj had put it. Finally, Isaac and Aaron relented on this matter, but they said they didn't really agree with me.

Photocopies were made of my passport and the children's for me to keep; the I Group held the originals. Joshua, the head of the organization, said he was going to take a second trip to Washington to see if he could get this matter resolved through another one of his contacts there. It was expensive, and it seemed hopeless to me, but I said nothing as I was afraid I'd grown too cynical about the State Department.

We deferred discussion about the recovery again as they reported that they hadn't gotten the material I'd requested on how the U.S. Witness Protection Program worked. I was very concerned about the recovery, but I was also looking ahead to the process of getting the children into the U.S., helping them get over the trauma of the kidnapping, and beginning to rebuild our lives.

I hadn't been twiddling my thumbs waiting for witness protection information from the I Group; I'd been working frantically with Mike and Sue to put in place plans for the next phase—the establishment of a safe harbor for my children and me. We had decided that I should go ahead with the sale of the house while we were investigating a new location for us. In the meantime we were trying to find a temporary safe house where we could hide until we figured out how to deal with the dangers of a reabduction by Iraj's relatives or hirelings or both. We also needed to experiment with living underground so we could make good decisions about our new life. And a new life it would be, because things could never be the same again. On the advice of people who had been through reabductions, our local law enforcement officers, and Drs. K and Cipriani, I was facing the fact that we might have to live with security and other precautions in an underground setting for a long, long time to come.

I reminded the I Group that I was also waiting to hear what they thought about my suggestion that we bring smuggling charges against Iraj in Iran or Turkey. I'd sent them a short memo on this subject, listing all the pros and cons I could come up with. I'd also questioned what, if anything, we might get by turning in Nasser, Jamshid, and Lelah to the Canadian authorities, since they were there under false pretenses, as well as having been conspirators with Iraj in the kidnapping. Bobek was in the U.S. legitimately on a student visa, but there was the matter of his role in the abduction to think about for the future.

The I Group said they hadn't really delved into this matter yet, which was okay with me if they'd made progress on recovery planning. I forced the discussion back to the primary issue.

And so we got to the point of the meeting, the recovery. This is what I believe I heard them tell us: I would meet Iraj and the children and whoever else accompanied them in Istanbul at the airport or hotel. We would share a happy reunion, and then I would tell Iraj that I'd noticed a small problem with Sara and Cy's passports. We would solve it and move on to Rome.

Hold on a minute. Small problem? This was a danger point. What would we do if it *wasn't* a simple matter of "we would solve it," what if Iraj did something drastic? After all, Isaac and Aaron had witnessed his bizarre and angry behavior; they knew from firsthand experience that I was not exaggerating his potential for violence. If the passport problem made him suspicious and angry, he might lock me up, beat me up, and sneak me out of the hotel and back to Iran. There were many, many potential hazards here, and I thought for my peace of mind I needed to have some ideas about how I'd be protected. They were sympathetic and sensitive to how frightened I must be but basically shrugged off the need for outlining the specific countermeasures they'd take. They went on then with the sketch of the scenario.

We would be on vacation in Rome—or Paris or Copenhagen—they said, and there'd be fun and laughter. Iraj wouldn't have the slightest suspicion that anything was amiss. While my little family was enjoying the sights, all of us would look for the opportune moment to grab the kids, run, and return with them to the United States.

I listened attentively, waiting for them to flesh out this skeletal plan, to go beyond this basic scenario, which was virtually the same as the one we'd come up with on the first day we had met the I Group and Rob had given them that large retainer. Where was the body of the plan? I was waiting to hear the detailed solution they'd been working out on the escape; we'd had several conference calls since our return about these specific problems. They weren't being addressed, and as for those that were, their plan didn't seem any better than the one we'd hatched in such a hurry just before going to Istanbul. I had the sinking feeling that we were going backward, not forward.

Sue spoke up, asking what they would do if it turned out that Iraj was surrounded by his cronies. They responded that they'd have to "go with the flow" and see what locals they could pick up as reinforcements. It would be much tougher, they conceded, to find a way to snatch the kids if Iraj had henchmen with him, but they believed this was a remote possibility, since they hadn't detected any people watching or working with him in Istanbul.

I reminded them that their locals had spotted and kept an eye on a couple of suspicious-looking characters hanging around the Hilton. Beyond that, I didn't feel that we had enough evidence from the Istanbul experience to conclude that Iraj had come and acted alone. Delays due to the earthquake, had prevented him from taking the flight from Erzurum, he'd said, but we didn't know that was true. Had they checked on the flights? Had they done anything to verify his story? The answer was no. What did surveillance after our departure reveal? They had not had him watched after our departure.

I was very troubled now. If no one had been doing surveillance on him in Turkey, maybe they hadn't done it on the Iranian side either, so we couldn't be sure of Iraj's story about the twenty-three hour trip or anything else. He could have been watching us tour the city with Isaac and Aaron for all we knew, because we had no corroboration of his story. We could have been living in a fool's paradise of certainty about the success of our trip all this time, with Iraj laughing up his sleeve and pulling my chain. I seriously doubted this extreme conclusion, but I didn't doubt that Iraj had had a couple of cohorts around the Hilton.

Rob inquired about the upcoming meeting in Istanbul with the children, which the group had glossed over. He wanted some good thinking on the issue of money, he said, which he was very sure Iraj would demand immediately. Once Iraj had a bankbook in hand, he might find out we'd set up a dummy account. Or, Rob went on to point out, if we'd financed a real bank account to throw him off, Iraj could take the money and run back to Iran. As the conversation proceeded, I could tell that Rob did not find the level of discourse on this issue from the I Group satisfactory.

I wondered if they would be able to watch the kids and

me all the time and how long they would need to set up the grab. They said they could guard us and they would make the grab on the spur of the moment. Nothing to it. I thought they were just leaving things out, so I prompted them to tell us about their plans in case they hadn't been able to satisfactorily "delay" Iraj. If Iraj were to get free and file a complaint with the Italian police, we would have to have safe houses along an escape route. We'd previously discussed the need for a set of false papers, and for disguises, maps of alternative routes, other safe houses, and tickets reserved at other airports in the names on the false passports. Since Iraj had just changed our meeting place from Paris to Rome, I didn't expect the I Group to have worked out specific plans for the new city. Undoubtedly Iraj would demand more changes, but surely, I said, some of the passports and backup tickets and things should be in process, as we'd have to have them no matter which city we did the recovery in. None of that, I was told, would be put in place until the very last minute, when everything was settled. But why? Identity papers could have been prepared already; we could have been looking at those backup—I hate to use the word *false*, though that's accurate—documents at this meeting!

I bit my lip. Was I too demanding? I have a problem with procrastinators in the best of circumstances. This was certainly not the best of circumstances, and I wondered if this wait-until-the-last-minute business touched off some deep-seated problem in me that clouded my judgment. I also have a problem with people who don't attend to details. But I concluded that this wasn't the difficulty. My confidence in the seriousness and thoroughness of the I Group was terribly eroded by this time, even though I really liked them. I decided to give them the benefit of the doubt as the meeting continued to unfold.

It did not unfold well. We heard virtually no specifics. And I felt, rightly or wrongly, that Sue, Mike, and I had done all the concrete, detailed work to date. They hadn't even done much thinking. This so-called plan was basically the scenario I had accepted when we were going to Istanbul and there was the off chance that Iraj might bring the children. But now we were about to take quite a few liberties with the laws of foreign countries, whose officials might not look too kindly on our activities. I wanted the I Group to be planning an operation that was as smooth and fail-safe as it was humanly possible to devise. I did not want to run any unnecessary risks whatsoever, especially not ones that might have us stuck in a Middle Eastern police station or courthouse.

As I sat there with my anxiety level rising until I was in a state of quiet hysteria, I surreptitiously looked at Rob. My God, he was shelling out a small fortune to these guys, and they were doing very little of the kind of hard work that would justify their fees. To be fair, however, I could see that we had a basic and very big conflict. We were novices, or as they called us, "amateurs," who wanted everything spelled out in advance. They had a vast amount of experience and self-confidence because they'd pulled off so many dangerous, tricky operations. But there was the rub. They had lots of experience—but *not* in recovering children abducted by an unstable, potentially violent parent. And I thought they were underestimating the dangers involved in the operation. My nightmare was that I'd find myself in a Turkish court with Iraj flourishing Persian papers that gave him a Muslim father's right to the children. *I'd* be viewed as the person attempting to break the law, and à la *Midnight Express*, my future would be down the drain. The real losers in that situation would be the kids. Italy or Greece or France; any other country wasn't so much better in my imagination. I doubted myself, but I needed to have my fears addressed. If I was to believe I was wrong about scenarios I imagined, I wanted darned good reasons why I was wrong.

Even though my family and I were only ninety-day wonders in terms of our expertise, we were probably up to speed with the I Group. That is, we knew more about abduction—and Iraj—and they knew more about covert and hazardous operations. So how did all this balance out? We were both right. What would tip the balance? There was my comfort factor, since so much depended on me and my performance. It was important that I feel as much at ease as possible in such a nervous-making set of circumstances. I had to know that I had full support and backup. I was sure to make some kind of big mistake if I believed I had to keep my eye on my helpers rather than dealing with the main issues. And when it came to actually taking my children out of Iraj's hands, I had to have full confidence in those who were doing the taking.

There was one other problem I was reluctant to face. The I Group seemed to believe that Iraj now trusted me about my honestly wanting a reconciliation. I wasn't so sure. In fact I suspected he might be engineering a really devious set of moves, and that we were somehow falling into a trap he was setting. I had the uneasy feeling that Aaron, Isaac, and Joshua were underestimating how cunning Iraj was, whereas they hadn't in the past. One of the most persistent ideas I'd had was that just as the first Istanbul trip was a trial run for us, so too it might have been for Iraj and the men who worked with him. They might have been putting together a very efficient and workable plan to get money and passports from me this time—and for Iraj to get his longed for revenge. I'd felt confident before, when the I Group was more apprehensive than I was. But I didn't feel confident at this juncture.

Our departure from the I Group's office was strained, awkward. We left them with clear direction: time was running out; a solid and polished plan had to be put in place.

The conversation in the car centered on the disappointment everyone was feeling about the I Group's casual planning. I tuned out. I felt as if a boulder had collapsed on me and I was being crushed under its weight. What would I do now, at this eleventh hour? I couldn't go it alone. Although Isaac and Aaron had said in the post mortem on my first meeting with Iraj that I had practically pulled it off by myself, I did not feel that was really the case. I had Sue and six men from the I Group. Whether or not Aaron and Isaac and their four locals had done anything, I'd felt their backing and protection. It had enabled me. I could not go it alone.

We had paid for expertise. Were we getting it? Was it just that our inexperience was misdirecting us into believing that we weren't? Rob wad obviously asking himself the same questions.

"What about that Buckman guy, Jess?" he asked. "You had a lot of confidence in him after you spoke with him. Why don't I call him, run the situation by him, see what he has to say?"

All of us thought this was a terrific idea.

And after he spoke to Patrick, Rob thought it had

been even better than a terrific idea! He'd presented a couple of problems that hadn't been satisfactorily addressed at the I Group meeting and asked Patrick what he would do in such a situation. The answers he got were very reassuring, constructive, on target.

We signed up Patrick as a consultant, asked him to meet with us, and arranged for him to fly in.

Maybe, I thought as I went to sleep that night, July 25 wouldn't turn out to be such a bad day after all.

Sue spoke with Patrick on the 26th. He was already on the job and had some requests. First, he wanted me to get the passports back from the I Group. Next, he wanted me to delay the trip and suggested I use my father's illness as the excuse. Patrick felt we needed some additional time to get our plans on track. He also felt I needed to get everything in order for our safety upon returning to the States.

"Don't forget for a second that Iraj could have his relatives on alert to steal the kids back," he said. "Or he could hire someone to snatch them, just the way you've hired people to reabduct them. You've got to have a secure place to stay until you can figure out a life-style that prevents Iraj from threatening you and Sara and Cy." I was delighted when Sue gave me these messages; Patrick was a take-charge kind of guy, and did I ever appreciate that. Of course I had been working on our life after the recovery, which Sue mentioned to him.

I doubly appreciated Patrick when I telephoned the I Group and asked for the passports back. In fact they'd made another trip to Washington and hadn't been able to get the extensions, but now their story had changed. They said they no longer believed the children's expired passports were a problem. My fears about their planning and performance were being confirmed very quickly.

The man who couldn't telephone me from Tabriz in April, May, and June was calling every other day at least. Iraj was suddenly full of directions. There were people I had to telephone on his behalf, things I was to collect and bring to him in Europe, including his American passport, which I hadn't been able to get before from Jamshid. (It amused me that Iraj had been nervous about entering his own country with his American papers on him.) There were reservations to be made and canceled for people he would add to his "guest list" on one day and take off three days later. Iraj was playing a very wicked game with me on the matter of my speaking with the children. During every call I asked to talk to them, and he always had a reason why that was impossible. They were out playing, over at a relative's house, asleep. At last, I realized, this was part of his psychological warfare against me. He was playing some sort of intricate game in which he was withholding even telephone contact with the children to make it plain to me that he now called every single shot. Complete dominance, absolute power over me was what he was after. I grew more and more suspicious about what he planned for me when we met in Istanbul.

Calls started to pour in from his relatives. Everyone of them had "a little favor to ask." Mostly they wanted me to do courier services for them; there was a little package to take over from Bobek, a little bundle of letters from Jamshid and Lelah. I was becoming a donkey for this selfish, thoughtless family—but pretending to be graciousness itself. It was reassuring, though. Iraj had been on the horn; he really did intend to meet me in Istanbul.

Meantime, we were working like crazy to get a new, safe situation set up for when we returned with the kids.

It was July 29, time for our crucial meeting with the I Group, at which they had promised to deliver the "final, complete plan."

This started off very badly.

"Say," Aaron offered, "we've been thinking that you should consider another option altogether. Actually, we think it's the best option."

"Yes," Isaac said, "we believe this is a brilliant idea, and it's based on how well you have been maneuvering your ex-husband."

It appeared to them that I could persuade Iraj to fly straight through to the United States. Then I could treat the relationship as if it were a legitimate reconciliation. Perhaps we could tour Europe first, cementing the charade by having that wonderful family vacation together. It shouldn't be too difficult with him in a happy mood, sexually satisfied, for me to get him to agree to return to the United States. We would live together for a few months until he was thoroughly lulled. One night, I could just disappear with the kids, and that would be that.

I almost fell off my chair.

Sue, Beth, Rob, and Mike were incredulous, speechless, mouths agape.

There wasn't anything to say. If knowing what a nightmare we'd been through for these last months and I'd lived through with that monstrous man for nearly a decade, they could make this suggestion, then they were not living on the same planet as we were. Live with him a few months? Absurd. We were divorced. Everything was in place to have Iraj arrested as the detestable law-breaker he was. Just disappear with the kids one night? Way beyond ludicrous. I don't believe they'd given a single thought to the psychological implications of this scheme. My children had been through more than enough; I wanted to rescue them and put an end to the turmoil and suffering in their young lives—not do something to prolong it. This crazy suggestion was almost as bad as saying I should simply let the whole matter rest until some day Iraj might be ready to bring or send the kids back.

"That's just—just totally unacceptable," I stammered. My words were almost drowned by a chorus of outraged comments from Mike, Rob, Sue, and Beth. The I Group seemed surprised, but they quickly recovered and moved on to the presentation of their plan.

It was little more than what we had heard before.

I recalled something that Patrick Buckman had said during our first phone conversation, in April. I had to satisfy myself by giving them a final test, based on that tidbit I remembered from the talk with Patrick. He'd said that one of the most crucial things in planning a recovery was determining how one was going to get out of the country with the child or children, and he'd mentioned that it always was the part of a plan on which he worked the hardest. He'd said something on the order of, "The means of exit must be unknown by the kidnapper and unknowable to the local authorities. Never ever," he'd said, and I remember this verbatim, "take a commercial airline out of the country where you are recovering a child."

So I asked the I Group what they thought our best bet was for getting out of Rome if we recovered the kids there.

"Airplane," said Isaac.

"I thought you'd already booked your return flight," said Aaron.

They'd failed the test. I felt betrayed. Despite our misgivings, we really had believed these warm, friendly, apparently well-qualified men were going to come through with a plan that was excellent, if not a stroke of genius. I couldn't bear to prolong the agony in their office and was fairly brusque and efficient about getting us out of there.

Disappointment kept us utterly silent for a long time on the ride home, then everyone started to speak at once. The consensus was that the I Group might be well-intentioned and good at other kinds of security work, but they sure didn't know what they were doing in this matter. And further, all of us felt ripped off. By now Rob had paid the I Group more than ninety percent of what the families in America earn in two years! We had an urgent need to speak to Patrick Buckman.

> All sunshine
> makes a desert.
> —Arab Proverb

I was in no danger of having my life turn into a desert; it was more like a rain forest on its way to becoming a swamp, with all the rain that was falling on my parade. In public I looked decisive, sometimes tough, always energetic, or so I'm told. In private with Mike I was my true self—often confused, scared, and full of self-doubt. At these times Mike was my sounding board and my backbone. I was in real trouble on the evening of July 29, and I'd never needed Mike more. We had twelve days until I was supposed to meet Iraj and the children in Istanbul. I'd been able to get him to go back to August 10, the date we'd originally agreed upon, instead of the new one he'd set, the eighth, but he just wouldn't budge when I suggested we make it later. I was frantic, petrified. I couldn't get it out of my head that we had one chance and one chance only to recover Sara and Cy. If we blew it, only God knew what might be the children's fate.

And I was terribly upset by the prospect of having to live underground for an indefinite period of time—if not forever. Everything I read and everyone I talked to brought home the dreadful necessity of disconnecting totally from one's real life. All my friends and family, my work and education would be gone! I'd have to be looking over my shoulder constantly, teaching the children to keep quiet, never speaking with anyone in the new setting about anything in my past. It was so brutally unfair. Fairness demanded that Iraj and his family be punished, so that Sara and Cy and I could go on with our lives amidst those we loved and who loved us, in familiar places and among familiar things.

"Jess, my love, forget that," Mike said. "Just ask yourself how much justice there can be in a world where Harry Chapin is dead because of a senseless car crash and John Wayne Gacy lives on?"

With insights like that and with infinite patience,

Mike saw me through this terrible night, as he saw me through so many other terrible nights and days.

We wanted to have a face-to-face meeting with Patrick Buckman, and Rob was able to schedule it for the thirty-first. Technically he was still our consultant on developing the plan with the I Group. But I believe that he knew he was coming in for a sort of a job interview, because we'd been candid in relating all that had transpired at our big meeting, and we'd made no secret of our disillusionment.

Still I had to come to grips with my feelings about the I Group. I was torn in many ways. I really liked these people and felt they were humane and intelligent. Was I underestimating them and their plans for the recovery? Should I try to get Patrick to take over the recovery, or should we go with the I Group? Patrick had credentials I could trust. He had recovered so many children, and just in the last few weeks I'd been in contact with parents he'd recently helped. He was completely honest on two points: first, he could give no guarantee of success; second, he would do everything in his power to avoid violence but urged us to keep foremost in our minds that the reabduction is often as traumatic for children, if not more so, than the initial kidnapping.

But the I Group had a lot going for it too. These men had tracked and located missing children; the organization had incredible references from important people; and they had agreed to go into Iran if I couldn't convince Iraj to come out, when no other person or group had committed firmly to that course. Who should I place my trust in? The fees for each were enormous, so using the I Group *and* Patrick was out of the question. Besides, they might trip all over each other.

The evening hours were filled with discussion of the pros and cons of each. My head was spinning. But always, always, those to whom I turned said the decision had to be mine. The children were my children. The outcome of the operation was one I would have to live with. No one could or would make the decision for me.

I felt like a dishcloth that had been wrung out by Arnold Schwarzenegger.

Patrick Buckman flew in from San Francisco for the meeting with me and my family. He earned our respect. He listened intently and asked intelligent questions based, I could tell, on his vast experience recovering abducted children. Patrick had handled more than 125 cases in the past fifteen years and had been successful in about a hundred of those, and he was scrupulous in his attention to detail. Dealing with the points I'd labored unsuccessfully to get the I Group to attend to was just second nature to Patrick. He had more details in mind than I did.

Patrick's personal and professional force were in perfect harmony with his appearance. Six feet three inches tall with a powerful build, he is an intense brunette, graying at the temples. His brown eyes are always expressive, and he is given to frequent piercing looks. He never once criticized the I Group, never denounced their plans. He merely asked the penetrating question, made the pointed suggestion.

He emphasized again that no individual or group could give any guarantees of success in an operation of the kind we were planning. These operations were growing more risky with each passing day, as drug smuggling became a bigger international business and terrorists roamed the world in ever growing numbers. Borders were getting much tighter, so crossing them had to be very well thought through.

If he were running the operation, he told us, he would set up two plans: one for Istanbul and an equally detailed one for the second city on the itinerary, whether Rome or elsewhere. He would invent reasons and help me to hang tough to prevent the trip from being scheduled in Paris, as France, he felt, was too oriented to the Iranian government and might honor any Iranian documents giving Iraj custody of Sara and Cy. This statement echoed my thoughts on the matter. He felt strongly that the reservations for the Hilton in Istanbul should be canceled immediately in favor of a smaller hotel that had a better layout for surveillance and communication. He suggested the Hotel Dedeman.

Oh, Tom, I thought, I hope you're able to go on being a saint of a travel agent. I could tell he was going to have to make a lot of changes—the hotel reservations were just the beginning!

Patrick said he would have to secure passports and visas in phony names for the children and me. He would rent two safe houses in Turkey, the first in Istanbul and another probably in Ankara, the Turkish capital, along with at least two other safe houses elsewhere in Europe where we could hide out for several days in case anything went wrong. He felt we needed to have rental cars reserved in Turkey and Italy and to plot main and alternate escape routes from both Istanbul and Rome.

"The odds are initially stacked against you in an operation of this kind," he said, "and you have to back up every plan just to try to get those odds bumped a little in the direction of even."

As Patrick ticked off item after item he believed was important to the plan, I felt a tight coil that had been deep inside with me for weeks slowly begin to unwind.

I fired the I Group. I hired Patrick.

·FOURTEEN·

I WAS BITTER AND I AM BITTER TO THIS DAY THAT LOOP-
holes in the law, along with official policies and attitudes
toward parental abduction, force decent, law-abiding
citizens like me to walk on the same path with drug
dealers and thieves. I had resisted even thinking about
reabducting Sara and Cy until I was sure that I had
exhausted all my options, and I resented feeling as
though I'd been pushed into a corner where illegal action
offered me the only possible way out. I resented Iraj first
and foremost, and his family of coconspirators, but I also
deeply resented federal law enforcement officials, and I
more than resented the Department of State.

One of the things about Patrick I most appreciated
was that he made no bones about the fact that in a
recovery one breaks many laws. While our intent was
radically different from a criminal's, our actions in many

situations might be the same. At some very basic level, the I Group either failed or refused to recognize that simple fact, and the consequence was that their planning was looser, less precise than I thought it needed to be. Not so with Patrick. He was as heedful as I of every aspect of the plan and as vigilant about things that might possibly go wrong.

Now the tables were turned. I wasn't bugging any one about details, I was being quizzed about them. Patrick had a yellow legal pad, and he would say, "Let's add that topic to our 'to do' list," or "Let's put that on the 'to check out' list." And he was reminding me that I should never trust Iraj for a second or give him an inch.

"Never have any faith in the word of a kidnapper," he would say. "Just remember that the man's a criminal who will use any means, including his own children, to get revenge and money." Or he would comment, "Don't forget, Jess, this guy is out for himself and his Iranian family. He doesn't give a damn about you or anybody else, probably not even Sara and Cy. He's an egomaniac, plain and simple, and a greedy son of a bitch as well." Thank God I had made the right decision—and I was very sure I had—in choosing to go with Patrick. He was tough, fast, experienced, and he understood the mentality of the kidnapper in general and of Iraj in particular. I gave him copies of photographs of Iraj, his brothers, and other relatives. A set of these had to go to everyone who would be working with us in Europe.

Just after this meeting I received another phone call from Iraj. He requested that I add a nephew to the reservation, taking care of both his flight list from Erzurum to Istanbul and his hotel reservation. Again, just another family member who was dying "to visit with you." Right.

So he wanted two people inside the Hotel Dedeman with us, his brother and his nephew, did he? And the expense? Didn't matter to him. As far as he was concerned, my family could take care of endless bills through the "borrowed funds." In other words, what I interpreted him saying was that I should have at his disposal the money from the sale of the house and the money he'd been told I had borrowed.

Then Iraj smacked me with his latest idea. He wasn't sure about Rome as the best vacation spot for us. Hmm, Holland, he mused. What about Amsterdam? Such a terrific city, one of the two capitals of the Netherlands.

"Iraj," I bellowed, "I've made a million reservations—flights, the hotels! Our trip is less than two weeks away, and it's the height of the tourist season. I don't even know if I could get a whole new set of reservations for Amsterdam at this late date."

I held my breath for fear that he would use the time factor against me and simply say that we should meet at the end of the month, or whenever it was that I could arrange the vacation that he wanted. Fortunately, he didn't pursue that line, yet still he didn't quite agree to go on with the plans for Rome.

"Well, I can manage such things easily from Istanbul, you know," he said haughtily, "I mean, in case I definitely decide we should go to Amsterdam instead of Rome."

"Of course," I murmured in a humble tone, "I'm sure you can handle all of that."

And I sighed with relief when I hung up.

Patrick insisted that I make very firm arrangements about the hotel rooms at the Dedeman in Istanbul. The brother and nephew had to be given rooms on a different floor from the kids, me, and Iraj. Patrick shook his head. "Sloppy of him to leave that up to you, Jess," he said. "He should make sure his bodyguards and strong-arm men have rooms right next door." And Patrick grinned.

The man Patrick designated to run my recovery operation was named Michael, and he was scheduled to fly in on August 6 to get to know me and go over the plans. Until then he would be working with Patrick by telephone, but the basic blueprint was in place.

We needed a communications link. Patrick proposed that we pull in a female associate of his, Linda, to serve that vital purpose. She would be on my flight to Istanbul. I would pretend that I'd gotten very sick on the flight, throwing up and feeling weak, feverish. Linda, posing as a nurse who was going to visit a relative in Turkey, would help me out and generously escort me to the Hotel Dedeman. Patrick gave me the responsibility of coming up with plausible reasons to continue a friendship with Linda, whom I'd "bump into," or better yet, plan to meet for a thank-you lunch or drink in Istanbul, which would give me an excuse to call her hotel, leave a message or two, and chat with her on the phone at least once to set up the date. A nifty little by-product of this scheme of Patrick's was that I might be able to avoid having sex with Iraj. A terrible hypochondriac, he would definitely want to stay away from me if he thought there was the slightest possibility I had the flu or anything else contagious.

Michael and Patrick would take care of getting passports under false names for the children and me. Patrick had been as concerned as I since he'd first heard about the passport problem. And as a man who conducted many escapes with recovered children, he knew there wasn't time to get passports extended at a consulate.

I supplied photographs of the children that would just barely do for the phony papers but had to get a new one for myself. These passports were only to cover us in an emergency. Patrick hoped that we wouldn't have to use them. His primary plan focused on taking the children from Iraj in Turkey and getting out of the country by private boat to Greece. We wouldn't need passports for that boat trip, and we would be much safer getting the extensions at a consulate in Greece than in a city where Iraj still could do his worst. His backup plan, which he and Michael were working on, would be to take the children in Rome—or any other city that His Lordship decided to travel to—in case something unforeseeable prevented us from acting in Istanbul.

This was more like it, I thought. A plan that made real sense, with everything falling into place. I'd be able to get some sleep in the coming nights and gather my strength for the taxing work I had to do in Istanbul. I was overly optimistic. Oh, not because of anything that was going wrong with the plan, but because of the pure bad luck of world events.

On August 2, Iraq invaded Kuwait. First an earthquake, now a regional war. I couldn't believe it. President Bush announced that the United States would stand firm in support of its friend and ally, Kuwait. Many commentators were writing about the region going on alert. Tension was building in Turkey because of the oil pipeline there. Security throughout the Middle East was being drastically increased.

Adrenaline surges were making me shake from head to toe. I was full of doubt that any plan could be successful under these circumstances, but Patrick's voice on the phone calmed me down.

"Jess," he said, "this is just a quick call to let you know that I'm nixing the boat from Turkey to Greece. Because of this Iraqi action, they'll probably throw a lot of navy security into all the waterways in that region, so I'm going to use a motor home instead. Much more effective and less risky under these conditions, but we'll have to use the phony passports. Can you handle that?"

I assured him I could.

He went over a checklist with me. I should pack very carefully. It was important that everything look natural and innocent, so my bags should include all the clothing that the kids and I would need for the vacation. There should be a bag of gifts for the kids, as well as toys, games, drawing materials, and anything else that normally I would take on a trip to keep them occupied and happy. Everything should be on for August 10. I had to force Iraj to keep to this date because tensions in the area made it imperative that we act as quickly as possible. Obviously Patrick was anticipating that the Iraq-Kuwait conflict was going to escalate, perhaps drawing more countries into the fight. We had to get in, get the kids, and get out before a war raised an insuperable barrier between me and Sara and Cy.

Iraj called to tell me to take his nephew off the flight from Erzurum. The nephew and the "other boys" who were coming with him had no papers and would have to drive across the border at an unchecked spot. Iraj and his brother and the children were sticking to the original plan to fly in on the ninth; I would be landing on the tenth. I was careful not to mention the Iraqi invasion of Kuwait. Iraj was notoriously uninformed about news and public affairs, living in his own little world of concerns, and I doubted the people around him were reacting in any significant way to the news of the day. I didn't want to give Iraj the slightest reason to start changing plans on me.

Then, agreeably, he mentioned that the continuation of our trip to Rome was all right with him. He'd decided that Rome, or even Paris, would be perfectly fine for our vacation, and he would decide there if we might go on to Amsterdam. Being this flexible about our destination was so unlike him that the hairs rose on my nape. Perhaps he didn't care because he had no intention of taking a step outside Istanbul with me and the kids. His stories and plans were getting more fishy every day. And Patrick agreed. No doubt Iraj was up to something, he said, probably planning to take the passports and money away from me by force if he had to and dump me somewhere in the wilds of Turkey.

Patrick chewed this over, concluding that he'd changed his mind entirely—or that circumstances had changed it for him—on the matter of Iraj. He no longer felt that my ex-husband was interested in getting me back as his wife to prove himself to me or to punish me. He had a gut feeling that Iraj was out for the money and the passports, which would enable him to set up anywhere in the world, with servants to take care of the children. Patrick felt he definitely would keep the children in his custody, not abandon them after taking money from me, because he wanted them as insurance. If he ever needed money in the future, he would try to extort it from me again by using the children.

"It's Istanbul, Jess," Patrick said. "That's it. We *have* to recover the children there, as early into the trip as possible. This guy is going to try to pull something in Turkey. I'll bet he doesn't have the slightest intention of going on to Rome or Amsterdam or anywhere else. Of course, we have to carry through on the preparation of the backup for Rome just in case I'm wrong."

Patrick had mentioned before that I had to be very tough when I first encountered Iraj again, refusing to turn over any money, paperwork, passports, or anything else to him until I saw the kids. He repeated that now. "Don't give this guy an inch. And start playing hardball with him, Jess. It's time he began to say yes to you for a change."

Easier said than done, Mr. Buckman.

I was internalizing my cover stories. I had to make them mine so deeply that I could play my role perfectly. Despondent over my father's condition, depressed because I was missing my children, I was to be in fragile health and stricken on the plane with a mystery illness with flulike symptoms. I went over and over the details, visualizing all this happening to me, and Linda befriending me so that I could be convincing. I reviewed the story about my dad being so ill and pleading to see the children, paying real attention to the details that Sue and I had invented about the exact nature of the cancer, how it was spreading, and his treatment. I was a little apprehensive about all this but psyched myself up to be the best actress I possibly could.

I was also making the arrangements for life after our return. I had the real estate agent working double time on showing the house—no small thing when we were going through such an agony of fast-paced work on the recovery and postrecovery. Sue, Beth, and Mike were wonders at packing up the contents of the house, only rarely having to consult me about what to keep out and what to box for storage. A number of friends offered apartments and houses where the children and I could stay. My darling father came up with the best place: a beachfront condo in Florida that belonged to one of his old business associates, who only used it for an occasional vacation and offered to "loan" it to us for as long as we needed it. There were family friends living nearby, too, which was reassuring. I had loaded up on books and articles about managing traumatic situations with children, and I fell asleep often over these works. I'm a fast study and was learning a lot, but when push came to shove, I trusted my own maternal instincts to guide me through to a healthy resolution for Sara and Cy.

Michael arrived for our meeting and stayed on so we could get acquainted. We needed to be as comfortable with each other as was possible to get in a short time, since we would be working under so much stress. It was easy to be comfortable with him as he's a very friendly, easygoing man who uses the latest cool expressions. His mother is Italian-American, his father a French-American, and Michael is a very handsome man, about six feet tall, a Mel Gibson look-alike, only with very dark hair and eyes.

How could I go wrong with two Michaels taking such good care of me? I teased my Mike, saying I thought of him now as the blond, bronzed, and beautiful one, while the new Michael was the tall, dark, and handsome one. There was also a local detective in the picture named Michael. So my Mike and I got a lot of chuckles out of the confusion over the name. And I kept saying, "It's an omen, I tell you. It's an omen!"

Tall, dark, and handsome and I set to work.

One of the things that Michael worked over with me were rendezvous spots around Istanbul. Using a large map of the city, we traced routes from the Hotel Dedeman and various landmarks that we undoubtedly would include on sightseeing tours to places where, if I could get the children away from Iraj, I could meet up— safely—with him or Linda or other members of the team they were putting together. We brainstormed about methods I could use to get Sara and Cy alone, for example, taking them for ice cream, to buy souvenirs, to see a place that wouldn't appeal to Iraj. A goal was to succeed in this nonviolent way. Unfortunately, Michael did not yet have the telephone numbers that I would have to memorize to reach him and other contacts so they could pick us up if I could get away. I'd have to learn these numbers and some addresses when they were given to me later. They had to be committed to memory; it would be too dangerous to keep them with me in writing.

On August 5 I called Iraj to tell him that all reservations were confirmed. He seemed to be taking notes, as he should, of all the airline ticket numbers for his "guests," and punctuated my list with uh-huhs. When we'd gone through the flight information, I started to mention the hotel. Iraj interrupted.

"I have decided we will stay at the Tashan," he said curtly. "It is a small hotel, less expensive. By far the best place for us."

"But—but you're leaving Iran day after tomorrow," I sputtered. "You'll be incommunicado. I can't even get back to you to confirm reservations at this other hotel!"

"I'm sure we can stay there. Don't worry about it. Now, about the money you should bring—"

"Iraj!" I was screaming now. "You just can't keep jiggling everything at the last minute like this."

"Why can't I?" he asked menacingly. "If I want things arranged a little differently to make us all happier, it should be."

There was a take-it-or-leave-it tone to his voice. I felt I had no choice but to take it.

"Very well," I said, "have it your way, but don't blame me if any of these arrangements get screwed up."

"Nothing will be screwed up because I will handle everything after I get to Istanbul."

I guess I was supposed to genuflect.

We got off the phone with the atmosphere far from sweetness and light between us, but with no ultimate harm done because he was going ahead with the trip.

Before I informed Michael and Patrick of this latest monkey wrench Iraj had tossed into the works, I thought I should talk to Jamshid under the pretext of a courtesy call just to see if I could get a little more information. Unfortunately Jamshid was out, and I got the obnoxious younger brother, Nasser. I explained that I'd just wanted the family to know the plans had been changed and we would be staying at the Tashan Hotel.

"Oh, I know this place very well," Nasser said excitedly. "It is a beautiful place where I stayed once with Iraj." Why did I get the impression that he already knew about the switch from the Dedemon?

"What's the Tashan like?" I asked, trying to sound casual.

"Very nice. The hotel's a small white building about a block from the Bosphorus, and it has pretty lace curtains at the windows."

I asked a few more questions and got the impression

that the Tashan was quaint and intimate with no more than eight to ten rooms—most of which, I feared, would be full of Iraj's relatives.

This brat had the nerve to lecture me about the money I was to take to Iraj "without fail." I didn't even try to hide my annoyance and got off the phone with Nasser fast.

But some of my anger at him and Jamshid and Bobek was assuaged in a conversation with Sue. She had been talking with our local detective, who had discovered the statute under the Uniform Child Custody Jurisdiction Act which would allow us to prosecute the brothers and cousin for "aiding and abetting in a parental kidnapping." They could be sued for recovery of expenses too. I *eagerly* looked forward to working with my lawyer to prepare to prosecute the Salimis!

> Forward, I pray,
> since we have come so far. . . .
> —William Shakespeare, *The Taming of the Shrew*

We had quite a lot of rain, but it didn't dampen my optimism. Patrick flew in on the sixth for our big meeting, immediately after which Michael was taking off for Istanbul. We reviewed the problems that arose from the change of hotel, which worried all of us. My goal was to get us out of there as quickly as possible, persuading Iraj that it would be much more fun to be at a more upscale hotel with full amenities, particularly a swimming pool which the children would enjoy. I was especially eager to get to a place with a pool, because while the children and I are good swimmers, Iraj did not know how to swim, and we might be able to leave him behind in the room while we went down to the pool. I didn't mind one bit making an escape with Sara and Cy and me in just our bathing suits!

Patrick felt the chances were slim that Iraj would agree to change the hotel yet again, but he encouraged me to give it my all. The first priority was to try to get Iraj to trust me, so that there might be some hope for me to get time alone with the children. He would be watching me very closely, we knew, but if I could dull his suspicions and pretend to be taking the children out for a treat, I was to watch for a car trailing us along the curb, walk as swiftly with the children as I could, and wait for the driver to shout at me to get in. If the three of us broke away from Iraj while touring a site and there was no car following us, I was to hustle the children into a taxi and make for the luxury hotel where one of Patrick's investigators would be staying. That hotel was our designated rendezvous point, to which I should flee at any hour of the day or night that I could get there with the kids. There also were the telephone numbers I'd be given to memorize, which I could use at any time to call for help. Our communications problems weren't solved by any means, however, since Iraj had put the whammy of the Hotel Tashan on us.

Another snag was that Linda, Patrick's colleague and my "nurse," couldn't stay in the same hotel now. (We'd decided it was plausible—just barely—that she also would have booked the Hotel Dedeman.) Still, I could go forward with the alternate plan of telephoning her, arranging to see her for the thank-you drink or meal. She also would be following us in Istanbul and could arrange to bump into me if a situation looked promising to her and Michael or their associates. Linda was coming in to meet me the next day so that we could rehearse our act.

Michael and Patrick gave me a couple of demonstrations of how they would separate Iraj from the children—if Iraj was ever alone with us. The problem was that nephew and his brother—and we had no way of knowing how many other men Iraj would have around him in Istanbul. I could only pray that they would party themselves into the ground, as Iraj had when I'd met him, and they'd all be so drunk that I could run away with Sara and Cy. There was the slim possibility that I might be able to sneak the children out late at night if all the men seemed to be sleeping very soundly. If that happened, Michael told me I could count on a man and a car being outside the Tashan for me and the kids.

We dismissed the idea of nabbing Iraj inside the consulate if he went with me to get the children's passports extended. Patrick wisely pointed out this was a very bad idea, since we really did not want Iraj returned to the United States. We'd much prefer him to be stranded in Turkey or back in Iran without his American passport, as he would then pose far less danger to me and the children. Michael reassured me that if Iraj grew violent when he found out about the passport problem, I was not to worry. He and Patrick had decided that if I should be out of sight for more than eight hours, they would have all their people storm the hotel, if necessary. They would get me out—and they'd raise holy hell while doing so, in the hopes of getting Sara and Cy out at the same time. This was a very last resort, however, as none of us wanted violence, or even much attention called to us. These were two tough customers, and I was glad to be in their competent hands.

Michael ran down a checklist of all the legal documents we would be filing within three days. All was set for the warrant for Iraj's arrest, which would be issued on August 9 as I left for Istanbul. Everyone in the police station was fully informed about how dangerous our situation was and had assured us there would be no leaks from that quarter. The paperwork for unlawful-flight-to-avoid-prosecution would be filed through the D.A.'s office by my lawyer, who would then request that Iraj's passport be revoked through the Immigration Service.

The revocation of passport brought with it a special alert to foreign immigration officials and embassies. Included were Iraj's physical description, photographs, and all the names he had used in the past. My lawyer would place liens against Iraj's property in Chicago and institute proceedings against Jamshid, Nasser, and Bobek for conspiracy to kidnap. All of this was geared to protecting the children from being reabducted by the Salimis, not to punish Iraj and his relatives, and not to get money from the property. I was thinking now of punishment and money only as welcome by-products, if we got them! Everything seemed to be in order, all the paperwork and the assignments about who was to do what at given times.

I hugged Michael good-bye at the end of the meeting, and Patrick and I agreed to meet at his hotel on the afternoon of the eighth. Michael would call me from Istanbul. I called Iraj to wish him a safe trip, which I meant with my whole heart, and he reminded me to look for him in the arrivals area of the Istanbul airport, where he said he'd be waiting for me with the children. Until then he'd be incommunicado. He had to leave with Sara, Cy, and his brother early on the morning of the seventh for the long drive to Erzurum. The border check might take up to eighteen hours, so they were scheduling enough time to get to Turkey by late on the ninth. Shudders of fear chased along my spine when I thought of Sara and Cy taking this journey. I was afraid that Iraj might be arrested and the kids returned to Homa and Nadir, and even if there weren't any trouble with the authorities, still I feared the hardship of the trip for my little ones, who were still suffering with stomach pains. The drive to the Turkish border was about one hundred twenty miles. From there to Erzurum was another two hundred or more miles. It would be long, hard, hot, and dusty driving, over very bad roads. I could only pray that Sara and Cy would be safe and well and not suffer too much.

While taking a deposition on the eighth, Rob met a man who, by a great stroke of luck, had a very close association with a highly placed lawyer in Istanbul, whom he agreed to call. Then Rob spoke to the lawyer, who, was more than willing to help us; Rob was able to reach Michael just after he landed in Istanbul to give him the name and number of this new resource. I was overwhelmed with this good fortune and claimed that it was another omen of our success.

Linda arrived on the morning of the eighth, and we hit it off right away. A tall blonde in her early forties, Linda is the kind of woman who inspires confidence right off the bat. She has a no-nonsense manner about her, yet a sympathetic air too. The perfect stereotype of a head nurse, I thought. This was going to work!

Linda and I talked, then rehearsed our scenes. Soon it was time to see Patrick and go over everything again. He wanted me to be strong and quick and sure of myself, so he gave me lots of encouragement. But he also wanted me to be on guard, because he was very, very sure now that Iraj never intended to explore a reconciliation or take a family vacation. Too much evidence had piled up, Patrick said, demonstrating Iraj's real intent. He might want to use me as a nanny, a translator, a secretary, and for sex and money, but Patrick firmly believed that my ex-husband now meant to exploit me to the fullest. He was bringing the children to Istanbul only for show; they were his bargaining chips for American passports and money. My blood curdled at those words. Bargaining chips. That's exactly how Iraj was using two precious human beings who were his very own children.

I was confident; I was scared. I truly believed that God was on my side and would see me through to successfully recovering the children. Then I would have visions of everything going wrong and my babies disappearing back over the border—away from me forever. I stanched such images and tried to have only positive thoughts. Nonetheless, dismal prospects would intrude. I might be whisked away by Iraj and never see my wonderful family and Mike again, so I wrote each of them a note to be opened after I left, telling them how much I loved them and appreciated how hard they'd worked with me on getting the kids back. I made Mike promise that if something happened to me he would go on with Sue and Beth and Rob to try to get the children home. And he swore that he would.

On the night of the seventh and the afternoon of the eighth Mike and I had scrubbed the empty house until it gleamed. We decided not to go to a relative's house or a hotel but to camp out alone on the bare floor. I might not ever see this house again. As the sun set, we went for a long walk through the woods and around the

neighborhood, saying good-bye to this place without
uttering a word. It was comforting to spend the night in
the house where our love had flourished and we had
known so much joy, then endured together so much
anguish.

Mike chose that place on that night to ask me to
marry him. And my answer was yes, yes, a thousand
times yes.

FIFTEEN

WE TOUCHED DOWN AT FRANKFURT, AND LINDA AND I shot off the plane, she to call Michael in Istanbul, I to take a fast walk along the halls that wound around the waiting area. We'd been bumped up to business class, a nice bonus, but even the larger seats hadn't helped me get comfortable. I was living on nerves, charged with energy that could go nowhere yet, and all the way across the Atlantic, I had felt the blood rushing beneath the skin of my forearms. How could I be still and calm when at any minute between the time we left the States and landed in Germany my children would be arriving in Istanbul?

Linda was smiling as she walked toward me, but I thought her eyes looked wary, and I tensed up. "What's going on in Turkey?" I asked.

"Lots of stuff," she said matter-of-factly. "Come on, let's get a coffee and talk."

From the coffee cart she led me to a lonely corner of the lounge to talk. "Look," she said, "don't worry, but Iraj didn't pick up the tickets in Erzurum. Not in Ankara either."

I'd had our patience-of-Job travel agent, Tom, flag the tickets for pickup in Ankara as well as Erzurum. I frowned. "Have they been spotted in Istanbul?"

"They haven't checked in to the Tashan, Jess." She glanced at her watch. "Let's see, with the time difference it's . . . well, he should have had the kids in the hotel and in bed last night and about to wake up this morning, but he hasn't even shown up and registered."

"Oh, God." I slumped in my chair, put my head back, and closed my eyes for a second.

Linda touched my shoulder. "Hey, let's not throw in the towel. You're worried that Iraj found out some way or other about the warrant, aren't you? Or about this whole operation or something? Don't, Jess."

I nodded weakly. "I know, I know. There's no way he could have found out, because the warrant won't be issued for several more hours and we covered all our tracks. But, Linda—"

"But nothing. We just have to figure at this point that they got held up at the border or some other place, but they're going to get to Istanbul, and we're going to go ahead as we've planned. It's important not to lose focus. We've got to stay optimistic about this. Right?"

I sat up. "Right." And I did try to feel optimistic, and strong, but all the way to Istanbul I worried incessantly that our operation had been blown, and I shook with fear that Iraj simply had backed out again. All the money . . .

all the time and preparation, and I might have to go through it *again* to try to get the kids back.

Now my cover story with Linda was coming true. I really was getting sick, feeling hot and nauseated. Fortunately, "my" nurse was up to her role, but she wouldn't let me give in to how sick I felt or how afraid I was. She had telephone numbers, names, and addresses Michael had given her over the phone that I had to memorize. I did so, with great difficulty, feeling my head would burst, then gave the papers back to Linda.

I had prayed throughout this ordeal. I'd prayed with Mike, and with my neighbor and dear friend across the street, Bessie, who'd come over almost every day to kneel with me and ask God to keep my children safe. And of course I'd prayed alone. But I'd never prayed as fervently as I did on that flight. I begged God to protect Sara and Cy and give me the chance to recover them. It was a glorious day, the sky a brilliant hard blue. The sun was dazzling, blinding. And I could feel its warmth through the plane's window, and its glory. It was a sign. I was sure of it. And my confidence returned in greater strength than ever before.

It was difficult for me to restrain myself and play my role. I wanted to bound across the runway and rush through customs. My babies could be within arm's reach, and my heart was thundering. Tricky as the situation was, I couldn't stop grinning, so I kept my head bowed as Linda, arm around my waist, pretended to practically carry me into the terminal. I got somber when we entered the building, though, for the importance of what I had to do in this situation hit me with great force.

We were approaching the baggage area inside customs, and off to our right was an alcove beyond which were rest rooms and water fountains. Linda nudged me, then steered me over to that area. Deep in a corner, just in front of a door to a service stairwell was Michael, who gave us a big wink.

"We're all set," he said, skipping any trivial small talk. "The kids and your husband and some guys arrived late last night. We're going to try to take the kids right here, Jess. Everything's in place, but just in case we miss, I've got a couple more numbers for you to memorize. And there are one or two things that have changed. Okay?"

"Okay," I said, thrilled and excited as he handed some notes to Linda. Sara and Cy were here! Close, so close. In just a few minutes I'd see them again, have them in my arms, and if we were very, very lucky, I might even have them safely away from Iraj.

With a quick whispered "Good luck," Michael turned and almost ran through the door to the stairs.

Linda and I went into the ladies' room where she went over the notes from Michael and handed them to me.

I was to drop the sick act, as it was no longer needed, and be ready to move on command. The only fly in the ointment was that they hadn't spotted Iraj here at the airport, but they were still hoping that he'd keep his word about meeting me. Other than that—which was no small thing, I thought anxiously—Michael said they were all set.

My mouth was bone dry, my hands shaking. I stopped for some long, deep swallows of water at the drinking fountain, then ventured into the arrivals area. Linda hung back, now prepared to act as though she scarcely knew me.

RESCUED

I got through passport control with amazing swiftness and was out in the lounge in minutes. My heart racing, I peered at the crowd on the other side of the huge plate glass divider. A thousand times I'd imagined the moment when I'd first catch sight of Sara and Cy's darling faces. But they weren't there. The faces of strangers seemed to mock me and my great high hopes. Looking around frantically, I spotted Michael. He was signaling to me, hand behind his back, indicating that I should go outside. He gave his signal several times—pointing toward the exit, then making a horizontal gesture. I felt the blood drain from my face. Michael had to be trying to let me know that the operation here at the airport was off. Apparently Iraj had decided not to meet me as scheduled. With a sinking feeling, I made my way through the crowd toward the main exit, looking everywhere and hoping against hope that the children were there and I'd see them any second.

I stepped out onto the sidewalk and saw a sea of orange taxis in front of me with only two or three broken-down, dark *dolmuses* swimming in their midst. The heat and noise were like a solid wall slamming into me, and for a few seconds I didn't think I could catch my breath. I hoisted the huge canvas bag I was carrying more securely over my shoulder, shifted my suitcase in my right hand, and started to walk, scanning the crowd ahead, twisting to glance behind me and to either side. No Sara. No Cy. No Iraj.

Taxi drivers were beckoning, people were banging into me. And suddenly I spotted Iraj. He was to my right, walking fast toward me. Alone. I raced over to him, dropped my suitcase, and gave him a hug.

"Where are the kids?" I asked breathlessly.

•

His response was little more than a snarl. "Later."

But through the din of shouting voices and honking car horns I heard a high, childish voice shrieking, "Mommy! Mommy!" Stumbling over the suitcase, I spun around and saw Sara running toward me through three lanes of heavy traffic. I jettisoned my canvas bag and raced to her, scooping her up at curbside. My beautiful girl. My beautiful, beautiful daughter! We were both crying and hugging each other so tightly that we choked the air out of our lungs. And then I heard that other wonderful voice, soft and poignant. "Mommy!" Cy was clutching my leg, looking up at me with tears running down his little face. I kneeled down, taking Sara with me, and scooped Cy into our embrace. Rocking back and forth, holding each other tight, the three of us sobbed with happiness and relief.

Abruptly, our wonderful reunion was halted. I felt a touch, then I heard Michael's voice shouting, "Get up. Get up and run. Run with the children!" I grabbed the kids' hands and started running for our lives. Almost dragging poor little Cy along the sidewalk, we tore past taxi after taxi. I saw orange blurs, nothing else; I felt the children's hands, nothing more. Sara and Cy were screaming; I was screaming. Then a hand smacked down on my shoulder.

"Oh, God, no," I howled.

I was spun around, the children twisting about my legs, and shoved hard in the opposite direction. But it wasn't Iraj or one of his henchmen. It was Michael.

"The cab! The cab! Jump into the cab!" he shouted over and over.

I desperately pulled the handle of the closest taxi, threw open the orange door, pushed the children into the back seat, and climbed in after them.

The kids were crying and so was I, and the driver, turning around in his seat, had a stunned look on his face.

"It's going to be all right," I crooned to the children, my arms wrapped around their small bodies. "It's going to be all right. We're going home. We're going home."

Movement, a blur of green startled me, and I stared through the window. The taxi was completely surrounded by policemen, with curious people staring over their shoulders and around their bodies at the three of us in the back seat. So this was what it was like to be a goldfish. Someone shoved my big canvas bag through the side window onto the seat next to me. More people came to see what all the excitement was about, and the green-uniformed policemen were pressed forward, closer and closer to the taxi. I felt trapped, panic rising. I squelched my own fears to worry about the children. I kissed and patted them, murmuring over and over that all was well, we were fine, safe, and we'd be driving off any second.

But where the hell was Michael—and what was I to do? All those policemen. Oh, dear Lord, we were in trouble, serious, serious trouble.

Suddenly, Michael yanked open the passenger door and leaped in.

"Police station," he said. "Police station."

The driver didn't move an inch. We sat dead still in that sea of people.

Then one of the policeman stuck his head through the window next to Michael and gave an order to the driver in Turkish. The taxi was off like a shot, people in front scattering like startled geese.

I cuddled Sara and Cy, saying reassuring things to them, and introduced them to "our friend Michael."

They looked at him wide-eyed as he smiled at them over his shoulder, then twisted around in the front seat to face us.

"Hi, guys," he said in such an all-American way that I grinned. "Don't worry about a thing. We're going to the police station to get everything straightened out so you can go home with your mom. You'll like that, won't you?"

Cy was nodding wildly and Sara was saying yes over and over again. I could see they were relieved, but very shaken.

Michael stared intently at me. "Jess, everything really is okay. No trouble. Went off like clockwork. You'll see." Then he gave me one of those winks of his and turned around again to stare through the windshield.

Now I could get a good look at the children's condition, and I didn't like what I saw. They had lost a great deal of weight and looked scrawny. They were dirty, their clothes rumpled and soiled. Cy's face was spotted with what appeared to be insect bites, and Sara's gorgeous hair had been hacked off and hung raggedly about her thin face.

We reached the police station and Michael paid off the driver. We were ushered into a large, virtually empty room inside. There was a single window, a table, and a long bench with broken rungs in its back and one leg shorter than the other three. I couldn't help myself. I laughed. What a heck of a place for the glorious reunion with Sara and Cy. They were able to smile, but they didn't budge an inch from my side.

We sat on the bench, the children clinging to me as though I was the dearest lifeline. And I felt their love as a tangible thing. I was the most fortunate woman in the world then. My big suitcase full of presents for them had been left at Iraj's feet at the airport, but that didn't matter to me. Things meant nothing; only people, especially the two little ones glued to my sides, were irreplaceable. Fortunately, though, I had a few small things for them and lots of food and candy in the big canvas bag that had been returned to me in the taxi. Sara and Cy ate hungrily, then amused themselves with the few little presents I had for them.

Michael tried to close the door to give us some privacy, but it was a sad thing, its hinges bent so badly that it stayed ajar despite his best efforts. That door suddenly and dramatically reminded me of Iraj and the damage he'd done repeatedly to several doors in our house, most notably the one to the powder room. I shuddered. God, please, I prayed silently and devoutly, let all that, let *him* be out of our lives forever.

A policeman eased into the room, a fat file folder in hand. He had a long muttered conversation with Michael, who spoke little, nodded a lot, and then left with him. He was back in a few minutes, which eased my mind, and he explained that the Turkish police were merely attending to a few formalities, reviewing our papers, and a complaint Michael had filed on my behalf. It had turned out that Rob's chance mention of our difficult problem to his fellow lawyer while taking a routine deposition had been extremely lucky, because the contact proved invaluable. The Turkish lawyer friend of that American lawyer had helped Michael through a legal thicket in the last eighteen hours, providing remarkable and speedy help. God truly was looking out for us. I would never believe that Rob's chain of association to this man was pure coincidence.

Our patience was strained to the breaking point and my nerves were frayed. I was hyperventilating because of the expired passports, scared that the police wouldn't simply "process" them but cause trouble. An hour went by without us seeing or hearing from anyone. During this time Michael told us that when the men with Iraj had seen the commotion at the airport and realized there was trouble, they'd piled into a white Mercedes and sped away. Eyebrows raised, Michael said, "We can only wonder where they went, right, Jess?"

I nodded, understanding too well what he was telling me, and that he didn't want the children to know: we could be in danger the minute we stepped out of this police station.

Suddenly the pathetic door to the room swung wide. There was a ruckus in the corridor just outside. Two officers, speaking in animated Turkish, were escorting Iraj to the interior of the station. I saw him try to shake off their hands and get them to listen to him. He literally couldn't get a word in edgewise as they continued to speak over him.

"He's being charged with smuggling, Jess," Michael whispered to me, and I saw a gleam of triumph in his eyes. I smiled at him for engineering that, then eased the children over to the window and told them to look out. I didn't want them to stare at their father being hustled through the station.

Iraj called out to me to come and speak with him. Without a word, I turned my back to him. I didn't wish to speak another word to him as long as I lived, and I hoped never to have to set eyes on him again either. Soon he stopped asking me to come talk to him. When there was complete silence, I glanced over my shoulder. Iraj had been taken away somewhere.

At last a policeman came in and told us we were free to go. I went weak with relief. Michael collected our passports and helped us gather our things and leave.

"If the children aren't too tired, Jess, I'd like to go straight to the consulate."

I nodded. "I think they'll be all right, and I'd feel better, too, if we got their papers in order."

The police assigned a man to drive us to the consulate, an arrangement that suited me fine, since I was worried about our safety. After all, we had no idea where Iraj's brother and nephew and the men working with them might be and what they intended to do.

At the consulate we were met at the door by a marine guard, sweet and brotherly, who led us into a big bright waiting room. I made straight for a large overstuffed sofa with the kids and bedded them down. It was evening now, and I was concerned about how tired they must be. There's nothing more enervating for a grown-up than waiting around, and since it's ten times worse for a child, I was feeling angry again at the State Department for making us go through this step. Damn their red tape; the passports should have been extended back at home!

In a few minutes the marine returned with cans of soda for all of us. It was a kind and generous gesture on his part, and I wish I could say the other consular staff members were as considerate. Unfortunately, it took them almost two hours to do this routine work that everyone in Washington and Philadelphia had assured us would be a breeze, would take no time at all. Then the consulate general himself came out to have a little chat with us. He didn't know our situation and questioned me about what was going on. I filled him in as swiftly as I could, then I had to endure a lecture from that stuffed shirt about the rights of all Americans, including my ex-husband, who might have been an Iranian national but was also an American citizen and deserved all the protection our country afforded. I somehow managed to hold on to my temper, thank him and everyone else, and get out of there.

Michael had excused himself shortly after we were settled in the consulate and he was sure our business was being attended to. But first he'd taken me aside while the marine kept the kids busy. He asked if I thought Sara and Cy and I could stand to travel that evening.

I frowned. "Michael, are you worried?"

"Not terribly, Jess. I can scoot you over to a safe house we've got on tap in the outskirts of the city, but I'd feel a lot more comfortable if we were well away from Istanbul."

I gazed at my vivacious and happy kids, then back at Michael. "Thanks for being calm and supportive, but I think I know what's on your mind. Maybe you've even got some information you're not sharing, about what Iraj's people might be up to. Yes, we can stand a drive. I think we can stand almost anything that's going to insure our safety."

Michael hugged me. "Good girl. Look, I'm going to get us to the Greek border. It closes at night, but we can stay in a small inn in the village of Ipsala, right on the border, then cross into Greece first thing in the morning. I got reservations for you and the kids for Athens."

Getting away tonight . . . Athens . . . that was more than fine with me.

Now Michael was back. He had a Jeep waiting for us at the back entrance of the consulate. He'd canceled the motor home reservation the day before when he'd finalized the plans for getting Iraj arrested for smuggling and had decided to take the kids from him at the airport. He wanted a nice, safe, fast Jeep in case we had to travel over bad roads.

It was dark and late, past ten, and we had to sneak into the Jeep. Actually the kids loved this and thought it was "like being in a movie," though I suspected that deep down they understood full well we were doing this for their protection. We snuggled together on the floor in the back of the Jeep, where Michael had heaped blankets for our comfort. And it was more than comfortable, it was heavenly to have my children in my arms. They chatted excitedly for a while, giggling about our situation. Every so often one of them would say something about an awful thing that had happened to them with their father.

As soon as we were clear of the city and sure that the only cars following were driven by our people, we stopped for a much needed hot meal. The kids were hungry enough but complained about the food. Their eyes glowed with excitement as they talked about getting back home and going to McDonald's for a Happy Meal or to Burger King for a flame-broiled burger. I cracked up as Cy, who has a very slight lisp, entertained us with his singsong repetition of "flame-broiled burger."

The road was very good, Route E5S, one of the two major arteries leading from Istanbul to Greece. As Michael sped us smoothly through the night, we got drowsy and nodded off. I was jarred awake as the Jeep pulled to a stop. Instantly alert, I looked at my watch in the light that streamed from the building in front of which Michael was parking; it was almost two o'clock in the morning.

"Sorry about this place," Michael apologized. "It's the only one near the border. Hope you can manage."

I nodded sleepily and stayed with the children until Michael checked in. Then we carried Sara and Cy, still sleeping soundly, up five narrow, steep flights of stairs to our room, supposedly a double with bath, but the bed was as narrow as a single and the bathroom was—well, odd. We found out just how odd a few minutes later when Sara awoke, complaining of the odor in the room and asking to go to the bathroom. We had put the kids down on the one bed, and Michael had secured the door with a chair pushed under the knob before arranging blankets on the floor for us to sleep on.

When Sara and I were washing our hands, a gush of water sprayed out over our feet and legs. The sink had no connecting pipe beneath it. The floor was flooded before we could turn off the faucet. We laughed hysterically, which brought Michael to the bathroom inquiring about what was so funny. Sara demonstrated at the sink, and Michael too started to roar.

Unfortunately, the terrible musty smell in the room kept the three of us awake, though Cy was sleeping through it all like a little log. Sara decided to "fix" the odor by sprinkling Michael's cologne around the place. He seemed to find my little girl a delight.

Soon everyone was fast asleep except me. I had a lot to thank God for, and it took me some time to do it.

Michael and I really only caught naps. A dawn symphony of crowing roosters, braying donkeys, barking dogs, and talking people woke us. The children slept soundly, though, so this gave us our first real chance to talk. I was eager to know what had gone on at the airport. I was amazed to learn what had transpired just inches from my very nose.

With backup agents poised in strategic spots, Michael had been ready to separate the kids from Iraj when they approached me at the airport. Of course, Iraj had left the children in the car. When Sara, Cy, and I met, Michael put himself between us as Iraj was reaching out to grab Sara's arm. Michael shoved him a couple of feet away from us, then punched him hard in the mouth. Meanwhile, I was running like crazy with the kids. Clutching his mouth, an absolutely petrified expression on his face, Iraj had fallen back against a taxi. Michael signaled the police with whom he was working, and they moved in to take Iraj into custody. The backup agents tried to keep track of the occupants of the Mercedes and were successful until it roared away. Because of the possibility of there being some difficulty getting me and the children safely away, they didn't pursue the car.

"Honest," Michael said, "I don't think I've ever seen a man as surprised and as scared as Iraj was. I don't think that rotten coward was ever hit before."

"Don't believe he ever has been," I agreed, smiling. Rotten coward. The perfect description for Iraj, I reflected.

Before we could share more about the previous day's events, the kids woke up and demanded some breakfast. We joined the backup agents, who'd stayed in a room one flight down, for a big meal. I was glad to see that even though we weren't having the American food the children craved, they no longer merely picked at what was set before them.

"Cy, Cy," Sara cried, "look at Mommy's wrist."

Not only the children but Michael and the other two agents were staring where Sara pointed. Around my left wrist below my watch was the good-luck bracelet I'd so often touched and twisted. It was actually two bracelets, not one, thin braids of colored string—the friendship bracelets that Sara and Cy had made for each other shortly before they'd been abducted and had left behind for me "to guard" for them while they were away. I'd worn these frail braids since the late morning of April 12. Beaming while blinking back tears, I carefully took them off and put them on Cy and Sara's wrists.

"You wore them because Daddy took us away," Cy said so wistfully and perceptively that even the tough men at the table had tears in their eyes. "You wore them until you could see us again, Mom, didn't you?"

I nodded and looked at Sara and Cy's bracelets, satisfied because they were back where they belonged, on their owners' wrists.

It was a little creepy passing through the border check, where we were stared at and quizzed. I couldn't decide if we were getting the third degree because the guards had never seen such a motley group of Americans—I'm sure we didn't smell any better than we looked, which was pretty awful—or because they'd been alerted to watch for fugitives. It was a huge relief when they waved us through.

The four of us had said good-bye to the backup agents just before crossing into Greece, right after Michael and I'd had a brief conference while the children played in the town square. He had been calling contacts in Istanbul, trying to learn Iraj's fate. Unfortunately, it was

RESCUED

Saturday, the day of rest in the Muslim world, and it was hard to reach anyone. We could only hope that Iraj was still being held in jail and wasn't directing his brother, nephew, and other men to follow and capture us. The possibility that Iraj had lodged a phony charge against us was also a worry. We had to behave as though both threats were real. The backup guys would retrace our route back to Istanbul, trying to make sure no one was in pursuit; once back in the city they'd find out everything they could.

We continued along the Greek part of E5S, the road hugging the coast of the Aegean. The children complained about how "ugly" the scenery was, saying it looked just like Iran. The hillsides were rocky, there was scant vegetation, and we saw only a few squat grayish buildings and the occasional shepherd with a small flock. Soon, though, Sara and Cy were much happier with what they saw, because the landscape changed and began to look more Mediterranean, with whitewashed houses and more greenery and flowers.

Alexandroupolos was the first sizable town we reached. Michael hoped that the airport there would be open and he could get us on a connecting flight so that the children would be spared more car travel. Athens, our destination, was about 1,100 miles from Istanbul, and he was very much aware of what the children had endured and how much they needed a good bed, food, and fresh clothing. Unfortunately, the airport was closed.

We had lunch picnic style, at a wooded area outside a charming little town, Kavala, I think, and the kids had the chance to run around and play ball with Michael. They were growing more fond of him by the minute. So was I.

Our next destination was Thessalonika. And once there, thank God, we were able to get a flight to Athens. Linda met us at the airport, with the suitcase I'd dropped and left behind in Istanbul. In it were clothes, of course, but Linda knew that it also contained dozens of presents, letters, and cards for Sara and Cy from their playmates, school friends, and relatives. Linda had made the special effort personally to retrieve and deliver it to the kids because, she said, "I knew it was full of the *most* important things—expressions of affection and love."

We'd made real friends of Michael and Linda, and we wanted to celebrate with them after we settled into the hotel. Unfortunately, though, Linda was booked on a flight back to Istanbul, so we had to say good-bye to her.

We checked into the Hilton. The very first thing that the children clamored for was not room service or to play with their toys. They wanted a bath. They were wild to get into a tub of warm soapy water because they hadn't had a bath since April 10. They said they hated the makeshift shower with only cold water that they'd had to use at the farm, and the less primitive one in Tabriz with warm water hadn't been much better. They played for an hour in the big tub in the modern Hilton bathroom. Then, rosy and clean and freshly dressed, we celebrated with Michael over club sandwiches and Coca-Cola in the coffee shop.

When the rich ice cream they hadn't had for the last four months arrived, it seemed almost a cue for them to start talking about their experiences. Rapt, Michael and I listened closely; I knew he understood as well as I did how important it was that they trusted him and that they were ready to begin to unburden themselves.

Recent events preoccupied them at the moment. They

shouted over each other, trying to get out every detail of what they'd gone through in the last five days.

Their father had crammed them into the Mercedes, along with their uncle, his son, and two young men they'd never met before. Sara pulled at my arm, many emotions flashing across her expressive face. She had been afraid because she'd overheard that her cousin had no papers permitting him to go across the border, and she was certain the "two boys," as Iraj called them, were also being smuggled out of Iran. Cy dragged at my other arm, saying excitedly, "Daddy was bribing the guards, Mommy. Bribing all those guys everywhere we had to stop."

"He gave them cigarettes and money," Sara chimed in.

"But this wasn't the first time, Sara," Cy told her. "You know how many times we've done this with Daddy."

"It was in the mountains then, Cy. We only went inside Turkey once or twice," she said.

They both sounded like little adults, which troubled me almost as much as the tales they were telling.

Sara said she'd not only been terrified about the bribes, but also because the men in the car had been drinking whiskey. Sara said she knew all about what happened to people in Iran who had whiskey or beer or wine with them—even if they didn't drink it and only kept it in their house or their car, it was against the law and they'd get killed for it. She and Cy had been taken to the central square in Tabriz to see the crane there from which people caught selling or drinking alcoholic beverages were hanged. I tried to hide the emotions I was feeling, but I couldn't restrain myself from asking one question.

"Who took you to see the hanging place?"

"Oh, we all went," Cy piped up. "Daddy and every-body. Practically the whole family."

I was furious with those miserable people for taking two little kids to such a place, but I promptly smiled, to encourage Sara and Cy to keep talking.

They had driven, the children said, straight through to Erzurum, and Iraj had allowed them to go into the airport with him, where he picked up the tickets I'd reserved. He went to another window with the tickets and got lots of money in exchange for them. Then he'd taken them for sodas before returning to the car to start driving again. They had slept in the car. When the cooler of food they'd brought with them from Tabriz was empty, they purchased food in a restaurant and ate it in the car. Cy said they'd had fun a couple of times when they'd made a fire and cooked food over it "just like Boy Scouts"—which prompted Sara to elbow him. "And Girl Scouts," he added hastily.

It was hard to keep from shuddering as I listened to them tell how difficult it had been to stay still in the car all those hours. I could scarcely believe that even Iraj would subject them to the hardship of four straight days and nights inside a cramped car. The bastard.

They'd fallen asleep. When they'd reached the hotel in Istanbul, Sara said, she woke up for a minute. Cy said he "hadn't waked up at all." But, she went on, they hadn't been there very long when Iraj got them up and said they had to go to the airport to pick me up. Once there, he'd told his brother and nephew to "hold on to the kids."

"I didn't want to be held on to," Cy complained.

"I didn't either, and we asked them to let us go. But they wouldn't! When I saw you, Mommy, I started to kick and punch to get free." "I did too," Cy said, "but I didn't yell like Sara did. Anyway, the second she got out, I did too and went running after her to find you."

I was weak with pity when they stopped, distracted by a waitress who meant well and had brought them some crayons and big paper place mats she'd found for them to draw on. While they bent over their coloring, Michael and I looked at each other, shaking our heads.

That night Sara and Cy left their own beds to crawl into mine, and with me snug between them, they slept soundly for over twelve hours.

We hated to say good-bye to Michael. He had to return to Istanbul to join Linda in "tidying up a few things" from the operation and couldn't fly home with us. Michael had done a superb job. He'd gotten the Turkish police on our side, walked them through the dossier he'd compiled on Iraj, which included a detailed account of his smuggling activities, in addition to his international arrest warrant, the UFAP, and copies of the liens, custody orders, and so forth; he'd convinced the police to handle the airport operation his way and agree to arrest Iraj on the spot.

He found a moment as the children were investigating the pool area to whisper to me, "You know, Patrick would have my hide for saying this, but I'd give up my fee on this case just for the memory of the look on Iraj's face after I punched him. He went white with panic, Jess, pure panic. Exactly what you'd expect from a bully, huh? Bullies don't like a taste of their own medicine."

I envied Michael. My knuckles tingled to slug Iraj in the nose. How I would have liked to have been the one to put that expression on Iraj's face—but, in a way, I guess I had! I'd had the guts to go for the recovery, to fire one group, and hire another. I'd worked hard, suffered a lot, and kept the faith. Yes, I too had turned the tables on the bully and put the look of pure terror on the face of Iraj Salimi.

Our time with Michael might have been short, but it had been deep and intense. And I believe that Sara and Cy knew as well as I did when we hugged him and said good-bye that he was a friend the three of us would cherish forever.

SIXTEEN

SARA'S HOMECOMING

BENJAMIN FRANKLIN WAS WAITING AT THE AIRPORT—
along with my aunts and my uncles and my cousins and
grandmother and grandfather—and I was so-o-o-o happy
I thought I might pop! Benjamin Franklin is the most
beautiful cat in the whole world. He's white and he has
gorgeous pale, pale, pale greeny-blue eyes. He cried and
meowed all the time Cy and I were gone in Iran. Mom
told me, so did Aunt Sue, and Aunt Bethie. They said he
just wandered around in our rooms and made all his sad
noises, but so loud sometimes he almost drove everybody
crazy. He really loves me and Cy a lot—like everybody in
my family does, especially my mom.

When Daddy and Cy and I got to Iran, it was okay for a
few days, because we thought we were only visiting there

for a real short time and then we'd be going home. And it was okay too for a little while because nobody looked after Cy and me, and we'd never been allowed just to run around with a bunch of kids and do whatever we wanted to—except there wasn't anything much to do—and then we missed having somebody grown-up around.

Everything smelled bad and all the food tasted bad, so we didn't eat any of that stuff, and we were hungry all the time. I ate candy bars, mostly Snickers, and Cy ate a few of them, but he'd have a little rice and fruit and stuff. I really started to worry a lot and to cry every night when Daddy told me he'd brought Cy and me to Iran because it was the only place in the world where Mommy couldn't get us.

He was very, very mad at Mom. Because of Mike mostly, I think. And he kept asking and asking and asking us what terrible things Mike did. Cy and I didn't know what to say, because Mike never did any terrible things. We wanted to make Daddy stop asking us and to keep him from getting angry all the time about Mike, so we made up things. But he never liked the stories we made up.

Anyway, I was scared and sad because I didn't know if we'd ever get home, which was very far away. I just felt awful any time I thought about my teacher at school. I was afraid I was in a lot of trouble because I didn't get back after Easter vacation. I knew I wouldn't get promoted to third grade. I worried about how far back I'd be and that I'd never catch up with my friends and have to go to school with kids a whole year younger than me, like I was some kind of a dummy or something. It really made me feel bad.

One day Daddy told me Mommy was dead. We'd been in Iran for a long time by then, and I'd been bugging him about when we were going to go home and asking him a lot of times if Mommy was going to come visit and take us home. And he'd get mad because he said I was a broken record and because I kept telling him everything in Iran was awful. So he'd punish me. But that day when he said—and he was very mad and had a terrible frown on his face—"Your mother is dead, Sara. Dead," I got really scared. For a couple of minutes I felt awful, like I'd die too. But then I started to think. Mom couldn't be dead, she just couldn't be, because I'd heard Daddy talking to her on the telephone. I got very upset, because it wasn't right for him to tell me something that was so awful and wasn't even the truth. I thought about it for a long time. Then I went running after him because he was going off on a trip, and I caught up with him and told him I knew he hadn't been telling me the truth and Mommy wasn't dead. Boy, did he get angry at me. And I got grounded—again! It seemed like I was getting grounded every single day. That meant I had to sit forever on this little pillow in the room downstairs. Sometimes from lunch until dinnertime. And Cy would stand outside the room, right by the door, and be sad and lonely and crying. Then I really felt awful. I tried to be Cy's mom when our mom wasn't there, but it was a real tough job, and we needed her a lot. She takes good care of us and she's a lot of fun and we love her very much.

I didn't think Mommy could ever get us back since we were so far away in a place where they did not like Americans at all. But she did! And, boy, did that make me happy!

We went to Disney World! It was the best. Then after a long time in Florida, Mom said she thought we'd be the safest from ever being taken away to Iran again, something that worried me a lot, if we lived in a fishbowl! She meant that back home all the neighbors and the police and everybody knew us, and we had the rest of our family, and everybody would be looking out for us. We went back home just before Halloween, which was pretty great too, and started school late. But, hooray, I was in third grade with all my friends! So everything turned out okay after all.

CY'S HOMECOMING

I love America. America is the best place in the whole wide world. I didn't know that until Daddy took us to Iran where everything is different and always kind of sad. I think everybody over there is *very* poor. They don't have hardly anything that we have at home. They don't have television or movies or many cars. And the ladies don't have any clothes at all! They just wear long black pieces of material that they cover themselves up with from their heads to their feet. The grownups have to work *all* the time so nobody takes care of the children. Sara and I were left by ourselves all day with only a very old lady who'd yell and shake a funny looking broom at us when we were bad, like the time we poured cups of water down from the roof on top of all these kids who'd been chasing us and were running around down there. The roofs of the houses were flat and Sara and I ran all over them, jumping across to the next house and the next and looking down at what everybody was doing. I felt like Superman. But I knew my mom would be yelling, "Come down from there this minute, Cy!" if she'd been there. So I felt a little bad about it.

•

There were lots of kids, but we couldn't play much with them because we didn't speak their language and they didn't speak ours. So we could only do things like play tag. And I felt really sorry for those kids because they didn't have any toys at all, *not any*. We didn't at first either, but we kept asking Daddy and finally he went out one day and came back with a Nintendo for us to play and then all the kids came crowding around and wanting to play it too, but they didn't know how. They hadn't ever even seen anything like it.

I missed my mom and my house and my friends. And I missed Benjie, that's my cat whose whole name is Benjamin Franklin. And Benjie missed me, and Sara too. And I don't think there was anything better ever than coming home. My aunts and my grandmother and my girl cousins kissed me and hugged me too much, but I guess that was okay, because they'd missed me as much as I'd missed them. And then the greatest stuff happened. My grandfather had borrowed this super plane from someone he knew. It was all ours for our trip to Florida, and it was like a little flying house. Sara and I could run all over the plane and we made a Benjamin Franklin room with his litter box and food and water bowl. And we got these little blankets out of a closet there and made a bed for him. And it was the best plane ever. Then in just a few days we got to go to Disney World!

Disney World was the best thing I ever saw!

The grossest thing I ever saw was in Iran when they killed the animals. I couldn't hardly eat anything at the farm. I felt sick all the time. It smelled really, really bad. And the worst thing was that they took Sara and me out to the shed to watch them killing the stuff for our dinner. The worst ever was killing the lambs. After they'd banged them on the head a lot or something, they put them up on hooks and cut them open right down the middle and blood dripped down into big puddles on the floor. And then my uncle would say things to his son and his son would get the hose and spray water all over the lamb's body and then he sprayed it hard on the concrete floor to make all the blood go away. I hated it. And I wouldn't eat any of the meat they cooked—ever.

One thing that was pretty neat, though, was when we saw all the army guys with guns. The guns were really, really long, and they kept the ammunition for them across their chests. We saw the army guys whenever we went into town or out on the big roads or when we went in the car with Daddy on his trips to get men out of there. The soldiers scared Sara, but not me.

For a long time I used to be worried that I'd get taken back to Iran and I'd never be able to find a way to get home again. But now I'm never worried about that. I used to get embarrassed a lot, though, when I thought about what I did at the airport in Turkey. I bit Michael's hand. I thought he was trying to take Mommy away or me away. But Michael and my mom say I should be proud of that, not embarrassed, because if anybody ever tries to grab me that's exactly what I should do again and any other kid that's being grabbed ought to do it too.

MY HAPPY ENDING

I was glowing with happiness at having the children back and with pride in having succeeded in the recovery. But I was looking over my shoulder all the time. We swam and built sand castles, and we went to Disney World. And

I've never seen Sara and Cy happier. They didn't want to talk about their abduction at first; they were having too much fun in the present. They betrayed their anxiety only by not letting me out of their sight for a second, and by constantly touching me. I didn't push them to talk; I hugged them and kissed them, read to them and played with them. My only goal at first was to cushion them, to make them feel very secure, very safe. And when they did feel safe, they began to talk—and talk, and talk. There was no stopping them.

One of the most difficult things for me to deal with was easing their sense of inadequacy. At first they really had believed they'd been taken on a brief visit to Iran and had no idea they'd been kidnapped; soon, though, they had realized something was very, very wrong, and they began to feel guilty that they didn't know how to escape. We had a lot to work through. Both children, but especially Sara, felt they were oddballs because they'd been abducted, something that never happened to other kids. They felt that a huge hunk of their lives had been pulled away and they fretted about what they'd missed that would set them back in school and with their friends.

One of the first things I'd done when we landed at Kennedy Airport was to call Mike, who'd wisely hung back. He felt strongly that the children needed time alone with me and it would be very wrong of him to intrude. Within a week I could see that they would welcome him. They talked about their father's obsession with Mike, what a nice guy Mike was, and how much they missed him. When he joined us, my happiness was complete. And I was terribly impressed too with how much the kids appreciated him. they loved playing with him, watching a cartoon with him, having him read to them—they just wanted to be around him at all times. Mike was providing them with a wonderful role model as a concerned, caring male. But still I looked over my shoulder.

As we'd been advised by people who'd lived underground, we didn't stay too long in the beachfront condo. We moved on to another "safe house." But soon our idyllic vacation had to end; we had to get on with our lives. It became a busy time. I looked into schools, Mike looked into employment opportunities. We practiced assuming our new identities. "Tracey" and "Peter" wouldn't answer to their names, however. And I would bring down the house when I'd say something like, "Cy—Peter—Cy, didn't you hear me?"

Anyone who thinks it's easy to adopt a new name or to fake a background, has not tried to pull it off! And it was very difficult to communicate with my lawyer (we had a lot of unfinished business!) and my family through third parties, always using aliases. When I didn't feel odd and uncomfortable, I felt vaguely fraudulent and silly.

I talked with Patrick Buckman and Michael, both of whom counseled that living underground was difficult, painful, often crazy-making, and sometimes dangerous. When Patrick told me how many children are reabducted from these underground situations, I said enough!

I decided it was much safer to live in a goldfish bowl—an expression Sara loves—where teachers, friends, neighbors, and police know the situation and give us a hundred more pairs of watchful eyes; where family is around to be loved as well as loving. And so we packed up in the late fall and we went home.

We are watchful, but not paranoid. We have lots of

security around us, but we are not afraid. We are living openly, joyfully—more joyfully than many people I see, because, I think, we are so aware of what we almost lost.

The last we saw of Iraj was in the police station in Turkey. We heard but do not know for a fact that he was released because of lack of evidence. Our assumption is that he returned to Iran. The liens on his property yielded nothing, because he'd cleverly got rid of almost everything or transferred ownership in ways that put it beyond our lawsuits. A cunning man, as I've said. And because of all sorts of complicated legal twists, we were never able to get the unlawful-flight-to-avoid-prosecution order issued or his passport revoked. (The Consular General in Istanbul demanded that I hand over his passport, which I did, though I'm told it was never given back to Iraj.) However, he is named as a fugitive, wanted on kidnapping and other charges, through the National Crime Information Center. He will have to travel, work, and live under an assumed name or face arrest and be returned to the United States to stand trial.

Canadian officials were very interested in the immigration of Jamshid, Lelah, and Nasser, but because of privacy laws I was never made aware of what if any action they took. Federal marshals frightened the devil out of Bobek when they served papers on him for his part in the kidnapping. He may have flown back to Iran; we're sure he alerted the entire Salimi family to the high priority I was giving to using every legal means to put up roadblocks to their having access to the children.

During the ordeal, when Sara and Cy were being held in Iran, I was full of anger and wanted revenge. Now I only want to make sure those people can never lay a finger on the children again. I have not forgiven them; I doubt I'll ever be able to forgive them. But I do not care to see them ruined. I do not care at all what happens to any of them.

Our stay in Florida was a time of great healing for the children and for me. I took long walks on the beach and thought about all we'd gone through in the last four months. I thanked God for giving me a host of supportive people and a family that backed me to the hilt. Tears came to my eyes when I thought of all those parents of abducted children who don't have my great good fortune. It is shocking that the fees and expenses for the recovery amounted to just over $179,000! I am one of the very privileged few who had relatives to borrow from to make it possible to get my kids back. Many children and their custodial parents will never see one another again because of the high cost of tracking down and recovering them. It is wrong that not everyone has the help I received. Laws must be passed to change all this . . . to help enforce the laws of our domestic courts, which awarded custody in the first place. As I walked the beaches, I vowed to do something to help less fortunate people who find themselves in my situation. And then an idea began to take form. I had to work to change things for abducted children and their custodial parents. I decided to share my experiences in a book, with the hope that it might help at least one parent, one child. And I had to do more, much more. . . .

I thought often, too, about the past, when I was a girl, then a young wife. And I realized how deeply I'd changed. I had been a nail for so many years, but I'd emerged to become a hammer. I was responsible for my own destiny and more than able to shoulder that responsibility. I would never again be passive and frightened but an active and unafraid woman. By this time my eyes had *not* fallen out, and I hadn't become loose in the joints, but I had become Real. And as the Skin Horse tells us, once you become Real you can't become unreal again. It lasts for always.

Together, Mike and I work through the nonprofit organization we founded, KID SAFE, to help protect all children from the trauma of abuse and abduction.

AFTERWORD

YEAR IN, YEAR OUT, NEARLY HALF A MILLION CHILDREN are wrenched from their homes, schools, playgrounds, and whisked away, many of them never to be seen again. Of these children, approximately 350,000 are abducted not by strangers but by members of their own family. If you can envision about six football stadiums crowded with boys and girls, you'll have a fairly good picture of about 350,000 kidnapping victims. But not a full picture. Behind each of the young victims stand others—grandparents, aunts and uncles, cousins, friends, and, of course, the bereft parent.

The U.S. Department of Justice's Office of Juvenile Justice and Delinquency Prevention commissioned a report on the problem of missing, abducted, and throwaway children in America, which was published in 1990. The statistics only apply through 1988, and the numbers break down as follows: 354,000 children abducted by family members and 114,600 attempted abductions by non–family members. The researchers recognized that family abduction appears "to be a substantially larger problem than previously thought." Indeed, it is a growing problem that we must address vigorously and without delay. No civilized society can allow so many of its families, particularly the children in those families, to suffer so much.

Once I recovered my own children, I wondered how I could give back something as a way of showing my appreciation. How could I, like so many others who have experienced something traumatic, turn it into something positive? I recalled the many voices that had been sources of information and hope for me. I too longed to be a voice for someone in need.

It seemed clear that we need better laws and law enforcement—help from the police, the FBI, the State Department and the UN—but experience had taught me that such changes would take time. Instead, I decided to go right to the source, focusing on the children and their parents. After much thought, I organized KID SAFE, a nonprofit organization established for the purpose of creating an educational program for preelementary and elementary children, to provide them with the skills and information they need to make judgments in potentially dangerous situations.

We are presently developing a multimedia educational tool with the express goal of teaching children and parents how to prevent abductions, and not just family abductions. We hope to empower all children with healthy lifelong survival skills. Nonviolent and non-threatening, our program teaches through interactive virtual-reality "edutainment." With participation and communication among parents, teachers, law enforcers, and children, we can combat abductions by strangers as well as family members.

I really would crawl across Turkey on my hands and knees to save my kids, and I know that almost all parents in a similar situation would too. When faced with a devastating act of revenge, you have few options but to act bravely for the sake of little hearts. I am an ordinary woman who has learned that when your children are threatened, there is no end to what you can and will do to rescue them. And there are thousands of ordinary men and women facing such challenges right now. They too can succeed.

There are many organizations and individuals committed to the ideal of protecting children from abduction and aiding parents who have been victimized by an abduction. I would be remiss if I didn't acknowledge the people who were instrumental in the recovery of my children, as well as those who continue to offer help and support. I wish to thank the following people:

Ms. Judith Drazen Schretter, general counsel, National Center for Missing & Exploited Children, for her encouragement and help with KID SAFE questions. Dr. Johnson and his conscientious staff, for you are all terrific! Michael Buben, Joe Bainbridge, and all the officers of LMT who helped with the cause and offered advice for safety and protection. Tom Heffernan, criminal investigator with the Child Abduction Unit of the Sacramento district attorney's office, for his keen insight and wisdom. (Tom Heffernan recently retired from the D.A.'s office and is now in private practice.)

Betty Mahmoody, for her emotional support and caring. Michael, for his continued friendship and desire to teach our KID SAFE program. The Edison gang, who brainstormed with us through hot summer nights, sharing laughter and tears. Angie, who has helped me work through so many really important issues and offered her creative insights. Jim White of White Marketing, who believes in our project and sees dreams become reality. Larry Cherba, senior deputy district attorney, for his willingness to learn even more than what was required. Bob Whitelaw, for his heart and soul, and patience. Dave Christian, for his wonderful, worldly advice. Bessy, Jules, and their families, and numerous friends who helped and never gave up hope. The doctors mentioned in the book, friends first, strategists always. Thanks to Joe for the use of his plane, which got us to Florida undetected. To Frank for the use of his condo in Florida, and to Nancy and Doug for sheltering us for so long.

Arnold Goodman, who believed *Rescued* was a story that should be told. Carolyn Nichols, for her talent of storytelling, and her heart-and-soul compassion. HarperCollins and Jessica Lichtenstein for the chance, for the help. My Mike, who supported me not only during our recovery of Sara and Cy, but also during these years of writing this book. And Sara and Cy, who are resilient and radiate warmth each day.

—J.D.

JESSICA DOYLE

A 1977 graduate of Pennsylvania State University, Jessica Doyle is spearheading an effort to protect children from abduction and its abuses through her nonprofit organization, KID SAFE. She is active in her local schools, where she is a substitute teacher, and in her community in suburban New Jersey.

CAROLYN NICHOLS

An editor and publisher for more than a dozen years, Carolyn Nichols is the author of seven published works. She lives with her teenage son in Manhattan.

WHAT'S IN IT FOR ME?

by Joseph Stedino with Dary Matera

Working with the Phoenix District Attorney's office, Joseph Stedino posed as a mobster out to legalize gambling in Arizona by buying votes. Once the word was out, legislators and lobbyists came running. The successful sting led to twenty indictments and shed glaring light on how politics in Arizona—and across America—really works!

THE KENNEDY CONTRACT

by John H. Davis

In 1979, the House Select Committee on Assassinations concluded that President John F. Kennedy's assassination was most likely the result of a conspiracy, and that the Mafia had the motive, means and opportunity to execute JFK. Including new information from key witnesses and shocking details surrounding the cover-up, *The Kennedy Contract* blows the lid off the most fascinating murder case in U.S. history. John H. Davis is an expert on the Kennedy and Mafia dynasties.

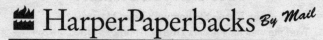